AF522364

INDIA *AND* AFRICA

INDIA *AND* AFRICA

LEGACY OF EXCHANGES AND CULTURAL AFFINITIES

EDITED BY
H.H.S. VISWANATHAN
K.N. SHRIVASTAVA

in association with

Konark Publishers Pvt. Ltd
206, First Floor
Peacock Lane, Shahpur Jat
New Delhi 110 049
+91-11-4105 5065
india@konarkpublishers.com, us@konarkpublishers.com
www.konarkpublishers.com

ISBN: 978-81-987405-5-7

Jacket design by Sourish Mitra

Typeset by K.K. Gusain

Printed and bound at Saurabh Printers Pvt. Ltd, Greater Noida

Contents

PART 5
Textile Traditions of Africa and India

PART 6
India–Africa Partnership

Foreword

This publication is the outcome of an international conference organised by the India International Centre (IIC) from 10 to 12 February 2020, with the theme "Understanding Africa: Continuity and Change". While writing this Foreword, I feel a great sense of sadness because the principal inspiration for and the moving force behind the conference, Dr Kapila Vatsyayan, is no longer with us. Ideally, this publication should have come out before she left us; sadly, COVID-19 prevented us from achieving that.

The IIC is well known for organising cross-cultural dialogues. The IIC-Asia Project was created in 1997 with the aim of fostering greater interaction with other Asian cultures. The experience gained inspired the Centre to develop the IIC International Research Division. Under the visionary leadership of Kapilaji, this Division put together many events exploring cultural links between India and Asian countries. In 2016, an international conference was held in collaboration with the Institute of Indo-Persian Studies (IIPS) to celebrate the 80th anniversary of the publication of Sadeq Hedayat's *The Blind Owl*. In the same year, there was a conference on "Linguistic Diversity in South and Southeast Asia". In 2018, we hosted a conference on "Pluralism in India and Indonesia: Diversity in the Quest for Unity", and one on "India and Central Asia". All these initiatives produced valuable publications carrying the papers presented.

This conference tried to expand the exercise to a continent whose relations with India go back many centuries. There is a feeling of solidarity, based on similar historical experiences, between India and this continent. Yes, I am referring to the great African continent. The timing of this discussion about Africa is also perfect. Today, Africa is in the news and for all the right reasons. Over the past two decades, there has been a tremendous resurgence in Africa. This resurgence is both political and economic. A few exceptions apart, most African countries have embraced multi-party democracy. We hear about transparent and successful elections leading to peaceful transfers of power. Violent conflicts, which were common a few decades ago, have become rare. On the economic front, there has been commendable growth in the GDPs of most countries. In the past decade, annual lists of the 10 fastest-growing economies in the world have invariably included five or six African nations. It is also timely because India–Africa relations are at an all-time high across all sectors: political, strategic, economic, commercial, technological and people-to-people.

It is not the first time that the IIC has hosted an Africa-centred conference. Back in February 1996, we held a conference with the theme, "Understanding Africa–India and South–South Cooperation," where many distinguished personalities, including Tanzanian President Julius Nyerere, were present. I have had the privilege of engaging with Africa on many occasions. I have been an ardent supporter of South–South Cooperation, and I believe the full potential of this idea has yet to be realised. I participated in the consultations held by the South African Government soon after the end of apartheid to decide the governance structures of the nascent nation. I have had the opportunity to visit Ghana, Burkina Faso and Tanzania. India and Africa share a bond due to our sufferings during the colonial days. As a result, our problems and aspirations are similar. We can work together to find common solutions, which is already happening in many areas.

Nonetheless, this conference was designed differently ab initio. In keeping with the traditions of the IIC, Kapilaji wished that the conference focus on the cultural and historical aspects and connections within those contexts. The experts who made the presentations were chosen with this focus in mind. The themes for the various sessions were selected after considerable discussion. All of them pointed to the glorious traditions of Africa in arts, culture, music, dance, textiles, crafts, language and literature. The sessions also brought forth not only the striking similarities with Indian traditions but also the vibrant exchanges that, unfortunately, are not well known. The sessions revealed gems of data on which scholars can do further research and create a substantial body of knowledge. The main objective of this publication is to encourage further in-depth studies on the themes of the conference.

Let me finally thank all those involved in organising the conference and in bringing out this publication. Neither would have been possible without the inspiration, encouragement and constant guidance of Kapilaji. We are greatly indebted to her. The success of the conference owes a lot to the participation of Ambassador Olabiyi Babalola Joseph Yaï, former Chairman of the UNESCO Executive Board. Despite his busy schedule, he responded to Kapilaji's invitation and delivered an unforgettable keynote address at the inaugural session. Unfortunately, he passed away in 2020, depriving us of having him as one of the editors of this publication. We cannot thank him enough for his contribution.

I must also thank Ambassador K. Raghunath (former Foreign Secretary of India) for bringing Kapilaji's idea to fruition. It was he who put together the team and guided them efficiently. The conference evolved from the concept paper prepared by Ambassador H.H.S. Viswanathan, who also coordinated all the various steps in organising the event. He, along with the Director, IIC, has edited this volume. I thank both of them for this great effort. Our gratitude also goes to the various participants, some of whom travelled long distances to be with us and contribute to the discussions and to this publication.

The Ministry of External Affairs (MEA), Government of India, was the pillar of strength behind the entire exercise. Foreign Secretary Shri Harsh Vardhan Shringla's Valedictory Address was one of the highlights of the conference. It is worth mentioning that he very kindly agreed to give the address despite having taken over the Foreign Secretaryship only a few days earlier. We also remember with gratitude the constant encouragement and support of Shri T.S. Tirumurti, Secretary (ER) in MEA, and Dr Neena Malhotra, Joint Secretary.

The views and advice of the various African Heads of Missions in New Delhi were taken from the initial stages of the preparation for the conference. They generously dedicated their time to engage with us. I express our heartfelt thanks to them.

I should not forget to thank Shri Ramachandran, who worked tirelessly to ensure the success of the conference and the realisation of this publication. Finally, I must thank Ms Malini Gupta for her translations of the French papers, and Dr Nandini Sen and her young colleagues for presenting the rapporteur's report.

It is my earnest hope that this volume will be a valuable addition to our knowledge store on Africa, particularly its rich historical and cultural traditions and the ancient links with India in these areas. Even if a few scholars take up these themes and do further research, the objective of this publication would be realised.

N.N. Vohra
Life Trustee, India International Centre

Preface

The international conference, "Understanding Africa: Continuity and Change", was the outcome of the idea of the late Dr Kapila Vatsyayan, who wished to have a conference on Africa along the lines of earlier conferences on Southeast Asia and Central Asia. This was part of the IIC's tradition of providing platforms for cross-cultural dialogue. The choice of Africa was natural because, with its political and economic resurgence, Africa has moved centre stage in the international scene. There is a general consensus that the 21st century will be one of African growth and development.

From the outset, Kapilaji was very clear that the conference should not follow the usual route of tracing India–Africa relations in the political, strategic, economic and commercial sectors, as there are already many fora for such dialogues. IIC's expertise lies in culture, tradition and people-to-people contacts. Hence, she visualised the conference as a dialogue on these aspects. Former Foreign Secretary Ambassador K. Raghunath kindly agreed to lead the team.

The areas for discussion were carefully chosen to include not only the glorious traditions of Africa but also the historical linkages with India in these sectors. The conference aimed to provide a holistic view of the evolution of these linkages. Some of the themes discussed were:

- **The African Narrative**

  This was the most important aspect of the conference. During the colonial and neo-colonial periods, the African narrative was suppressed, and what we heard about Africa came only from outsiders, which was distorted and untrue. There is a famous African proverb that says, "Until the day the lions have their own storyteller, the story of the hunt will glorify the hunter". Fortunately, the situation has changed. Thanks to the resurgence of Africa, the continent's stories today are heard more and more from Africans themselves. Many of the old African narratives are also being revived. The conference provided a platform for some of these narratives.

- **Continuity across Time**

  A correct understanding of Africa must take historical continuity into account. Compartmentalising Africa into the "old" and the "new" would mean missing out on the vital linkages that the Africans are very proud of. An analysis of Africa based solely on the old and the new only reinforces prejudices and ignores the finer nuances in historical developments. The same holds true for India–Africa ties. The specifics of such ties may have changed with time; however, the underlying factors that have influenced each other have endured. The engagement between the two has gone on for centuries. Long before the colonial era, both exchanged not only goods but, more importantly, knowledge, ideas, techniques and traditions. Millet, for example, is an African crop introduced to India centuries ago. While continuing our current robust engagement with Africa on issues of today's relevance, it would be educative and more productive to explore the historical two-way flow of knowledge, information, and linguistic and cultural influences.

- **Oral Traditions in History and Literature**

  Both India and Africa have a glorious tradition of passing on history and literary works orally. India's Vedas, Upanishads, Ramayana, Mahabharata and the Puranas were passed down through generations for centuries only because of the oral tradition. Similarly, in Africa, the histories of various empires, tribes and villages were sung and passed on to the next generation. Luckily, some talented griots have kept the art alive and continue to practise it even today. It was a misconception of the West that only written history is authentic. In fact, the opposite is true: oral historical traditions are able to capture a more multi-dimensional view of history. It is also said that the African continent is home to more than a million proverbs. These proverbs are the compressed wisdom of generations, distilled over many centuries. The world would profit a great deal if there were wide dissemination of these proverbs. The session on "Languages and Literatures of Africa" dealt with these aspects in great depth.

- **Indigenous Knowledge Systems**

  Closely associated with the above is the question of indigenous knowledge. India and Africa have developed indigenous technologies and concepts over centuries. The idea of sustainable development, which we talk about today, was the fundamental pillar of lifestyles in both India and Africa. Traditional medicine and medical practices stressed the twin aspects of prevention and cure. Living in harmony with nature led to a holistic approach towards life itself. Discussions on this theme included the examination of "endogenous knowledge" in Zarma-Songhai societies (cross-border communities in Niger, Mali, Burkina Faso, Benin and North West Nigeria), and the recognition of the contribution of culture to understanding the contemporary world. In today's context, there is also the danger of business interests in the developed world appropriating traditional knowledge from Africa and India and patenting it, leading to huge financial losses for the countries concerned.

- **Art, Music, and Cinema**

  How can one discuss Africa without talking about music and dance, which are synonymous with African culture? The continent's contribution to the world in these fields cannot even be measured. There is no nation in the world today whose music and dance have not been influenced in some way by Africa. Rhythm and percussion are natural to Africans. To this, we should also add visual arts like drawing and painting, where Africa has some unique techniques and influences. Modern African cinema has drawn heavily from their traditional folklore and drama. Their narrative styles, symbolism and acting techniques bring a breath of fresh air to contemporary world cinema. The discussions also covered mutual influences in these areas between India and Africa.

- **Textile Traditions**

  Both India and Africa have very rich textile traditions going back millennia. In both geographies, every region and sub-region had its own techniques of weaving, dyeing and motifs. In pre-modern times, after agriculture, textiles provided the bulk of employment opportunities. Sadly, much of this tradition was lost during colonial times. Fortunately, there is now a conscious effort to revive this sector of the economy in Africa as well as India. However, the biggest impediment to these efforts comes from cheap, machine-made textiles that are imported in bulk.

  The exchange of textiles and techniques between India and Africa has been significant throughout their histories. Scholars explained the importance of textiles in the early interactions between Gujarat and Tanzania. Similarly, the *khanga/kanga* textile was a bridge between India and the Swahili Coast. While on the subject of textiles, one must also mention the other crafts that were highly advanced in Africa and India centuries ago. All household gadgets were handcrafted, and many continue to be produced even today.

- **India–Africa Partnership**

  To cover the continuities in India–Africa engagement, one session was devoted to the contemporary state of relations. There was a clear consensus that India–Africa relations have blossomed in the last few decades and are poised for greater growth. There is solidarity and mutual respect. Having gone through similar historical experiences, such as being colonised, both realise that much can be learnt from each other for mutual benefit and development. There is no fundamental conflict of interest between the two geographies. Many new ideas also emerged on how the engagement can be further strengthened.

These themes informed the structure of conference sessions, and evolved into the sections of this book. The real challenge for the conference was to get the appropriate experts and scholars for the sessions. Fortunately, we were able to identify the best of them, who very kindly agreed to participate. The biggest achievement was securing the participation of the late Ambassador Olabiyi Babalola Joseph Yaï, former Chairman of the UNESCO Executive Board who, despite his very busy schedule, consented to travel to New Delhi to deliver the Keynote Address at the inaugural session.

H.H.S. Viswanathan

Coordinator of the Conference,
Distinguished Fellow,
Observer Research Foundation,
New Delhi

Contributors

A. RACINE SENGHOR is a professor, literary critic, author of French textbooks and a poet and novelist for children. He hosts literary programmes and publishes cultural and educational articles. He has held various significant roles, including Director of Secondary Education, Director of the Arts, and Director of Cabinet of the Minister of Culture. He also coordinated the ARCHES Teaching Project and served as an expert for UNESCO and the OIF (Organisation internationale de la Francophonie). Senghor teaches at the National School of Administration in Senegal and Gaston Berger University. He is also a guest lecturer at Seoul National University, among others. He was the Administrator of the African Renaissance Monument, and is now the President of the Museum of Black Civilisations in Dakar.

AJEET N. MATHUR is a Professor of Practice at the Department of Management Studies in the Indian Institute of Technology Roorkee. He previously served as Professor of Strategy and International Business at IIM Ahmedabad, as the EU-TEMPUS Professor of European Integration and Internationalisation and held Faculty positions at K.U. Leuven in Belgium, the University of California at Berkeley, Helsinki School of Economics and University of Tampere. He was also the IFCI Chair Professor at ICRIER, New Delhi. He has published 29 books and over 150 papers in scientific journals and anthologies and is one of the authors of the *International Encyclopaedia of Laws*. Mathur has served as Director and CEO of the IAMR in the Planning Commission of India. He has been consulted by the ILO, the Asian Development Bank and the European Commission. He has authored a Country Case on Togo in West Africa and was involved with research in Egypt and South Africa.

GEORGE DANFORD NAHIMIANI is a Lecturer in the Department of Creative Arts at the University of Dar es Salaam, Tanzania. He received his PhD in Fine Arts from the same university for his thesis titled "Stylistic Evolution of Tingatinga Painting School from 1968–2011". He also holds an MA in Fine Arts studies and a BA in Fine and Performing Arts, both from the University of Dar es Salaam.

HARSH VARDHAN SHRINGLA is a Member of Parliament, Rajya Sabha. He has served as Foreign Secretary of India, Ambassador of India to the United States of America, High Commissioner to Bangladesh, and as Ambassador to Thailand. He has served in France (UNESCO), the USA (UN, New York), Vietnam (Hanoi and Ho Chi Minh City), Israel, and South Africa (Durban). He has published on conflict prevention, economic diplomacy, the Indian diaspora, and India–Bangladesh relations.

JOSÉ LUÍS MENDONÇA is a writer, journalist and teacher of Portuguese at the Agostinho Neto University, Angola. From 2012 till 2020, he worked as editor-in-chief of *Cultura*, a bi-weekly newspaper on literature and arts. He was a Press Counsellor at the Angola Permanent Delegation to UNESCO in Paris (2008–12), and a Communication and Information Officer at UNICEF in Luanda (1990–2007). Mendonça has published three novels, and several books of poetry, including *November Rain* and *A Flight of a Butterfly in the Inert Mechanism of Time* (which was awarded the Angola 30 Years Prize in 2005). He has also been honoured with the Children's Book Prize and the Lusophone General News award in 2005. In 2015, he received the National Prize for Culture and Arts.

K. MATHEWS (PhD, JNU) is a Professor of International Relations at the Addis Ababa University, Ethiopia. Previously, he was Professor of African Studies at the University of Delhi. He has held teaching and research positions at several prestigious institutions, including the Universities of Nigeria, Nsukka, Dar es Salaam in Tanzania, Oxford

University, Carlton University in Ottawa, the Africa Institute of South Africa in Pretoria, China Foreign Affairs University in Beijing and the United Nations Institute for Training and Research (UNITAR) in New York. He has over 100 publications to his credit, including two edited books, book chapters and journal articles. He is also a former Editor of *The African Review* (Dar es Salaam) and *Africa Quarterly* (ICCR, New Delhi). He is the founder and President of the African Studies Association of India (ASA).

KOFI ANYIDOHO is a poet, educator and literary scholar. He is currently serving on a post-retirement contract as Professor of Literature in the English Department at the University of Ghana-Legon. He has served as the Director of the CODESRIA African Humanities Institute Program, Acting Director of the School of Performing Arts, and Head of the English Department. He has lectured and performed his poetry in English and Ewe globally. He has published several books of poetry, journal articles, book chapters and edited books on African literature and the humanities that are recognised as major contributions. He was President of the US-based African Literature Association (ALA), the first occupant of the Kwame Nkrumah Chair in African Studies, and is a Fellow and past Vice President (Arts) of the Ghana Academy of Arts and Sciences.

MALA PANDURANG is the Principal at Dr BMN College, Mumbai. She is a postdoctoral fellow of the Alexander von Humboldt (AvH) Foundation, Germany, and was nominated as its "Ambassador Scientist to India" in 2019–2022. She has taught as a Fulbright Visiting Professor at the University of Texas in Austin. Her other research grants include the Charles Wallace In-UK Research grant, a major research grant from the University Grants Commission (UGC), the Aroon Tikekar Fellowship in Social Sciences from Asiatic Society (Mumbai), Associateship at the Indian Institute of Advanced Studies (Shimla) and NET/JRF from the UGC. Her areas of research include postcolonial writing, diaspora theory, and gender studies. She has published seven books and 45 research papers. She serves as the Series Editor for *Postcolonial Lives*, published by Brill.

M. OLABIYI BABALOLA JOSEPH YÄI was elected Chairman of UNESCO's Executive Board in 2007. Prior to this, he was the

Permanent Delegate of Benin to UNESCO. In the 1970s and 1980s, he was a consultant for culture and language policy in Benin, Burkina Faso, Nigeria, Togo and Mozambique. A specialist in African literature and languages, literacy, oral poetry and the cultures of the African diaspora, he was Director of the Institute of Cultural Studies, University of Ife, Nigeria, and Chair of the Department of African and Asian Languages and Literatures, University of Florida, USA.

MAMOUDOU DJIBO is an Associate Professor at Abdou Moumouni University, Niamey, Niger. He holds a PhD in Contemporary History from the University of Montreal. He served as the Chairperson of the Nigerian National Commission on Human Rights and Fundamental Liberties (2008–2010) and as the Minister of Higher Education, Research and Technology (1999–2000). He has published three books and several papers in academic journals, and was made Commander of the Order of the Niger.

MANJARI SINHA is a classical music and dance critic and musicologist. She has an MA in Sanskrit from Allahabad University, an MA in Music from Vikram University, Ujjain, and the degree of Sangeet Prabhakar in Hindustani Vocal, Tabla, Sitar and Kathak dance from Prayag Sangeet Samiti, Allahabad. She had further training in Sitar under Guru Pt. Arvind Parikh in the lineage of Ustad Vilayat Khan. She is the author of *Ustad Bade Ghulam Ali Khan* (1996), and contributed the chapter on Kathak for *Indian Dance: The Ultimate Metaphor*, ed. Shanta Serbjeet Singh (2000). A regular broadcaster on AIR and Doordarshan, Sinha has given lecture-demonstrations on Indian music and dance at the A.B. University, Zaria, Nigeria. Her articles in English and Hindi on the performing arts feature regularly in leading journals and periodicals. She writes columns on music and dance for the *The Hindu* and *Narthaki* web magazine.

MARTIAL ZE BELINGA is an economist, editorialist and sociologist regularly featured in influential European and African media; an associate member of the International Scientific Committee of the General History of Africa (UNESCO, vol. 9); and a member of the Executive Board of the African Community of Culture (formerly the African Society of Culture). From 1998 to 2008, he was the Editor of

Africana.com, an influential cultural and alternative French-speaking website. He teaches in vocational high schools and in institutes of higher education in France.

MICHÈLE RAKOTOSON is the author of numerous prize-winning novels, short stories and plays in French. She is also a translator and notably translated *The Diary of Anne Frank* into Malagasy. As the coordinator of the "Les Inédits de RFI-ACCT" competition, she launched several French-speaking authors. She served as an advisor to the Minister of Culture, Madagascar, and was the President of both the "Synergy of Authors, Publishers and Booksellers of Madagascar" and the "Bokiko Operation" association, both dedicated to promoting books. In these roles, she organised book fairs, literary events, and writing workshops. Rakotoson was responsible for the literary section of the *Revue Noire*, and is currently a columnist for the newspaper *Les Nouvelles* in Antananarivo, while also featuring on RFM radio. She was awarded the Grande médaille de la francophonie by the Académie Française in 2012 and the Grand Prix of the Indian Ocean and the Pacific by ADELF in 2006. In 2023, she received the Orange Prize. She is a Commander of Malagasy Arts and Letters.

NIVEDITA RAY is the Director (Research) at the Indian Council of World Affairs (ICWA), New Delhi. She completed her PhD from the School of International Studies, Jawaharlal Nehru University. She has conducted research on foreign policy and security issues in Sub-Saharan Africa. Her areas of research interest include Indian foreign policy, India–Africa relations, BRICS, IBSA, South–South development cooperation, the Indian diaspora, maritime security, gender and conflict. She has edited the books, *India and Africa Looking Ahead: Contemporary Realities and Emerging Prospects, India and Africa: The Road Ahead, Africa and India: A Partnership for Development and Growth* and *Tagore the Eternal Seeker: Footprints of the World Traveller*, and has authored *India's Engagement with East Africa: Opportunities and Challenges*.

N.N. VOHRA, Life Trustee (and past President) of the India International Centre, Delhi, is a recipient of the Padma Vibhushan. During his service in the IAS (1959–94), he held various important positions in the Government of India, including as Defence and Home Secretary, and, after retirement, as Principal Secretary to the Prime Minister. He has extensive experience in the security management arena. After the India–China conflict, he joined the Special Services Bureau, received training with the SAS of the UK, and served in the Western Himalaya theatre. Later, he served as Home Secretary of Punjab during the turbulent period after Operation Blue Star. He also served as Governor of the erstwhile State of Jammu and Kashmir during 2008–18. Author of Safeguarding India (2016), he has edited over a dozen books on varied themes.

OGUNDIRAN SOUMONNI is an Associate Professor of Innovation Policy and Management, and Programme Director of the Master of Management in Innovation Studies at the Wits Business School, Johannesburg. His research interests include the plural epistemological paradigms that underpin innovation domains, with a view to clarifying conditions under which more just societal outcomes might be attained. He obtained his PhD in Public Policy from the Georgia Institute of Technology in Atlanta, Georgia, USA, where his research focused on innovation studies and energy policy, and has held visiting research fellowships at the University of Edinburgh (2023–2024) and at the University of Ghana, Legon (2020). He is a co-editor of the multidisciplinary journal, *Black Histories: Dialogues*.

OKPEH O. OKPEH, JR. is a Professor of African History at the Department of History and International Studies, Federal University of Lafia. He is a Fellow and the current National President of the Historical Society of Nigeria. He is also a consultant on gender and development studies. Okpeh is well-published in both national and international peer-reviewed journals and currently serves as the Editor of the *FULafia Journal of History and International Studies* and the *FULafia Journal of Heritage and Development Studies*.

OUSMANE MAHAMANE TANDINA has been teaching Literature since 1984 and is currently a faculty member in the Department of Modern Languages at Abdou Moumouni University, Niamey. He has studied in Mali, Senegal and Ivory Coast, and has travelled to the

USA, Malaysia and other parts of Africa. Tandina has authored three books on epic traditions (critical studies, recordings and translations), and has published over 30 articles in international journals.

PENINA MUHANDO MLAMA (PhD) is a retired Professor of the University of Dar es Salaam, Tanzania, where she had a distinguished career as a Professor of Creative Arts. Throughout her tenure, she held numerous significant positions, including Associate Dean of Research, Dean of the Faculty of Arts and Social Services, and Deputy Vice Chancellor for Academics. She played a key role in developing the Tanzanian version of the Theatre for Development model. Mlama co-founded the TUSEME Girls' Empowerment for Gender Equality model, which uses theatre as a tool for social change. She also established the Gender Responsive Pedagogy model, aimed at improving teacher training. In 2016, she received the UNICEF Change Maker Award for girls' empowerment in recognition of her work with TUSEME. She is one of the most distinguished female authors writing in Swahili today. In addition to her plays, Mlama has written several scholarly works in English on Swahili literature.

RAJEN HARSHÉ has taught Political Science and International Relations for more than four decades at universities such as the University of Hyderabad, and South Asian University. He is the founder and former Vice Chancellor of the Central University of Allahabad (2005–10). He also served as the President of the G.B. Pant Social Science Institute (2014–20) in Allahabad. He has written extensively on African and International Affairs. His latest work is *African in World Affairs: Politics of Imperialism, the Cold War and Globalisation*, published in 2019.

S. SHAJI is an Associate Professor in the Department of Political Science at the University of Hyderabad. He was a Guest Professor at the Institute of Political and Social Studies, University of Würzburg, Germany, in 2012 and 2014, and a US Foreign Policy Fellow at the SUSI Program at Bard College, New York, in 2013. His research interests include India's relations with developing states, particularly in the Afro-Asian region, technology transfer and the foreign policy of developing states. He teaches courses such as "Global Politics", "India in World Affairs" and "International Relations of Emerging Powers".

SALOME MSHAI MWANGOLA is affiliated with the African Leadership Centre in Nairobi and is also associated with the Orature Collective and Performance Collective through advocacy and arts practice. Her current research focuses on "African fabric as a gateway to the world" for the UNESCO General History of Africa, vol. 9. Mwangola has published extensively on the arts, performance, culture and national liberation. In 2018, she was an Art and Literary Arts Fellow at the Bellagio Center, Italy, through a grant from the Rockefeller Foundation.

SANJUKTA BHATTACHARYA (PhD, JNU), now retired, was a Professor of International Relations at Jadavpur University, Kolkata. She has received the prestigious Fulbright Award twice and has published four books and over 80 articles and chapters in international and national journals and edited volumes. She has also presented over 150 papers at national and international conferences. Currently, she is a member of Academic Councils, Boards of Studies, and Doctoral Committees of universities around the country, an Executive Board member of several prestigious academic bodies and Member, Advisory Board, Jadavpur Association of International Relations and Visiting Professor, IMPRI, New Delhi. Her research interests include bilateral and multilateral international relations, African studies, American studies, women's issues, medical ethics and human rights. Her latest work is an English translation of the novel, *Maa*, by Anurupa Devi, one of Bengal's pioneering women writers.

SUHAS BORKER is the founder of *Citizens First TV* (*CFTV*), established in 1981, and has been making documentary films since 1980. He was the Head of *CFTV NEWS* from 1993 to 2024, and covered/interviewed world leaders, including former South African President Nelson Mandela, former Namibian President Sam Nujoma, former Malaysian Prime Minister Mahathir Mohamad, former Secretary-General of the 1955 Bandung Conference Roeslan Abdulgani, former South African Foreign Minister Alfred Nzo, former Egyptian Foreign Minister Amr Moussa and former Vietnamese Foreign Minister Nguyen Dy Nien. His major films include *Tees Janvari: Jagaran aur Gavahi* (1991)—a documentary on Gandhiji's martyrdom, and *The*

Unfinished Revolution (1998)—a documentary on the history and relevance of the Non-Aligned Movement (NAM) for the NAM Durban Summit, 1998, which was telecast by South African Broadcasting Corporation (SABC) in 1998.

SUKRITA PAUL KUMAR was born and brought up in Kenya. A poet, translator and painter, she translated Joginder Paul's novel *Blind*. Currently, she is the Editor of *Indian Literature*, the journal of the Sahitya Akademi (India's Academy of Letters). Her critical books are *Narrating Partition* and *Conversations on Modernism*. She held the Aruna Asaf Ali Chair at the University of Delhi, and was a Fellow of the Indian Institute of Advanced Study, Shimla. She was honorary faculty at the Durrell Centre in Corfu and an invited poet at the International Writing Programme, Iowa, and the Hong Kong Baptist University. She was awarded the Rabindranath Tagore Prize for Literature, 2023 for her book of poems, *Salt & Pepper*. Her latest publication is *Yellow*, her book of poemlets, brought out by Sahitya Akademi, New Delhi.

Chapter 1

Understanding Africa: African Perspectives and Epistemological Considerations

Keynote address
M. Olabiyi Babalola Joseph Yãi

My first duty is to humbly and confidently congratulate the Government of India and the India International Centre for the choice of the theme for this colloquium: "Understanding Africa: Continuity and Change". In many international circles nowadays, the very concept of Africa carries the semantic weight of being "taken for granted". We are thus confronted with the paradox of Africa being a sempiternal problem because she is un-problematised by the same impenitent "experts" who claim to know and understand her. Remember Tagore:

> Alas, Africa of shadows,
> your human face remains unknown
> to the darkened vision of contempt.
> (From "Africa". Composed in 1937, this poem was included in his collection *Patraput* published in 1938)

In the context of epistemological arrogance in international circles when Africa is concerned, the gerund "understanding" in the title stands out as a humble (pre)disposition to learn through an ideally collective and consensual process. This attitude, in itself, warrants optimism about the outcome of our colloquium, and I do believe that our conference will mark the beginning of a long journey for African and Indian scholars and decision-makers.

Allow me to re-enact the gesture of Yoruba women poets called *yùngbà*. These are court poets who, like all poets in Yorubaland, enjoy poetic licence. They ritually begin their court performance by saying:

> *Kabiyèsi, E jé n sààlo tán*
> *Kí n tóó sàfojúdi*
> (Your Majesty, first I'll be courteous
> Before being rude)

This terse distich needs an exegesis. The women poets are, in effect, warning the king that while they will certainly praise him and his ancestors, they will also unflinchingly interject caustic, critical remarks about his administration during their performance. They are able to do this because, as permanent court residents, they are privileged observers of the conception and implementation of royal policies. In addition, they routinely send young girls of their suite to the market to gather information from the populace. The women court poets are thus the vox populi, the voice of the people, in the very heart of the kingdom.

I have always admired the sophistication and noblesse oblige approach of these women wordsmiths. I, therefore, intend to emulate them in my opening remarks. However, in doing so, I will invert their tactics while endorsing their strategy. In other words, in the first part of this address, I will briefly yet critically assess the overall performance of African governments over the last 60 years. More than occasionally, I will be unapologetically caustic in my assessment.

I take it as axiomatic that an understanding of the complex symbol called Africa must be predicated on a knowledge of Africa that is acceptable and agreeable as such to Africans.

Thus, adopting a longue durée perspective, I shall endeavour to examine the felicitous conditions for acquiring knowledge of Africa. This constitutes the second part of my presentation. I will conclude my remarks with some suggestions as to what I see as the specific responsibilities of India and Africa in our era of uncertainties and faltering globalisation.

The period between Bandung (1955) and the Tricontinental Conference (Havana, 1966) is often referred to as the African independence decade. Most "modern" African states became independent during this period. Even those that became independent after this time drew inspiration from these two landmark global conferences of the oppressed peoples. Indian political thinkers and activists played a critical role in the conception and organisation of both gatherings.

Galvanised by the Independence of India and the Bandung Conference, Kwame Nkrumah, the first President of Ghana and a leading advocate of Pan-Africanism, addressed the African people with his celebrated *cri de cœur* in biblical style: "Seek ye FIRST the political kingdom, and all other things shall be added unto you".

The African people responded massively and enthusiastically, following Nkrumah and their other leaders. The most cultured literati among the patriotic African youth everywhere chanted the first line of a poem by Tagore, "Blessed am I that I am born to this land and that I had the luck to love her".[1]

Irrespective of whether they were characterised by political analysts as leaning towards the left or the right, all African governments signed a minimal social contract with their people at independence. This included:

- Political freedom and independence from the colonial power
- A commitment to economic and social welfare, especially food security and health for the rural masses, with special attention to women and the youth
- Mass education and literacy in African and European languages
- African unity and solidarity
- Neutrality and non-alignment
- Friendship with the people of the world, particularly formerly

1 *The English Writings of Rabindranath Tagore*, ed. Sisir Das (1994), p. 341.

or still colonised people, and solidarity with the oppressed people under apartheid

Today, 55 years after Bandung, it is intellectually sound and fair to assess the performance of African states against the socio-political Bandung-Tricontinental template. The overall performance has been appallingly disappointing.

Political freedom has proven to be evanescent almost everywhere. Instead, we have witnessed neocolonialism and, indeed, recolonisation in Libya, Mali, Burkina Faso, Côte d'Ivoire, Niger and the Democratic Republic of the Congo.

Instead of food security, we have famine and the massive importation of frozen and dangerous food from European, American and some Asian states.

Instead of being dressed in African attire dyed with indigo and natural dyes, our youth roam the streets in jeans made of African cotton but manufactured in Bangladesh, and T-shirts made of synthetic fibre with alienating sentences in languages they oftentimes cannot read.

At independence, our people wanted states based on *sui generis*, endogenous African political thought, enriched with other political ideas that were critically examined and compatible with our values. Instead, the political elite imposed on our people the "democracy of the others", to borrow Amartya Sen's phrase, complete with its inevitable rigged elections, violence, one-party systems, life presidents, and ... one emperor, at least so far. Remember the infamous emperor Bokassa I!

At independence, there were dreams of industrialisation and of an African socialism that would ensure minimal economic justice. Instead, the elite have imposed an economic system centred on the extraction of our natural resources and total extraversion of the economic system. As a result, our youth try every imaginable route to migrate to a mythical European Eldorado, with massive hecatombs in the Sahara Desert and the Mediterranean Sea.

In the realm of religion, African endogenous religions, Islam and Christianity, jointly welcomed, celebrated and blessed independence. But nowadays, African religions and spiritualties are demonised.

Islamism, jihadism and other travesties of Islam and Christianity are the order of the day, promoting intolerance, violence and obscurantism, while favouring cultism. Tartuffery is rampant across religions, with the worship of Mammon becoming the common denominator.

Despite triumphalist declarations in Addis Ababa, the reality of African unity and integration is appallingly disappointing. Today, it is easier for a West African citizen to go to London or Paris—depending on who their former colonial power was—than to visit any capital in Central or East Africa. Worse still, at least two thirds of the salaries of African Union workers come from the coffers of the European Union. This fact is shameful by any standard. But the clearest sign of our governments' lack of commitment to the ideal—or the idea of—African unity is that the headquarters of the African Union in Addis Ababa was not built through the collective effort of our states, as one would naturally expect. Instead, it was a gift from the PRC (People's Republic of China). In all African traditions, building a house is a collective effort of the community, whether from a lineage or a village. No one expects their house to be built by outsiders. While I appreciate the generous intention of the PRC authorities, I join the African youths in blaming our leaders for their collective dereliction of dignity. Solidarity should not be confused with mendicity.

As the Yoruba poets would put it, "I could speak until tomorrow" on the subject of the failures of Africa's ruling classes since independence. But suffice it to say, that compared to other bourgeoisies around the world, who played the role of midwives of modernity in their respective societies, ours is an unimaginative, consumerist *lumpenbourgeoisie*.

But I fear that you may accuse me of being an Afro-pessimist, which I am not. In fact, I am an inveterate Afro-optimist. Understanding Africa involves much more than simply chronicling the turpitudes of African states over a mere half-century, when that represents just a small fraction of millennia of African history. We must turn our gaze from the *lumpenbourgeoisie* to the feelings, thoughts, practices and actions of other, more creative Africans—both past and present—if we are to do justice to this GRANDE DAME of world history called Africa. (I can only imagine Africa as a noble and beautiful lady.)

Yes! Grande Dame Africa lives! Her heart and spirit are intact. She is a Mother Courage who can sing, laugh and dance despite all odds. She is alive and vibrant because she *reinvents* herself daily, although not much is said about her remarkable ability to rise like a phoenix. This resilience explains why those who really know her can only be inveterate Afro-optimists.

Despite the calamitous picture I have just painted, some African states, such as Ethiopia, Namibia, Botswana, Rwanda, Ghana, and Mauritius deserve commendation for trying to meet the needs of their people. They are often described as "success stories". But success on whose terms? These nations are labelled as "good students" of the Bretton Woods institutions, which renders their success stories somehow suspicious. The real issue is whether when envisaged in the longue durée perspective and judged against African criteria of human-cum-nature well-being and progress, their success stories can be deemed credible and sustainable. Therefore, "Allegro, ma non troppo", to borrow from musicological terminology, should be our judgement of these success stories at this juncture in African history. Let us wait and see.

However, Africa provides us with daily reasons to remain optimistic. Success stories in all walks of life abound at the village, association and individual levels. The daily inventiveness of Africans is truly phenomenal, though it often goes underreported. For example, I can mention alternative and innovative agricultural projects like the Songhai Project in Porto-Novo, Bénin, started by Dr Nzamujo and replicated across West Africa, the Women Artisans Cooperative Centre in Mali, initiated by Aminata Dramane Traoré, and many others. Scholarly attention is now being turned to these unsung success stories. Just two years ago, in 2017, the University of São Paulo, Brazil, organised a symposium titled "*A África de que não se fala*" ("That Africa about which No One Speaks"). There are thousands of young inventors in Africa who are now coming together in regional, continental or even global networks. Electronics and computer engineering are their domains of predilection, but they are also making strides in areas like drone manufacturing. In 2012, four Nigerian female teenagers were reported to have devised an electricity plant working with urine.

At this juncture, I must point out a blind spot in African historical studies, or at least an area that has been insufficiently researched. We have yet to undertake a thorough investigation of systemic entities in Africa, as opposed to her enslavers, as alternative societal models. We need detailed studies of the economic and social dimensions of maroon societies, compared with their ancestral African counterparts. Haiti, frequently described as the only successful slave revolt in human history, has oftentimes been described as a failed state. However, it is pertinent to recall that in the early days of the Haitian nation, there was a debate among the Haitian élite about what form the state should adopt after the end of slavery. Those who argued that the new state should beat Europe on its own terms prevailed over those who wished to adopt an African ancestral state structure. From an African historical perspective, Haiti, therefore, represents a double failure: the failure of the early Haitian élite for betraying the African majority by opting to adopt their oppressors'—the French—model; and failure again because they were not successful in implementing the chosen model.

In retrospect, Haiti must be seen today as a rejection by the African people, as opposed to the élite, of the European model of societal arrangement. I want to emphasise that we cannot begin to understand Africa unless we critically re-examine our knowledge claims about the continent. The first intellectual gesture in this reassessment is to acknowledge the AFRICAN EXCEPTION.

Africa is the birthplace of humankind. As the eminent African thinker Joseph Ki-Zerbo once said, she physically, biologically, intellectually and spiritually gave birth to humankind.[2] This fact, this seniority and its possible implications have not always been given their due weight by analysts of African affairs. Now, as we know, seniority ranks high in African worldviews.

---

2 "The Cradle of Man", in *Africa and its History: A Continent Viewed from Within: The UNESCO Courier* August–September (Paris: UNESCO, 1979), p. 39.

Another characteristic of the African exception is that no other continent, no other human group, no other "race"—to use a term with no scientific value, but with cruel efficiency—has been subjected to the level of dehumanisation, racism, discrimination and *thingification* that Africans have endured.

Yes, in a theological controversy, the infamous Valladolid Controversy staged by Christianity in Spain (1550–1), we were denied a soul by the Christian doctrine so that we could be used like animals without guilty conscience on the part of the Christian nations. We were called "peça" in Portuguese, meaning "object", "piece", "ebony wood"—therefore, and henceforth, *thingified* for:

- Many centuries of human traffic and slavery through the Sahara and the Mediterranean by Arabs and Europeans
- Many centuries of slavery across the Indian Ocean
- Five centuries of traffic and transatlantic slave trade by Europeans
- Two centuries of colonialism, neocolonialism and apartheid

Yet, part of the African exception is that the African people emerged from these long centuries of denial of humanity as "magnificently resilient" (as Christiane Taubira puts it), bearing "the Muse of Forgiveness" (as Wole Soyinka described it). They came out with "flowers of evil" long before the French poet Charles Baudelaire coined the expression.

An expected consequence of long centuries of slavery and *thingification* is a problematic identity and naming. This is an epistemological issue, as the act of identifying and naming is the very beginning of knowledge. The power to name is bestowed upon the "namer" or baptiser, granting them control over the one being named or baptised. So, who named Africa? Borrowing *Ifriqiah* from the Berbers, the Romans gave the name *Africa* to the coastal fringe of the north of the continent. The faithful inheritors of the Roman Empire later applied this name to the whole continent.

Nevertheless, despite being in bondage in the Americas, enslaved Blacks discovered and embraced their shared heritage and resisted the violence of Euro-baptism. Using synecdoche as a device from

African languages, they called their continent "Aruanda" in Brazil and "Guiné" in Haiti. The most expressive and significant of these names is "Ilú Ayé" in Brazil, a Yoruba phrase which translates as "the abode of life", in stark contrast to the servitude endured by our enslaved ancestors in the Americas, which they experienced as "the abode of death".

Lamentably, these subtle African coinages were not adopted by the Pan-Africanist élites of the 19th century. Therefore, African intellectuals of our generation have inherited the task of naming as adequately as possible our unique and complex experience, for "name thyself" is the implication of the so-called Socratic and universal dictum "know thyself". This is why the International Scientific Committee of the General History of Africa has now come up with the new concept and appellation of "Global Africa".

However, before embracing this concept, an effort at "de-baptising" is absolutely necessary. We must reject those appellations imposed on us by our racist enslavers and colonisers: White North Africa, White South Africa, Black sub-Saharan Africa, Brown Horn of Africa; or Anglophone, Francophone, Hispanophone and Lusophone Africa. (Would India ever endorse the appellation "Anglophone Asia"?)

Taking this a step further, the idea and ideals of Pan-Africanism—now reframed as Global Africa—take stock of our shared experience as the African exception, while highlighting the African presence in the world.

It allows us to craft an African and diasporic common vision of history, free from Eurocentric chronologies. It opens the possibility of restoring a transversal cultural continuum between the continent and its diasporas, emphasising different circulations within the Afro-diasporic spaces (circulation of people, ideas, technologies, and know-how). It proposes a dynamic and textured mapping of Africans' contributions to diverse forms of modernity (cultural, political, intellectual, and scientific).

In addition to being in consonance with the African Union's important decision to recognise the African diaspora as its sixth region, the concept of Global Africa is expected to provide researchers with a new acumen, both endogenous and universal. It is a welcome concept in a context of contestation of Eurocentric models and narratives, calling for paradigm shifts, epistemological pluralism and the emergence of new knowledge from the people and intellectuals of Asia, Latin America and Africa.

Aimé Césaire, one of Africa's best sons and poetic voices, likened Global Africa to a river and painted her in unforgettable colours:

> ... River
> to which all is permitted
> above all wash away my banks
> widen me
> that an ear I might auscultate
> the new coralline heart of the tides
> and let the whole horizon venture forth
> vaster and vaster before me
> and take off from your snout
> henceforth
> swirling
> and liquid
> ("Your Portrait", in *Lost Body*)

Once the "Name thyself" condition is satisfied, even if provisionally, several other hurdles appear on the road of the quest for a knowledge that bears the stamp of credibility in the eyes of Africans.

We cannot pretend to forget the fact that "Africanism", or the collective body of knowledge and knowledge claims, known as "African Studies", was originally a peripheral branch of "Orientalism". In the history of European ideas, African Studies as a collection of disciplines is a *colonial science.* Yes, I did say colonial science. This supreme oxymoron betrays the Eurocentrism of constituted knowledge.

For a long time and in haughty tranquillity, France had an Académie des Sciences Coloniales. The name has changed, but certainly not the content. The USA took African Studies from European states and brought them to their apogee during the 1960s and 1980s with the creation of "Area Studies" in a bid to counter the spread of communism in Africa. As one can see, Africa has always been an "object of study" not for herself, but for external interests, foreign to the continent and its people. In my opinion, even with the American involvement in African studies, we are still, epistemologically speaking, within the purview of a colonial science.

Congolese philosopher and author Valentin Mudimbe coined the phrase *bibiothèque coloniale* (colonial library) to describe the collective discourse of the missionaries, explorers, colonial administrators, ethnologists, anthropologists and other commentators on Africa during the colonial period (Mudimbe 1988). But we do know that colonial discourse did not magically stop with the independence of African countries. The truth is that African Studies—in its essence, orientation, telos, and funding—remains a colonial science par excellence.

The concept of "coloniality", introduced by theorists from Latin America and Asia, allows us to expand the notion of "colonial library" to include much of the discursive production on Africa far beyond independence, perhaps including the writings of Mudimbe himself, especially since they are not known to be rooted in an African intellectual tradition. At the very least, the concept of the "colonial library" has to be revisited, and its content and scope thoroughly examined. While waiting for this necessary epistemological overhauling, as recommended by our International Scientific Committee, all concepts drawn from the colonial library must be regarded as suspect and provisional.

If we cannot base our understanding of Africa on the colonial library, what alternatives do we have?

The first epistemological posture and gesture is to be convinced that *another knowledge of Africa is possible and necessary.*

The content of this new understanding must be the collective effort of our generation and those to come, for destroying the old colonial library and building a new one is not an easy task. The creative destruction of the colonial library and its replacement by a new body of knowledge in tune with the interests and intellectual traditions of Africans must be done by both non-alienated Africans of

Global Africa and non-African scholars who align with the intellectual agenda of Global Africa.

Before I proceed, I would like to quote an important section from the Preamble of the Constitution of UNESCO:

> The governments of the state parties to the present Convention, on behalf of their peoples declare:
>
> That a peace based exclusively upon the political and economic arrangements of governments would not be a peace which could secure the unanimous, lasting and sincere support of the peoples of the world, and that the peace must therefore be founded, if it is not to fail, upon the intellectual and moral solidarity of mankind.

This strong statement is foundational and speaks more of the mission and purpose of UNESCO than the often-quoted section: "Since wars begin in the minds of men, it is in the minds of men that the defences of peace must be constructed..." which is more circumstantial and inspired by the aftermath of the Second World War.

More importantly, it refutes and dissolves the idea of cultures as "soft power" serving another, presumably superior, power. Another knowledge, as a prerequisite to understanding the people of Global Africa on their own terms is, therefore, a constitutive part of the "foundations of the intellectual and moral solidarity of humankind".

Paramount in acquiring that kind of knowledge of Global Africa is the learning of her endogenous languages on the African continent. How can one claim to respect people as humans and yet refuse to learn to speak and study their languages? The issue is not a choice between African or European languages. Precolonial African states have developed a culture of accumulation rather than substitution in the area of languages. They encouraged and practised polyglotism and multiculturalism for centuries. Professor Joseph Ki-Zerbo, in his characteristic profound and pedagogical style, likened African languages to the homes Africans live in, and European languages to bridges that link us with the global world. He concludes by saying, "European languages imported into Africa may be bridges toward the globalised world, nonetheless it is difficult to leave one's home to go and live under or on a bridge".[3]

The literature on African languages as a prerequisite for African Renaissance is abundant, and I need not dwell on what African linguists and other literati have always taken for granted (UNESCO, AU, Ngugi Wa Thiong'o). Suffice it to say that African languages are a *sine qua non* condition for truly understanding Africa.

We cannot begin to know and understand Africa without listening to the messages and teachings embedded in her worldviews, philosophies and sagacity, which are expressed through a variety of texts, discourses and forms.

This implies an epistemological and methodological approach that revisits classic texts such as Egyptian hieroglyphic inscriptions, Kurukan Fuga, Ker Issa, Ifá, Kaidara, the Ubuntu teachings, the Mvet, etc., usually dismissed as "folklore" or "oral literature". But African worldviews are also encapsulated in art forms like Makonde, Kongo and Yoruba sculptures, Igbo women's *uli* drawings, *adire* indigo textiles, Haitian *Naïf Art*, the paintings of artists like Wifredo Lam, Mestre Didi Santos, Abdias do Nascimento, Onabrakpeya, and Malangatana and installations by Peju Layiwola.

Surely a comprehensive African understanding of the messages within these texts cannot be achieved without first *indisciplining* the disciplines we have inherited from Western institutions and approaches to knowledge. If we truly believe another kind of knowledge is possible, if we want to critique the colonial library, and if we want to remove, in Wole Soyinka's words, the "layers of visual cataracts [that] accumulate and harden over centuries, obscuring a truthful apprehension of the continent"[4], then, in other words, if we truly desire to understand Africa, *we must be prepared to learn to unlearn.* I am tempted to risk the following formula: "Unlearning from the colonial library is the beginning of wisdom."

---

3 Quoted by A. Samassékou in "From Eurocentrism to a Polycentric Vision of the World: Advocacy for a Paradigm Shift", *Diogenes*, vol. 58, no. 1–2 (2011): pp. 149–50.

4 Wole Soyinka, *Of Africa*. Ithaca: Yale University Press, 2012, p. 26.

I now would like to foreground a feature of the African exception that I deliberately left out earlier. Because we Africans are "*les fils ainés du monde*":

> Truly the elder sons of the world
> permeable to all the breaths of the world
> fraternal compass points for all the breaths of the world
> deep lake bed for all the waters of the world
> spark of the sacred fire of the world
> flesh of the very flesh of the world,
> palpitating with the very movement of the world!
> (Aimé Césaire in *Journal of a Homecoming /Cahier d'un retour au pays natal*, tr. by N. Gregson Davis)

Xenophilia has become a basic feature of our cultures. We have opened our doors to all manners of foreigners, welcoming their creeds, arts, philosophies and religions. As Wole Soyinka aptly put it, "Put simply: politically, technologically, commercially, and in religion, Africa has never posed a hegemonic threat."[5] Africa was "unconcerned to vanquish, but playing the game of the world", as Césaire observed.[6]

Tolerance, openness and solidarity have always been central to Global Africa, even in the face of persecution and bondage. It is, therefore, profoundly African to recognise that "'Understanding Africa" today—more than ever before—cannot be fully dissociated from "Understanding the universe". As President Kwame Nkrumah once said, "The independence of Ghana was meaningless without the independence of the rest of Africa". In the same vein, a Global Africa Renaissance is inconceivable without a vision for the global reimagining and reordering of our universe, ideally into a *pluriverse*. Our era is defined by "globalisation". Yet, those who coined the term "globalisation" did so carefully—and deceptively—in the intransitive.

Globalisation never tells, never confesses that which it globalises. Instead, it presents itself as something ineluctable, driven by inexorable

---

5 Ibid., p. 25.

6 Aimé Césaire, *Journal of a Homecoming/ Cahier d'un retour au pays natal*, translated by N. Gregson Davis. Durham: Duke University Press, 2017.

logic—a desirable and inevitable stage in the world's development. But we know better. Those who, for the last five centuries, have been—and continue to be—globalised know that intransitive globalisation means hegemonic Westernisation of the universe, of its lifestyles and deathstyles. And we know that this does not augur well for humankind, as this type of globalisation produces more victims than beneficiaries, and it is not sustainable. Fearing that its days or years may be numbered, intransitive globalisation seeks to survive by passing the mantle to powers in the Global South. As a result, a new discourse emerges among some intellectuals in the North, proposing that the 21st century will, or should, be South-hegemonic.

Theories now abound in the North regarding the future emergence of a "Chinafrica" "Indiafrica" or even a "Chindiafrica" as the next hegemonic powers—new robes and disguises of intransitive globalisation. The real question, however, is this: must we perpetuate the "hegemonic temper" of the West? Do the enslaved, by necessity, have to envy their enslavers and continuously reproduce their misdeeds and lifestyles?

To these questions, I believe the philosophies and worldviews of India and Africa will respond negatively. For centuries, perhaps even millennia, African cultures engaged in dialogue with India and the Orient in general. Even far-away West African cultures participated in this exchange, as evidenced by Indian loanwords in West African languages. For instance, *tanga* refers to the smallest coin in Yoruba, Hausa and other West African languages. I have been reliably informed that its origin is a Hindi word. However, with the onset of the Atlantic Slave trade, Europeans literally "dis-Oriented" Africa. The West then colonised India. Ever since, India and Africa have been in the same boat, both metaphorically and, sometimes, literally. Like Siamese twins, we found ourselves together in countries such as Mauritius, South Africa, Kenya, Uganda, Tanzania, La Réunion, Suriname, Guyana, Trinidad and Tobago, as well as cities like London, Birmingham, Amsterdam, and Paris.

While, as Tagore emphatically reminded us, "Alas! the Man of the East never meets the Man of the West", the Man and Woman of Africa *did* meet the Man and Woman of India. From this meeting, we produced and shared the legacy of Mahatma Gandhi, who, in turn, inspired figures like Madiba Nelson Mandela, Martin Luther King, and Kwame Nkrumah. None of them would recommend an *Indiafrica* with a Western hegemonic temper.

In a broken world where liberal capitalism desperately clings to survival by promoting the idea of man-robot alloy—at a time when we precisely need a new human alloy—I trust that Gandhi and his disciples will call us to a radically different responsibility. That responsibility, I believe, is for African and Indian intellectuals to start putting together novel ideas with a view to fixing a broken world. And those ideas must be rooted in our ancient philosophies, worldviews and sagacity—"our pure multi-coloured selves", in Césaire's words.

I, therefore, would like to suggest that each India–Africa summit be preceded by a summit of Indian and African artists, women and men of culture, economists, writers and intellectuals.

Among the powers that organise regular summits with the African Union, India stands out as the closest to African hearts for understandable historical and cultural reasons. It is therefore expected that India would not harbour the same hegemonic intentions towards African states as do some Euro-American and Asian powers. None of these states has so far shown interest in hosting a non-economic summit that focuses on culture and intellectual matters.

India could pioneer this experiment, showing her willingness and determination, and—I need to quote Tagore again—to apprehend Africa's "human face which remains unknown".

My senior brother and friend, Wole Soyinka—an iconic herald of Africa's human face—echoed Tagore's words nearly a century later:

> The value of Africa to the world remains its untapped source—but source for what? As an 'invisible continent'—invisible as in Ellison's parable of invisibility—populated solely by much coveted inert, material assets? Or, alternatively, as a humanized resource for continuing self-transformation that will place an enlightened face on a renewed Scramble for Africa (Soyinka, *Of Africa* 2012, p. 26).

Understanding Africa—whether driven by pragmatic reasons or a gesture of human solidarity—requires discovering not only Africa's "human face" (Tagore) and "backup heart" (Césaire) but also those of the people of the world.

In this domain, Chinua Achebe encourages us with: "Morning yet on Creation Day." And though Ayi Kwei Armah, another African writer, realistically but optimistically advises us that, "The beautyful Ones are not yet born", Tagore—the Eldest and the Great Global Optimist—will have the final word:

"I know that the flower one day shall blossom crowning my thorns".[7]

References

Achebe, Chinua. *Morning Yet on Creation Day*. New York: Anchor Books, 1976.

Armah, Ayi Kwei. *The Beautyful Ones are not yet Born*. Boston: Houghton-Mifflin, 1968.

Baudelaire, Charles. *Les Fleurs du Mal*. Paris: Auguste Poulet-Malassis. 1861. Available online: https://fleursdumal.org/1861-table-of-contents (accessed on 4 March 2025).

Césaire, Aimé. *Journal of a Homecoming* (*Cahier d'un retour au pays natal*), translated by N. Gregson Davis. Durham: Duke University Press, 2017.

Mudimbe, Valentin Y. *The Invention of Africa: Gnosis, Philosophy and the Order of Knowledge*. Bloomington: Indiana University Press, 1988.

Soyinka, Wole. *The Burden of Memory, the Muse of Forgiveness*. New York: Oxford University Press, 1999.

———. *Of Africa*. Ithaca: Yale University Press, 2012.

7 The references are to Chinua Achebe's collection of essays, *Morning Yet on Creation Day* (1976), the novel by Ghanaian Ayi Kwei Armah, *The Beautyful Ones are not yet Born* (1968), and the first line of a poem by Tagore first published in 1914, and reprinted in *The English Writings of Rabindranath Tagore*, ed. Sisir Das, vol. 1 (1994), p. 347.

Ki-Zerbo, Joseph. "The Cradle of Man", in *Africa and its History: A Continent Viewed from Within: The UNESCO Courier*, August–September. Paris: UNESCO, 1979.

Samassékou, A. "From Eurocentrism to a Polycentric Vision of the World: Advocacy for a Paradigm Shift", *Diogenes* vol. 58, no. 1–2 (2011): pp. 147–58.

Tagore, Rabindranath. *Patraput*. Kolkata: Visvabharati Granthalaya, 1938, pp. 63–65.

———. *The English Writings of Rabindranath Tagore*, volume 1, 'Poems', ed. Sisir Kumar Das. New Delhi: Sahitya Akademi, 1994.

PART 1
Africa–India Connections Across Time

Chapter 2

Historical Linkages between Africa and India

Okpeh O. Okpeh, Jr.

Introduction

Very little has been written or known about Africa–India relations prior to modern times, even though they have had a history of close contacts and interactions dating back centuries. Even in modern times, scholars who have attempted to document this history often trace its origins to the centrifugal forces of colonisation (Jenkins 1961, pp. 291–6; Isaacs 1972; Stanley 1906). However, such a history is surely inadequate because these narratives were never told from the standpoint of the races directly involved in and affected by the making of that history. Instead, they were written from an obviously particular and grossly limited perspective, with the aim of justifying certain actions or even inaction (Davidson 1972).[1] However, the denial of agency this entailed for Africa and India makes it necessary to review this perspective based on new evidence on the subject.

1 As colonies, Africa and the Indian subcontinent were victims of Eurocentrism, and early European scholars documented only the activities of European colonialists in these societies. Such prejudiced notions shaped the way these Europeans understood African and Indian societies. For more on this, see Basil Davidson, *The Growth of African Civilization: East and Central Africa to the late Nineteenth Century*, London: Longman Publishing Company, 1972.

Our purpose in this chapter is threefold: first, to explore the historical linkages between Africa and India, with the aim to correct certain assumptions about their nature, pattern, and implications for both societies; second, to examine the contours and sinews of these historical linkages as a foundation for understanding Africa–India relations and their strategic role in South–South cooperation; and third, to assess the prospects of these relations in the competitive and globalised world of the 21st century.

My arguments are divided into five mutually reinforcing sections, including the introduction and conclusion. Following this introduction, I attempt to establish the basis of Africa–India relations by showing that geographical proximity, variations in ecosystems and resource endowments, and, to some degree, common historical experiences underpinned Africa–India relations both in the past and in the present. On the basis of a careful examination of these variables, I proceed to interrogate Africa–India relations from a temporal perspective, arguing that linkages between them have never been episodic. On the contrary, the relationship has evolved over time, thriving through centuries of disruptions and adjustments. In the fourth section, I will map out the prospects of these linkages, particularly against the backdrop of the challenges posed by the globalising world of the 21st century. I advance far-reaching recommendations on how India and Africa can leverage their demographic and other advantages to extract favourable concessions from the Global North. I conclude my arguments in the fifth section.

Understanding the Basis of Africa–India Linkages: Key Assumptions

It is possible to make some preliminary assumptions about Africa and India and, on that basis, explain their historical affinities and complementarities. The first is their geographical proximity. Throughout history, geography has determined how people lived with and related to each other. It is critical to the ecosystem and underlies the biodiversity of nations. In the case of Africa and India, geographical proximity and variation in resource endowments were two factors that brought them close from the remote past to the present. It also determined the character and pattern of economic relations between Africa and India. Secondly, both Africa and India are multicultural, home to diverse ethnicities, cultures and social systems. The term "multiculturalism" is loosely used here to underscore the existence of a mosaic of ethnic groups brought together by the contingencies of history.

Related to this multicultural diversity is the fact that both Africa and India share demographic buoyancy and advantage, which have been considered both a blessing and a curse. India's population is estimated at 1,374,529,581, representing 17.7 per cent of the total world population, while the combined population of African countries stands at 1,327,346,413, representing 16.72 per cent of the global population.[2] Of the world's most populous countries, in 2020 *Worldometer* ranked India second, Nigeria seventh, Egypt 14th and DR Congo 16th. Some analysts argue that during the 20th century, high population growth rates in both Africa and India failed to create and accelerate the expected pace of development.[3] As a result, both regions have long struggled with poverty and other challenges associated with rising populations in the midst of plenty.

Africa and India have a common history of being victims of Western imperialism. Starting with the 15th-century "voyages of discoveries", made possible by advancements in naval technology, Spain and Portugal reached Africa and India, among other places. This was soon followed by the slave trade and, later, colonialism, which left both societies ravaged by alien forces (Rodney 1976). The conquest and sequestration of land that both regions suffered under colonialism in the 19th and 20th centuries remain important episodes in their histories. Although colonialism was eventually wrestled down, the problems it created in India and in the countries

---

2 See https://www.worldometers.info/world-population (accessed on 5 February 2020).

3 It is argued that such quantitative growth in population which was not matched by qualitative improvements in the standard of living of the people foregrounded the high level of poverty which haunted Africa and India during the century under review (Falola and Odey 2017; Okpeh, Jr., 2018; Harrison 1960; Jalan 1992; Crosette 1993; Tharoor 1997).

of Africa still persist. The colonial experience, along with their struggles against it, as well as their membership of supranational organisations like the Commonwealth of Nations and the United Nations, have continued to pull Africa and India closer. Their common colonial experience has always been a factor in how they respond to international politics at the UN and the Commonwealth of Nations, and it continues to shape their foreign policy decisions. We will explain the many ramifications of this later.

Africa and India belong to and have always championed the cause of the Global South. This geopolitical region comprises countries once derogatorily referred to as the "Third World" and whose economies were generally categorised as "developing" in Western scholarship. The term "Third World" implied that these nations were largely distinguished by the indices of neocolonialism and underdevelopment. The countries of the Global South have the unfortunate experience of being pawns in the hands of great powers in global politics. Due to their large populations and shared history as victims of colonialism, Africa and India are key actors in Global South politics at the UN.

During the Cold War, many Global South countries, particularly India and the majority of the African nations, remained nonaligned (Gaddis 1987; Johari 1993). Using platforms such as the Non-Aligned Movement (Calvocoressi 2001), these countries sought to remain relevant in the bipolar global politics of the Cold War. In the current era of globalisation and the rise of regional economic blocs, Africa and India continue to push for a more inclusive UN, advocating for the democratisation of the Security Council and other key organs of this supranational body. It is important to note that India has always supported the representation of Africa on the UN Security Council as part of the widely publicised calls for UN reform.

Historicising Africa–India Relations

Africa–India linkages present a rich picture of sustained economic and socio-cultural relationship going far back in time. For the purpose of this ongoing analysis, we have categorised these interactions into two broad phases: pre-modern and modern. Each phase was shaped by a complex cluster of events that influenced the nature and character of the relationship between Africa and India.

(i) The Pre-Modern Phase, 100–1700 CE

This was a period during which both regions were evolving, and in which documentary evidence was deliberately preserved. Archaeological data shows the depth of Africa–India relations predating 100 CE, but it is from this date onwards that extensive documentary records of their relationship begin to emerge. Sailors' diaries and travel guides contain copious details of the Indian Ocean trade network and the active participation of both Africans and Indians. Ade Ajaye, for example, argues that between 800 and 1000 CE, this trade significantly matured, leading to a robust socio-cultural intermixture between Africans, Indians and Arabs, among other people who were part of the economic hub (Ade Ajayi 1966, pp. 75–91).

The period also witnessed the infiltration of two new forces: (i) Muslim adventurers, missionaries and traders who helped spread Islam and Arabic culture in parts of Africa; and (ii) early European explorers, who acted as advance parties of Western imperialism. Evidence gleaned from the records kept by the Venetian traveller Marco Polo and, particularly, Ibn Battuta, the African Muslim traveller, documents the activities of Indian Gujarati and Saurashtrian merchants on Africa's East Coast. They also referred to African traders visiting parts of western India.

What is important to note about the period under review is that interactions between Africans and Indians were primarily economic. Trade relations were based on the exchange of goods over which trading parties had a comparative advantage. Thus, Africans traded gold, ivory, iron, rhino horns and later slaves, in exchange for a variety of Indian textile products, metal implements, foodstuffs like wheat, rice and jaggery, as well as porcelain and glassware. The trade in slaves left permanent legacies in both societies and their people. The displacements and forced migrations which were common features of slavery and the slave trade created multicultural settlements on the coasts of Africa, with significant numbers of Indians (Anene 1966).

By the end of the 1700s, the Africa–India relationship had taken on a definite pattern.

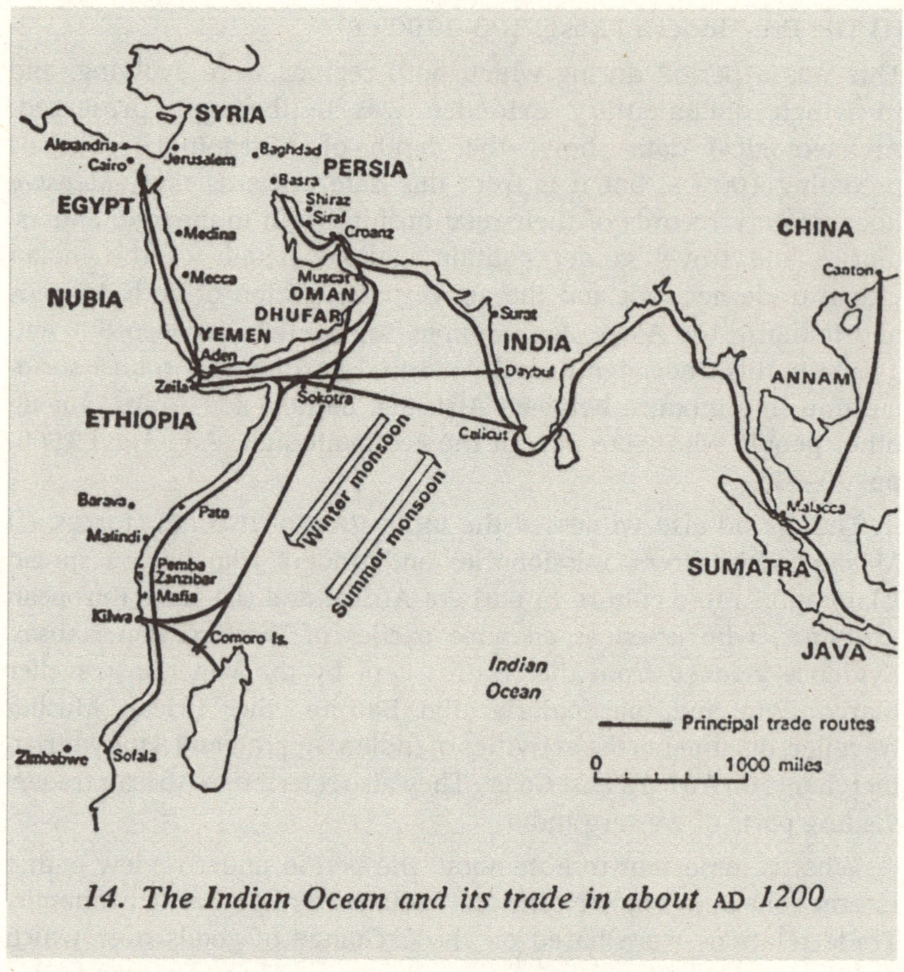

14. The Indian Ocean and its trade in about AD *1200*

Fig. 1: The Indian Ocean Trading Network, AD 1200.

Source: Davidson 1969, p. 95.

Although the pre-modern linkages suffered disruptions, first by the Portuguese conquests and their eventual monopolisation of the Indian Ocean trade, and later by the slave trade, they survived and even thrived beyond European colonisation.

(ii) Modern Phase, 1800 to the Present

(a) The Colonial Period

The modern phase was ushered in by the abolition of the slave trade, the introduction of the so-called "legitimate" trade and the advent of European colonialism. The fundamental economic objectives of European imperialism deeply affected African–Indian interactions in several ways (Okpeh, forthcoming). First, it disrupted the relative autonomy that had characterised precolonial interactions between Africa and India, as both polities lost control over the forces that had shaped their very close and robust connections. Second, colonialism introduced certain strange conditions and elements that complicated trade and other relations (Okpeh, forthcoming). For example, the establishment of artificial boundaries and tax regimes regulated trade between African societies and India. Third, under colonialism, the control of the economy was completely removed from the indigenous peoples of both regions, negatively impacting pre-existing patterns of trade and other forms of interaction. In the final analysis, the colonial period provoked changes with far-reaching consequences.

For example, the modernising influence of colonialism triggered the second wave of massive migrations from India to parts of Africa. Following the colonisation of Africa and the rise in demand for labour in construction and mining, British colonial authorities initiated the mass-scale transfer of Indians to South Africa, Madagascar, Mauritius, Uganda, Kenya, and Tanganyika, to mention but a few African countries. These Indians came in millions, as voluntary and/ or indentured labourers, and remained in parts of Africa even after colonialism ended, forming Indian diasporas across the continent, as shown in Table 1.[4]

4 This was particularly the case in South Africa, Kenya, Uganda and Mauritius, where large Indian migrant settlements were established and well developed throughout the period under review.

S. No.	Country	Population
1.	Kenya	110,000
2.	South Africa	1,300,000
3.	Tanzania	60,000
4.	Uganda	50,000
5.	Malawi	4,000
6.	Zimbabwe	9,500
7.	Zambia	13,000

Table 1: Indian Diaspora in Selected East and Southern African Countries.

Source: Author's compilation from several sources, 2020.

The period was also marked by the struggle to regain political independence. After the Second World War, the writing was already on the wall that colonialism was seeing its final days. The war had left European nations battered and economically in ruins. The resulting power vacuum was filled by the US, which supported nationalist movements in Africa and Asia as a strategy for making economic inroads into these regions. Africa–India relations received a tremendous boost as nationalists from both regions forged common ground against colonial imperialism through their participation in the Pan-African movement. Pan-Africanism provided the platform for this new political consciousness and collaboration efforts between Africa and India.

India's independence in 1947 undoubtedly influenced developments in Africa. Indian leaders actively supported the struggles against colonialism in Africa as a major plank for the liberation of Indian immigrants under white minority rule in South Africa. The philosophy of peaceful resistance, espoused by Mahatma Gandhi, became a dominant ideology of nationalist struggles in several parts of Africa. There was a strong Indian presence in the titanic struggle against white minority rule in South Africa, leading eventually to the downfall of the apartheid regime and the establishment of a multi-racial polity by 1993.

By the time the winds of independence were blowing across Africa, the Cold War had divided the world into a bipolar system, with socialism and capitalism vying for global dominance. The Non-Aligned Movement (NAM), led by Indian leaders like Jawaharlal Nehru, became the major platform where countries of the Global South subsumed their interests and sustained relevance in the emerging post-war world order. Following the Bandung Conference of 1955, many soon-to-be-free African countries tailored their foreign policies towards the fundamental realist posture of the NAM. They could hardly do otherwise because of the contentious character of the prevailing global system into which they were introduced as emerging state actors, and its obvious contradictions and unfairness to the developing nations of the world.

(b) The Postcolonial Period

The first three decades after 1960 witnessed the deepening of the Africa–India relationship on all fronts. In particular, India consolidated her bilateral and multilateral economic and other agreements with individual African countries, extending beyond East and Southern Africa. The effectiveness of these close diplomatic relations could be gleaned from the unified stance they took when engaging with their counterparts in the Global South in the United Nations. For example, after the Lusaka Conference of the NAM, India and African countries jointly called for a fairer deal for Global South nations. The demand for a reordering of the global economy provoked a historic debate following the declaration of the New International Economic Order at the UN General Assembly in 1974. The Declaration, in part, called for a new economic order that would be:

> ...based on equity, sovereign equality, inter-dependence, common interest and cooperation among all states, irrespective of their economic and social system which shall correct inequalities and redress existing injustices, make it possible to eliminate the widening gap between the developed and developing countries and ensure steadily accelerating economic and social development and peace and justice for present and future generations (P.J.I M. de Waart, cited by Ikoni 2003, p. 104).

The Declaration identified the remaining vestiges of alien and colonial domination, foreign occupation, racial discrimination, apartheid and neocolonialism in all forms as the greatest obstacles to the full emancipation and progress of developing countries. It called for a just and fair world order in which all nations are considered equal and cooperate with one another for the development of humanity.

One of the immediate fallouts of this Declaration was the South–South Cooperation Initiative, primarily driven by Africa and India. As a practical demonstration of this initiative, there were a deluge of trade agreements between India and African countries in subsequent years. One of the direct results of this growing relationship was the explosion of the Indian immigrant population in Africa.[5] Indian textile exports found their way into major African markets. In West Africa, for instance, Indian textiles and goods were found in markets in Kano, Kaduna and Sokoto in northern Nigeria; Lagos, Ibadan and Ogun states in western Nigeria; the Kotoko and Kumasi markets in Ghana; and others in Madagascar, Uganda, Kenya and Southern Africa, to mention just a few places. In these markets, Indians acted as middlemen, in addition to owning their own shops and stores. The Indian film industry (Bollywood) was equally popular in Africa during this period. Virtually all cinema houses were dominated by Indian films through which Indian culture and ways of life permeated different parts of Africa.

From the mid-1980s to 2000, the world witnessed rapid changes with far-reaching implications for Africa–India relations. The unification of East and West Germany in 1989 and the disintegration of the Union of Soviet Socialist Republics (USSR) in 1992 signalled the end of the Cold War and the emergence of another world order, initially characterised by terms such as "Unipolarity", "New World

5 Beyond their traditional radius of operation in East and Southern Africa, Indian traders and expatriates migrated to Central and West Africa. In countries like Nigeria, Indian migrant engineers dominated the Nigerian Railway Corporation, while many others entered the education sector as instructors and bookkeepers, and the manufacturing sector as plant managers and salesmen.

Order" and/or "The End of History". This new order was dominated by the phenomenon of globalisation under which the world's economies and nations were (and continue to be) integrated due to advances in information technology, the acceleration and complexification of cross-border trade and population movements, and the consequent division of international trade between three regional power blocs: North America (dominated by the US and Canada), Europe (dominated by Germany, Britain and France), and Asia (dominated by China and Japan).

Against this backdrop, it is important to note that the flourishing of Africa–India relations was threatened by the intensification of development gaps between the Global South and the Global North under the New World Order (NWO) and the globalisation process. The diminishing of the sovereignty and therefore of the principal role of the State as a regulatory institution increased the vulnerability of African countries and India in the neoliberal world of the 21st century. Like previous international orders, the NWO has so far perpetuated an unequal relationship between the Global South (including those in Africa and India) and the Global North. Contrary to the popular narrative that globalisation, which is a major plank in the NWO, offers developing countries limitless opportunities to "catch up" with their developed counterparts, these countries are unfortunately still pawns in the hands of the latter.[6] Finally, the NWO has brought about new patterns and bases for interaction between nation-states in the global system. In one context, cultural forces are said to be dominating world politics, accounting for the upsurge in racial contradictions, antagonisms and conflicts. Ali Mazrui and Samuel P. Huntington predicted this, and it has since come to pass. According to Huntington:

---

6 For instance, roughly 75 per cent of the world's population in the Global South accounts for less than 25 per cent of the world's productive output and less than 15 per cent of global trade. In addition, poverty levels range from 65 to 75 per cent in most countries in the South, and over 70 per cent of the population in these countries is threatened by hunger and starvation. The prevalence of diseases is also on the rise, affecting well-being, while a good number of them suffer severely from the impact of climate change.

> ... The fundamental source of conflict in this new world will not be primarily ideological or primarily economic. The great divisions among humankind and the dominating source of conflict will be cultural. Nation states will remain the most powerful actors in world affairs, but the principal conflicts of global politics will occur between nations and groups of different civilisations. The clash of civilisations will dominate global politics (Huntingdon 1992, p. 22).

At another level, globalisation has sparked massive regional counter-response (Okpeh 2013, pp. 153–4). At the dawn of the 21st century, and in response to the above, Africa and India recognised the need to draw closer to each other as a way of reawakening and strengthening the largely moribund South–South cooperation. It was partly to achieve this goal that, in 2008, the India–Africa Forum Summit (IAFS) was inaugurated to discuss areas of potential economic collaboration and deepen previous socio-cultural ties. Although initially attended by just a handful of African countries, the summit led to far-reaching decisions on how to surmount the many challenges that India and African nations would face in the emerging NWO and globalisation process.

A significant milestone was achieved in 2015 when 54 heads of state, representing all African countries, participated in the third edition of the IAFS. With the theme, "New Hopes, New Horizons", the summit unveiled a dynamic and transformative agenda anchored on mutual empowerment and resurgence between African nations and India. This has since translated into many bilateral trade agreements and other collaborations, which are yielding positive results. The Delhi Declaration, issued after the IASF III, addressed the key development concerns of the African continent and aligned strategically with Africa's Agenda 2063. In principle, both parties agreed to commit resources to capacity-building, knowledge exchange and tackling issues such as poverty, disease and global terrorism. They also pledged to collaborate on UN reforms and generally assist each other in consolidating their comparative trading advantages in the increasingly competitive globalised world. A major trend in all these agreements is the relative ease with which nationals from India are settling in Africa, resulting in their huge population in parts of the continent (see Table 3). In the years ahead, these figures are expected to double, and the Africa–India relationship is poised to grow from strength to strength.

4. Africa–India Linkages: Mapping the Prospects

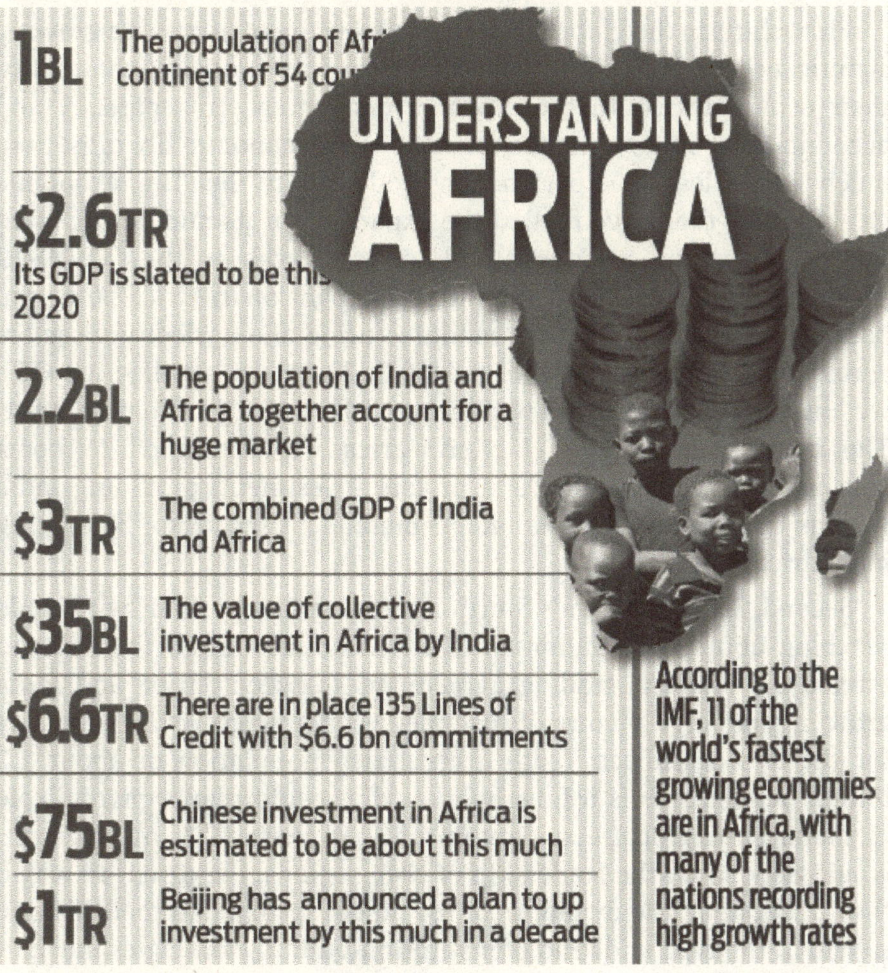

Fig. 2: The Prospects of Africa and India Economic Relations in the 21st Century.

Source: Adapted from the *Indian Express*, 2019.

To better understand and appreciate the prospects of the Africa–India relationship in the 21st century, we must elaborate further on why both regions would need each other. As is obvious from the preceding paragraphs, closer and sustained ties between Africa and India could be beneficial to peoples of both regions. The reasons for this are clear.

First, shifts in the global economic environment affirm the growing significance of both Africa and India and the positive changes in their economies. With the dawn of democracy, transparency and accountability in governance, coupled with economic liberalisation, much of Africa is experiencing moderate to healthy economic growth rates that have fuelled the expansion of its middle class and increased demand for goods and services. Prior to the COVID-19 pandemic, evidence shows a significant expansion in Africa's tourism, banking, telecommunication, manufacturing and agriculture sectors across the continent. By the end of 2020, Africa's collective GDP was projected to reach $3.6 trillion, up from $2.1 trillion in 2011. The burgeoning middle class in Africa has continued to boost consumption, construction and private investment, providing India with an opportunity to stimulate its manufacturing sector by tapping into African markets.

Second, India is Africa's fourth largest trading partner, with trade reaching about $72 billion in 2014–15, after China, the UK and France. As bilateral trading agreements between Africa and India grow in number, a picture of sustained economic growth is emerging for the decades ahead. With a combined population of about 2.2 billion people, this is a huge market that could play a pivotal role in shaping the global economy in the 21st century. A lot, however, would depend on the leadership of both regions: the extent to which they understand the dynamics of the global system and their historic role in it, the type and kind of institution-building strategies they put in place, and the extent to which they are committed to the project of nation-building during this century.

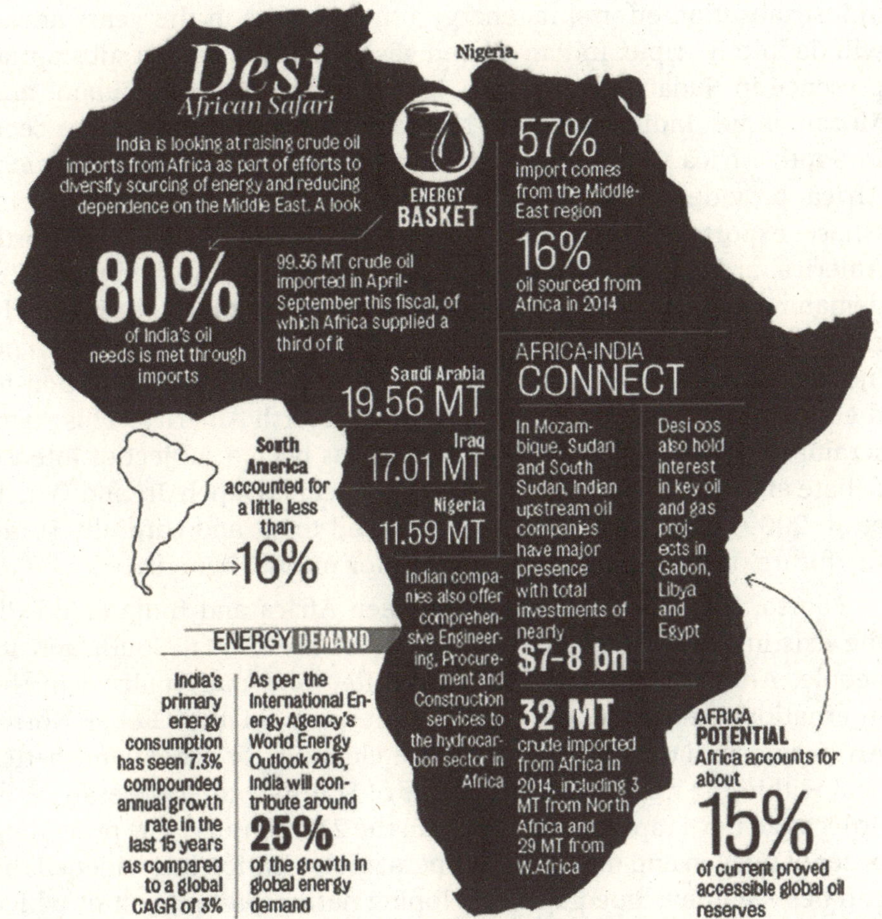

Fig. 3: India's Energy Demands on Africa, 2019.

Source: Adapted and modified from the *Indian Express*, 2019.

Third, sustained Africa–India relations in the 21st century have the potential to deepen their comparative resource advantages in the international market, a development that could positively impact their domestic economies. For Africa, this would mean more foreign investments and better spinoffs in terms of employment generation for its burgeoning and agile youth population. Figure 3 provides rough estimates of India's energy needs from Africa and other oil-producing countries of the world. As India continues to expand its industrialisation efforts, its energy requirements in the years ahead will definitely triple. Indian oil and gas companies have a substantial presence in Sudan, Ivory Coast, Libya, Egypt, Nigeria, Gabon, and Mozambique. Indian interests in coal and other minerals are seen in South Africa, Mozambique, Tanzania, Zimbabwe and Botswana. Africa provides an alternative market for Indian manufacturers, whose exports to traditional destinations like Europe and North America are on the decline. This is happening at a time when demand for resources is rising globally, particularly from newly emerging industrialising countries in Asia (such as Malaysia and Indonesia), as well as from Brazil in South America, in addition to the older industrial powers in Europe and North America. This "new scramble" for Africa by these countries has been a subject of intense debate among African scholars in recent years (Okpeh Jr. and Wuam et al. 2009). Africa and India would need to sit and carefully study the future of their economic relations for mutual benefit.

Fourth, a strong partnership between Africa and India could tilt the existing economic order in favour of the Global South and its people. After centuries of being exploited and marginalised in the international economy by their counterparts in the Global North, Africa and India could champion the clamour for a new and better deal within the framework and ideals of South–South cooperation, in order to achieve rapid development in the 21st century. The prevailing order of uneven and unequal neoliberal globalisation has widened the gap between developed and developing nations, as a result of which the economies of the latter have remained vulnerable. Sustained economic cooperation between Africa and India would undoubtedly renew the South–South ideals of more balanced development and contribute to a peaceful and progressive world in the 21st century.

Fifth, the exploration of the prospects of the "Blue Economy" by the leadership of both regions in recent years is a step in the right direction. It should be recalled that in pre-modern times, the Blue Economy was the core of the economic relationship between India and some East and Central African countries. We have already seen how the trading networks of the Indian Ocean trade catalysed economic and socio-cultural changes in parts of Africa, India and the Middle East. It is in this specific regard that the inclusion of the agenda for the development of the Blue Economy during the 2018

IAFS is important. The plan covers the development of the marine resources of India, the East African coast, as well as other states with littoral coastlines. If and when this is eventually actualised, it is hoped that this project would further consolidate India–Africa marine commerce and transform both into leading economic hubs. As India's Prime Minister Narendra Modi observed:

> We will cooperate for sustainable development of the Blue Economy that will become important future drivers of our prosperity. For me, the Blue Economy is part of a larger Blue Revolution to reclaim our blue skies and blue waters, as we move on the path of clean development (Modi 2020).[7]

Pursuant to the above, a number of bilateral agreements have been entered into between Indian and some littoral and coastline states in East and Central Africa. It is hoped that, in the not-too-distant future, the dividends of these agreements will begin to be manifest.

Conclusion

It is clear that Africa and India will need each other in the globalised world of the 21st century. Undoubtedly, such a relationship would improve the diplomatic bargaining power of both countries in the prevailing world order and, at the same time, strengthen the prospects and well-being of their citizens. Given their vast resource endowments and demographic potential, a closer relationship between Africa and India could make their economic relevance on the global stage a concrete reality. Already, India has a head start in technology and medical tourism, from which African nations are immensely benefiting.

Moreover, in line with the pristine ideas of the NAM and the South–South cooperation, both regions have defended their interests at the UN General Assembly on a wide range of issues, including the democratisation of the Security Council, UN protocols on climate

---

7 Speech at the Inaugural Ceremony of the Third India–Africa Forum Summit in New Delhi (29 October 2015), https://www.mea.gov.in/Speeches-Statements.htm?dtl/25977/Speech_by_Prime_Minister_at_the_Inaugural_Ceremony_of_the_Third_IndiaAfrica_Forum_Summit_in_New_Delhi_October_29_2015 (accessed on 5 July 2025).

change and the global war on terrorism. Undoubtedly, these issues are at the very core of the development of both centres of civilisation. It is hoped that in the not-too-distant future, these historic and recent links will encourage leadership in both regions to remain steadfast and committed to the dreams and aspirations of their people.

To achieve this, the foreign policies of these countries should adopt a pragmatic and dynamic approach, translating agreements into concrete realities. Indeed, they can hardly do otherwise in a world economic order that is deliberately skewed by the Global North against the Global South. South–South cooperation, therefore, can hardly survive without stronger and more sustained collaboration between Africa and India in the 21st century.

Africa and India should similarly strive to broaden and deepen their cultural ties as a foundation for streamlining and expanding their economic interactions. In this sense, the leadership of both regions should leverage the opportunities provided by their longstanding cultural diplomacy. The advantages that this legacy offers will greatly enhance and strengthen Africa–India relations in the decades ahead.

Beyond these, Africa and India could explore the potential of sustained intellectual interaction through initiatives such as those championed by the India International Centre. In this regard, credible institutions in both regions could be identified to host global conferences on select themes of mutual interest and benefit. It is hoped that through such initiatives, the critical question of how to deepen Africa–India relations in the neoliberal era would be broached from time to time, with scholars from both regions formulating strategies for the way forward.

Finally, we must emphasise the point that Africa and India share a common destiny shaped by geography and history. In many ways, this fortuitous closeness has not yet been tapped to the fullest by the people of both regions. In the face of daunting global economic challenges, accentuated by the COVID-19 pandemic, there is no better time than now for Africa and India to come even closer, team up and maximise their comparative advantages and thus to change the narrative. This would positively impact the lives of people in both Africa and India and greatly improve their prospects in the globalised world of the 21st century. The time to take that bold step is now!

Table 2: Africa–India Linkages in the Pre-Modern Times, 100 CE–1500 CE

Eras/Events	Nature of Linkages	Outcomes
• **Pre-100 CE:** A thriving trade between India and the Western Indian Ocean region, as evident from the first-century merchant sailors' guide, *Periplus of Erythraean Sea.* • **800–1500 CE:** Trade between Africa and India increased in volume. • **1500–1700 CE:** International slave trade, activities of merchants and religious adventurers, and explorers.	• Merchant adventurers took advantage of the monsoon winds in the Indian Ocean, leading to the exchange of goods between African, Indian and Arab traders. The Chinese relied on Indian traders to access parts of Africa. This period was the Golden Age of Indian Ocean trade, before the advent of the Portuguese, who sought to seize and monopolise the trade. • This era witnessed the deepening of interactions and the fusion of cultures and indigenous knowledge systems. • Diplomatic relations with parts of India emerged around the Horn of Africa, the East African Coast and in some North African polities.	• The slave trade had profound consequences on the demographics of Africa and India. Slaves from Africa were often seen in parts of India. Some, like Malik Amber, rose to influential positions. • The Siddis formed a significant part of the population in parts of Gujarat, Karnataka and Hyderabad. • Indians were found in reasonable numbers in the Horn of Africa, the Maghreb, and, above all, East and Central Africa. Some of them were slaves. • Intermarriage between African immigrants and local Indian communities led to the rise of a new generation of Afro-Indians.

Source: Author's compilation from several sources, 2019.

Table 3: Africa–India Linkages in Modern Times, 1800–the Present

Eras/Events	Nature of Linkages	Outcomes
	(i) The Colonial Period	
1. **1800–1860s:** Aggressive infiltration of African and Indian territories by European countries, signing of treaties and massive conquest and sequestration of lands.	1. Africa–India relations lost autonomy to the colonialists. Close contact was maintained but under a new arrangement.	1. The violence that characterised the colonial penetration of Africa initially dislocated linkages between Africa and India. However, based on precolonial trade connections, new patterns of interactions began to emerge. Indian textiles and cuisine thrived in parts of Africa.
2. **1860s–1900:** Establishment of colonial rule and the laying down of administrative and socio-economic infrastructures of exploitation.	2. African and Indian merchants and traders continued to exchange trade items. Socio-cultural interactions trudged on despite intense pressure from colonialists.	2. Precolonial trade connections persisted, based on which, new patterns of interactions began to emerge. Indian textiles and cuisine thrived in parts of Africa.
3. **1900–1945:** Demand for labour on construction sites and emerging minefields encouraged the migration of labourers across international boundaries.	3. Massive migration of Indians to parts of Africa as indentured labour resulted in the explosion of the Indian population in Africa.	3. Indian diasporas emerged in South Africa, Tanzania, East and Central Africa, Madagascar and Mauritius. The social processes this ignited fused African and Indian cultures and civilisations, with profound consequences.

Eras/Events	Nature of Linkages	Outcomes
4. **1945–1960:** Vigorous anti-colonial struggles in Africa.	4. African and Indian nationalists forged common grounds as victims of imperialism. Pan-Africanism provided the platform for this new political consciousness and collaboration.	4. India's independence in 1947 influenced developments in Africa. Indian leaders supported the struggles against colonialism in Africa. They also protested against the apartheid system in South Africa. African countries eventually regained their political independence in the 1960s, and the apartheid system ended in early 1990s.
5. **Cold War:** Creation of a bipolar world, with the Socialist Eastern bloc led by the USSR and the capitalist Western bloc led by the USA.	5. **Cold War:** The Non-Aligned Movement, led by Nehru from India, spread to the continent of Africa with resounding success, especially following the Bandung Conference of 1955. From this period, African leaders integrated their interests with the politics of the Global South.	5. The foreign policies of emerging independent African countries adopted the realist posture after India. They understood the global system into which they were introduced as emerging state actors in terms of its inherent unfairness to the developing countries of the world.
(ii) The Post-colonial Period		
1. **1960s–1990s:** African countries regained political independence in the 1960s; anti-	1. By virtue of its civilisational links with the continent and the plight of the Indian diasporic	1. India's independence in 1947 influenced developments in Africa, with Indian leaders supporting

Eras/Events	Nature of Linkages	Outcomes
apartheid struggles in South Africa continued till the 1990s.	community in South Africa, India's foreign policy during this period supported anti-apartheid struggles in South Africa, as well as struggles against racial minority rule in Namibia and South Rhodesia.	struggles against colonialism in Africa.
2. **1970s**: The Lusaka Non-Aligned Submit provided a platform for member countries to reject the structural imbalance in the prevailing global economic order.	2. In an uncommon alliance, Indian and African countries championed this cause in all UN conferences during this decade, making them the most vocal in the developing world.	2. Foreign policies of emerging independent African countries adopted the realist posture after India. They understood the global system into which they were introduced, as emerging state actors, in terms of its inherent unfairness to the developing countries of the world.
3. **1980s–2000:** Collapse of the USSR and the emergence of a new world order characterised by unipolarity and neoliberal globalisation.	3. Africa and India championed greater South–South economic cooperation, the democratisation of the UN and supported agitations against climate change.	3. Developing countries called for a reordering of the global economy on the basis of South–South cooperation. The debate for a New International Economic Order (NIEO) was tabled at the UN General Assembly.

Eras/Events	Nature of Linkages	Outcomes
4. **2000–Present:** Responses from countries of the Global South to neoliberal globalisation agenda include clamour for involuntary integration into the emerging globalised world, a greater civilisation consciousness and an upsurge in regional impulses. India emerges as the fifth-largest economy in the world after France.	4. Greater and more vigorous cooperation between Africa and India on all fronts, including bilateral trade agreements between individual African countries, the promotion of UN reform and increased visibility for Africa in its critical organs.	4. Inauguration of the India–Africa Forum in 2008, with its third summit in October 2015 attracting scores of African countries. The Delhi Declaration announced greater partnerships with African countries in areas of economy, investment in capital projects, human capital, healthcare and solar energy.

Source: Author's compilation from several sources, 2019.

References

Ajayi, J.F. Ade. "A Survey of the Cultural and Political Regions of Africa at the Beginning of the Nineteenth Century", in *Africa in the Nineteenth and Twentieth Centuries*, eds. Joseph C. Anene and Godfrey Brown. Ibadan: Ibadan University Press and Nelson, 1966, pp. 75–91.

Anene, Joseph. "Slavery and the Slave Trade", in *Africa in the Nineteenth and Twentieth Centuries*, eds. Joseph C. Anene and Godfrey Brown. Ibadan: Ibadan University Press and Nelson, 1966, pp. 92–109.

Calvocoressi, Peter. *World Politics, 1945–2000*. South Asia: Pearson Education, 2001.

Crosette, Barbara. *India Facing the Twenty-First Century*. Bloomington: Indiana University Press, 1993.

Davidson, Basil. *The Growth of African Civilization: East and Central Africa to the late Nineteenth Century*. London: Longman Publishing Company, 1972.

———. *A History of East and Central Africa to the Late Nineteenth Century*. New York: Anchor Books, 1969.

Falola, Toyin and Mike Odugbo Odey (eds.). *Poverty Reduction Strategies in Africa*. London: Routledge, 2017.

Gaddis, J.I. *The Long Peace: Inquiries into the History of the Cold War*. New York: Oxford University Press, 1987.

Harrison, Selig S. *India: The Most Dangerous Decades*. Princeton: Princeton University Press, 1960.

Huntingdon, Samuel J. "The Clash of Civilizations?", *Foreign Affairs* vol. 72, no. 3 (1993): pp. 22–49.

Ikoni, Ukooh D. "The New International Economic Order and the Developing Countries: A Revisitation of the Concept", *Journal of Globalization and International Studies* vol. 1, no. 1 (2003): pp. 103–20.

Isaacs, Harold R. *Images of Asia: American Views of China and India*. New York: Harper and Row, 1972.

Jalan, Bimal, ed. *The Indian Economy*. New Delhi: Penguin, 1992.

Jenkins, Wilfred J. *The Way of World History*. Exeter: Wheaton, 1961.

Johari, J.C. *International Relations and Politics: Theoretical Perspective in Post-Cold War Era*. New Delhi: Sterling Publishers Private Ltd, 1993.

Okpeh Jr., Okpeh O. and Terhemba Wuam, et al. (eds.). *China and Africa: Opportunities and Threats*. Makurdi: Aboki Publishers, 2009.

Okpeh Jr., Okpeh O. "Globalization and Regional Impulses from the Global South: A Comparative Study of ECOWAS and ASEAN", in *The Political Economy of Development and Underdevelopment in Africa*, eds. Toyin Falola and Jessica Achberger.. New York: Routledge, Taylor and Francis, 2013, pp. 147–75.

Okpeh Jr., Okpeh O. et al. (eds.). *Poverty and Social Policies in Africa*. Lagos: Integrity Publishers, 2018.

Okpeh Jr., Okpeh O. "Colonialism and the Changing Nature of Relations between Africans", in *Colonialism and Relations in Modern Africa*, ed. Okpeh O. Okpeh Jr.. Lagos: Yavnelle Publishers.

Rodney, Walter. *How Europe Underdeveloped Africa*. London and Dar-Es-Salaam: Bogle-L'Ouverture Publications and Tanzanian Publishing House, 1976.

Modi, Narendra "Speech at the Inaugural Ceremony of the Third India–Africa Forum Summit in New Delhi (29 October 2015)" 2020. Available online: https://www.mea.gov.in/Speeches-Statements.htm?dtl/25977/Speech_by_Prime_Minister_at_the_Inaugural_Ceremony_of_the_Third_IndiaAfrica_Forum_Summit_in_New_Delhi_October_29_2015 (accessed on 5 July 2025).

Stanley, H.M. *Through the Dark Continent*. New York, Harper and Brothers, 1906.

Tharoor, Shashi. *India: From Midnight to Millennium*. New York: Arcade, 1997.

Chapter 3

India–Africa Relations: A Historical Overview

K. Mathews

"The darkest thing about Africa has always been our ignorance of it."

—George Kimble (1951)

Introduction

The emergence of India and Africa as formidable economic and political forces on the global stage in the 21st century is a subject that deserves thorough study and analysis. This chapter aims to provide a historical overview of the relations between the African continent and the Indian subcontinent, to facilitate a better understanding of their age-old connections. I confine myself to select historical linkages, and do not address contemporary developments. Interactions between these two ancient civilisations have spanned various fields, from trade and religion to architecture, language and food. Until the 20th century, India's contacts with Africa were primarily cultural and economic, with very little political engagement for understandable reasons. These contacts antedated the establishment of European rule in Africa and India. For a broader understanding, we may briefly examine some of the background developments.

Background

For many people outside Africa, its history and culture remain as obscure as they were to 19th-century Europeans, who once described it as the "dark continent". However, in recent decades, there has been a decisive shift away from this Eurocentric approach. Historians, linguists, archaeologists, geographers and other scholars have, both individually and collectively, undertaken the task of reconstructing African history, culture and civilisation. The result has been a clear confirmation that Africa was far from being one of the least advanced regions at the beginning of modernity. Historians and anthropologists now recognise Africa as "the cradle of humankind", where the earliest known civilisations emerged.

When the supercontinent Gondwanaland split up in geological times, one segment drifted west and became Latin America, while the other floated east, crashed against Asia, and became the Indian subcontinent (Reader 1998, p. 22). In other words, Africa is the "Mother Continent". It was Charles Darwin who first speculated that evidence of the evolution of the ancestors of *Homo Sapiens* would be discovered in Africa. Louis Leakey proved this hypothesis when his team discovered the earliest then-known remains of human species in Olduvai Gorge, located in the Serengeti Plains of northern Tanzania, dated to 3.8 million years Before Present. In Ethiopia, the fossil of a 3.2–million–year–old skeleton of a young girl, named "Lucy", was discovered. This remarkable fossil is on display at the National Museum of Ethiopia in Addis Ababa. These discoveries, along with other studies and findings, confirm that the genesis of humanity was in Africa, more precisely in Eastern Africa (Carmichael 1993, p. 31).

Some three decades ago, scientific studies of the DNA of living humans confirmed that all humans share a common family tree (Hamid 2019, p. 96). It was found that all people outside Africa are descended from ancestors who left Africa more than 60,000 years ago. These first modern humans reached Australia 50,000 years ago and, about 45,000 years ago, they ventured into Europe, having travelled through the Middle East. By 15,000 years ago, they had reached South America. As they spread into different parts of the world, they formed groups that became geographically isolated from one another and, in the process, acquired their own distinctive set of genetic mutations. Genetic and linguistic theories are supported by archaeological findings. The general consensus among scholars is that modern humans originated in Africa. Given the current state of knowledge, there is truth behind the declarations that humans were born in Africa or that "We are all Africans!"

Africa has played a crucial role in moulding world history, learning, and science for centuries. Although we lack continuous written records of its political and economic history, available evidence suggests that as far back as 5,000 BCE, large and highly sophisticated civilisations had come up. There is evidence of democratic governance and well-developed socio-economic organisations. Great kingdoms on the continent influenced the world's economic, social and political developments. African General Hannibal Barca famously conquered parts of Europe. Africa is also home to the majestic pyramids of Egypt, the ruins of Great Zimbabwe and the famous city of Timbuktu. Historians and archaeologists have unearthed evidence that the ancient kingdoms of Ghana, Songhai (Niger/Burkina Faso), Timbuktu (Mali), Nubia (southern Egypt, northern Sudan), Aksum (Ethiopia), the Democratic Republic of Congo and Munhumotapa (Zimbabwe/Mozambique) established contacts with distant communities. The Kingdom of Ghana, in particular, was known for its shrewd traders who had contacts with countries as far away as China and India.

There was trade from very early times between India and the eastern seaboard of Africa. Spices, crockery, hides and skins, dress material, bangles and beads, pots and animals were among the commodities traded between Africa, India and the Gulf. India's cultural influence on the eastern seaboard of Africa extended to food and music (Mazrui 1977, p. 114). Even today, the food cultures of places like Zanzibar, Dodoma and Dar es Salaam in Tanzania, and of Lamu and Mombasa in Kenya bear traces of Indian influence. Some of the spices used, and even the names of particular dishes, suggest a cultural convergence between Eastern Africa and the other shores of the Indian Ocean. Undoubtedly, on those other shores, there are also important cultural influences from Eastern Africa. What we see along these coastlines might be referred to as the "civilisation of the

Indian Ocean", marked by contact and mutual influence in music, food, architecture, language and the realm of ideas. We now turn to examine the development of India–Africa relations from antiquity.

India–Africa Relations from Antiquity

According to R.K. Gupta (2014, p. 4), India has more than 3,000 years of cultural and commercial relations with Africa. Sources indicate trade between the Dravidians and Babylonians as early as the 7th century BCE. These Indian merchants likely visited South Arabia en route, and most probably the eastern Horn of Africa as well (Richard Reusch, cited in Gupta 2014, p. 4). These ancient linkages continued to flourish during the medieval period through trade and were later exploited by European powers in the 15th century, as they looked for new routes to India (Gupta 2014, p. 4).

The Indus Valley Civilisation, which flourished between 2,600 and 1,700 BCE in what is now north-western India and Pakistan, was contemporary with the ancient Chinese, Mesopotamian and Egyptian civilisations. There is strong evidence that the Indus Valley had active trade links with the outside world, particularly Mesopotamia. Archaeologists have uncovered a sophisticated system of docks for sea-going vessels in the port city of Lothal in Gujarat. The Indus Valley Civilisation began to decline around 1,000 BCE for reasons that remain disputed, with some suggesting that climate change may have contributed to its downfall.

Historical sources tell us that centuries ago Indian sailors sailed in wooden dhows to African countries circling the Indian Ocean. Indian sources reveal that ebony, ivory, and textile goods including cotton and silk (meant mainly for wrapping Egyptian mummies) were supplied to Egypt in the second millennium BCE by Abyssinian and Somali traders who transported them from India (Karmwar 2010, p. 2). Egypt and India appear to have shared a long history of vibrant interaction, which continued into the modern period. India's links with Egypt, under Pharaonic, Greek and Roman rule, as well as during the great age of Islam from the 10th to the 14th century, unfolded a far-reaching process extending to neighbouring African lands along the Red Sea (Dubey 2016, p. 11).

Early works provide evidence that Indian ships sailed regularly to the coast of East Africa. The *Periplus of the Erythraean Sea,* a sailor's guidebook dated variously from 60 to 266 CE, remains a major source for the early history of East Africa and the Red Sea Coast. It throws much light on ancient India's sea-faring activities (Ali 1987, p. 6). Benefitting from the monsoon winds, merchants traded cotton, glass beads and other goods in exchange for gold and soft-carved ivory. The *Periplus* offers a valuable account of the Horn of Africa's foreign trade (Pankhurst 1972). As mentioned above, Indian commerce with the Horn of Africa was vital due to its location on the trade route from India to Egypt and the Roman Empire. Observers noted that as many as 120 vessels sailed from Egyptian Red Sea ports. Over a millennium and a half later, James Bruce highlighted the significance of the trade winds, which had long facilitated trading connections between India and the Red Sea (Karmwar 2010, p. 6). It was said that from ancient times, providence had been "kind to India", as it enjoyed a superabundance of three export commodities highly prized in Africa: pepper, silk and cotton. The Kingdom of Kush in Sudan, one of the gold-producing regions in the ancient world, also had trade relations with India.

Evidence of Indian contacts with the Aksumite Kingdom of Ethiopia rests on solid foundations. It is established that the Indian maritime presence in the Red Sea had impressed the Aksumites by the fourth century CE (Chatterji 1968, p. 53). The bonds between Ethiopia and India extended from commercial and social to political and cultural realms. The influence of Indian architecture on Aksumite structures further highlights the strength of these bonds. Ethiopia is one of the oldest civilisations in the world, with a recorded history that stretches back to Biblical times. Both Ethiopia and India are civilisations with histories spanning at least 5,000 and 3,000 years, respectively. Historians have noted that in ancient times, large numbers of people migrated from the west coast of India and settled in Ethiopia, Egypt and Nubia (modern-day Sudan). Ethiopia was a major source of gold, ivory, rhinoceros horn and slaves, all of which were in great demand in India. In return, India supplied cotton and silk, pepper and other spices, which were equally in demand in Ethiopia. Indian spices

Fig. 1. Map of the Indian Ocean World.

Source: University of Texas Libraries, University of Texas at Austin (Downloaded from the University of Texas Perry-Castañada Library Map Collection, and cropped).

greatly influenced Ethiopian cuisine. The slave trade was also an important aspect of early Indo-Ethiopian trade.

In the case of the littoral and island states of the West Indian Ocean region, the probability of intra-continental cultural interaction in a broader sense cannot be overlooked, as both peoples became integral parts of the Indian Ocean "circuit of trade", facilitated by favourable trade winds and the development of suitable maritime technology (Dubey 2016, p. 12). It is observed that trade provided contact with the outside world, bringing new ideas and concepts, and promoting material prosperity, which in turn stimulated advances in political organisation as well as in social and cultural life (Yadav and Baghel 2009, p. 287). In his travelogue, Marco Polo writes about encountering merchants from Gujarat and Saurashtra on Africa's East Coast and praises them as the best and most honourable in the world (Marco Polo 1903, p. 363). Subsequently, as Indian trade with East Africa expanded, the Indian rupee replaced European currencies as the principal currency in the region.

More concrete evidence of exchanges between India and Africa dates to colonial times, owing to their shared colonial masters—the British, French and Portuguese. Mozambique became the staging ground for the Portuguese presence in Goa, while the British East Africa Protectorate, which included Kenya and Uganda, was initially administered from Bombay, a city that the British had acquired from another European power as part of a royal dowry. The British unwittingly facilitated India's presence in Africa by sending thousands of Indians as indentured labourers to work on plantations in South Africa, Mauritius and other African destinations. The next sections will explore the population exchange between India and Africa over the centuries.

African Diaspora in India

According to Purnima M. Bhatt (2017), the migration of Africans to India may have begun as early as the first century CE. From the 13th to the 17th century, western India witnessed massive migration of Ethiopians and other East Africans, known as "*Habshis*" or "Siddis". Slaves were transported from the east coast of Africa to the Persian Gulf and Red Sea ports and from there to India. Many of these migrants converted to Islam, which facilitated their assimilation into Indian society. Today, Siddis comprise scattered communities along the western coast of India, mainly in Gujarat, but also in Goa, Karnataka, Andhra Pradesh and Telangana, Sri Lanka and in Sindh (Pakistan). Their ancestors came to India largely as slaves, but also as soldiers, sailors, merchants, mercenaries, crewmen and pearl divers (Bhatt 2017).

As observed by Bhatt (2017), a number of Afro-Indians rose to high positions at the courts of Sultans, wielding considerable power. Some became trusted commanders, while others founded dynasties. Many amassed great wealth, gaining prestige and influence, and even commissioned monuments like mosques and tombs. One well-known example is Malik Ambar, an Ethiopian born in Harar in 1550. His original name was Shambu, and he was sold as a slave in his early childhood to a buyer from Baghdad who had him educated. Later, he was sold to one Changez Khan, who trained him in military strategy and administration. Eventually, he was brought to India, where he became a great warrior, fought against the Mughals, and became the Prime Minister of Ahmednagar. Malik Ambar was also a highly successful diplomat.

Indian Diaspora in Africa

From the dawn of history, Indians have been migrating and settling abroad, just as India has been receiving people from abroad. The pastoral *Beja* tribe of Sudan, which represents about five per cent of the country's population, claims origins from India, and the language they speak shows affinities with Prakrit, which was prevalent in ancient India. It is said that the earliest settlers in East Africa around 650 CE were from India.

In the 19th century, large numbers of Indians migrated to Mauritius, South Africa and East Africa as indentured labourers, traders and free passengers. The construction of the railway line between Mombasa and Kampala in the late 19th century brought around 34,000 Indian indentured labourers and led to greater cultural interpenetration. Subsequently, many Indians also went as traders, particularly from Gujarat, and settled down in different African countries, although they had closer affinity with the states that were or had been under British colonial rule.

After India gained independence in 1947, many Indians went to Africa as skilled workers on contract. Along with entrepreneurs, a growing number of Indian professionals such as doctors, teachers (educationists) and engineers have established a presence in Africa. Of the approximately 30 million Persons of Indian Origin (PIOs) across the globe, around three million reside in Africa, serving as a vital link between India and their new home states.

Mauritius is the only country where nearly 70 per cent of the population is of Indian descent. After the abolition of the slave trade in 1834, and until 1922, thousands of Indians were brought to Mauritius by the British colonialists to work as "coolies" on the sugar plantations, replacing African slaves. These workers endured conditions similar to slavery. Indian culture remains vibrant and alive in Mauritius, earning it the nickname "Land of Ramayana"! Politics in Mauritius is largely dominated by people of Indian origin. No wonder the country is known as "Little India".

The case of PIOs in South Africa is unique. There are about 1.5 million Indians, mostly living around KwaZulu-Natal and Durban. Indians initially went to South Africa as indentured labourers in the latter part of the 19th century. The historic struggle led by Mahatma Gandhi against racial discrimination there (1893–1914) is well known. The cause of Indians in South Africa has remained a significant focus of Indian foreign policy over the years. The end of apartheid in 1994 brought about a new era in South Africa.

The PIOs in East Africa offer another interesting case study. Permanent Indian settlements in Kenya, Uganda and Tanzania date back to the 19th century, when the British colonial administration recruited Indians to work on the railways. By the 1950s and early 1960s, when African countries were gaining independence, around 3,80,000 Indians, or "Asians", settled in these three countries. In terms of economic development, the Indian community's contribution has been disproportionate to their numbers. On the whole, Indians in East Africa have never made up more than two per cent of the total population, and most have been involved in trade, seldom taking any interest in the political affairs of these countries.

Conclusion

The relationship between India and Africa since India's independence in 1947, and more particularly after the wave of African independence in the early 1960s, has been discussed at multiple forums. Most of these discussions have focused on the roles played by Gandhi and Nehru, as well as instances of Indo-African cooperation in the struggle against colonialism, apartheid and other forms of political oppression. However, there have been only paltry efforts to explore the less-known historical background of Indo-African relations. Changes in international attitudes towards Africa and its past have added new significance to India's relationship with the continent. As this chapter has shown, there has also been a distinct shift away from the view of Africa as a continent illuminated only after the arrival of the Europeans.

Being next-shore neighbours across the Indian Ocean, India and Africa have had regular interactions through their communities and traders for thousands of years, especially in East Africa, the west coast of India and parts of South India. Indo-African relations date back to the ancient Indus Valley and Nile Valley Civilisations. The *Periplus of the Erythraean Sea* refers to trade between Aksum and India in the early first millennium. Relations attained deeper levels during the medieval times, with the documented presence of Africans in India as early as the 8th century CE. Several Africans played important roles in regional kingdoms across India. Mahatma Gandhi's stay in South Africa from 1893 to 1915 is one of the historic episodes that paved the way for modern-day political relations.

It is in the 20th century, however, that we see, at least for a while, the full flowering of political interaction between India and Africa as a whole. As the present Indian Prime Minister Narendra Modi observed at the Third India–Africa Forum Summit in New Delhi in October 2015, "This partnership between India and Africa is not a new journey, nor a new beginning. But this is a new promise of a great future for an ancient relationship."

References

Ali, S.S. *India and Africa Through the Ages*. New Delhi: National Book Trust, 1987.

———. *The African Dispersal in the Deccan: From Medieval to Modern Times*. New Delhi: Orient Longman, 1995.

Baptiste, Fitzroy A. "The African Presence in India", *Africa Quarterly* vol. 38, no. 2 (1998): pp. 75–126.

Battuta, Ibn. *Travels in Asia and Africa 1325–1354*. Translated and selected by H.A.R. Gibb (First Indian Edition). New Delhi: Oriental Books Reprint Corporation, 1986.

Bhatt, Purnima Mehta. *The African Diaspora in India: Assimilation, Change and Cultural Survivals*. London: Routledge, 2017.

Carmichael, J. *African Eldorado*. London: Duckworth, 1993.

Chakravarti, Ranbir. *Exploring Early India: Up to c. AD 1300*. New Delhi: Primus Books, 2016.

Chatterji, S.K. *India and Ethiopia from the Seventh Century B.C.* Calcutta: Asiatic Society, 1967.

Chauhan, R.S. *Africans in India: From Slavery to Royalty*. New Delhi: Asian Publication Services, 1995.

Collins, Robert, O. "The African Slave Trade to Asia and the Indian Ocean Islands", *African and Asian Studies* vol. 5, nos. 3-4 (2006): pp. 325–46.

Davidson, Basil. *Africa in History*. London: Penguin Books, 1974.

Dubey, Ajay. *Indian Diaspora: Global Identity*. New Delhi: Kalinga Publications, 2003.

———. "India–Africa Relations: Historical Goodwill and a Vision for the Future", in *India and Africa's Partnership: A Vision for a New Future*, eds. Ajay Dubey and Aparajita Biswas. New Delhi: Springer, 2016, pp. 11–40.

Dowden, Richard. *Africa: Altered States, Ordinary Miracles*. New York: Public Affairs, 2009.

Gupta, Aniruddha (ed.) *Minorities on India's West Coast: History and Society*. New Delhi: Kalinga Publications, 1991.

Gupta, Rajneesh Kumar. "Indian Diaspora in Africa: A Profile", *Africa Trends* vol. 3, no. 2 (2014), pp. 4–9.

Hamid, Mohsin. "In the 21st century, we are all migrants". *National Geographic Magazine*, August 2019, https://www.nationalgeographic.com/magazine/article/we-all-are-migrants-in-the-21st-century (accessed on 28 November 2024).

Harris, Joseph. *Global Dimensions of the African Diaspora*, Washington, Howard University Press, 1994.

Hawley, John (ed.) *India in Africa, Africa in India: Indian Ocean Cosmopolitanisms*. Bloomington, Indiana University Press, 2008.

Karmwar, Manish. "India's Relations with East Africa: A Historical Study", 1 & 2. (2010), pp. 78–88, https://www.researchgate.net/publication/334284675_INDIA'S_RELATIONS_WITH_EAST_AFRICA_A_HISTORICAL_STUDY (accessed on 6 November 2020).

Kimble, George. "Africa Today: The Lifting Darkness", *Reporter*, 15 May 1951.

Kosambi, D.D. *Ancient India in Historical Outline*. New Delhi: Vikas Publishing House, 2002.

Marco Polo. *The Book of Ser Marco Polo, the Venetian, Concerning the Kingdoms and Marvels of the East*, vol. 2, translated by Henry Yule (3rd ed.), London: John Murray, 1903.

Mathews, K. "Indian Diaspora in East and South Africa", *Indian Horizons* vol. 47, no. 4 (2000): pp. 1–22.

Mawdsley, Emma and Gerard McCann (eds). *India in Africa: Changing Geographies of Power*. Nairobi: Pambazuka Press, 2011.

Mazrui, Ali A. *Africa's International Relations: The Diplomacy of Dependency & Change*. London: Heinemann, 1977.

———. 1986. *Africans: A Triple Heritage*. London: BBC Publications.

Meredith, Martin. *The Fortunes of Africa: A 5,000 Year History of Wealth, Greed and Endeavour*. London, New Delhi: Simon & Schuster, 2014.

Mutharika, Bingu Wa. *The African Dream: From Poverty to Prosperity*. Limbe: The Guardian Publications Ltd., 2010.

Pankhurst, Richard. "The history of Ethiopia's Relations with India prior to the Nineteenth Century", *Accademia Nazionale, Problemi Attuali di Scienze e di Cultura*, 191 (1974), pp. 281–9.

Panikkar, K.M. *India and the Indian Ocean*. London: George, Allen & Unwin, 1945.

Patel, J.K. "African Settlements in Gujarat", *India Quarterly* vol. 42, no. 1, 1986.

Rao, S.R. *Lothal and the Indus Civilisation*. Bombay: Asia Publishing House, 1985.

Reader, John. *Africa: Biography of the Continent*. London: Penguin Books, 1998.

Richard, Oliver and J.D. Fage. *A Short History of Africa*. London: Penguin Books, 1972.

Sanyal, Sanjeev. *The Indian Renaissance.* New Delhi: Penguin, 2008.

Thapar, Romila. *The Penguin History of Early India: From Origins to AD 1300.* London: Penguin Books, 2002.

Tharoor, Shashi. "India–Africa Partnership" (Foreword), in *India–Africa Enduring Partnership: Emerging Areas of Co-operation,* ed. Aparajita Biswas. New Delhi: Gyan Publishing House, 2013.

Vohra, N.N., and K. Mathews (eds.). *Africa, India and South–South Cooperation.* New Delhi: Har-Anand Publications, 1997.

Yadav, S.N. and Indu Baghel, "India–Africa Strategic Partnership", in *India's Foreign Policy: Opportunities and Obstacles in the Post-Cold War Era.* New Delhi: Global Vision Publishing House, 2009, pp. 287–311.

Chapter 4

Recapturing Defining Moments in India–Africa Relations since India's Independence: Themes and Issues

Rajen Harshé

This chapter offers a bird's eye view of India–Africa relations by recapturing defining moments in their ties since India's independence on 15 August 1947. Any defining moment signifies a milestone that invariably brings about perceptible and long-lasting change in an existing relationship. Given the complexity of the central theme, I will try to handle it by being sensitive to the diversities among African states, taking into account factors such as their colonial past, geopolitical significance of their locations, resources, and varying levels of their economic, technological and educational development.

In fact, history, as a continuous process, is witness to all kinds of events, but only a few of these stand out as milestones. These events are defining moments, and hence cannot be overlooked. With this in mind, I propose to highlight two defining moments in the context of how India employed the apparatus of non-alignment, and the remaining two by underscoring how they unfolded after India began to negotiate with the era of globalisation.

Independent India opted to pursue non-alignment as its foreign policy strategy by steering clear of two adversarial power blocs led by the then two superpowers, namely, the United States of America (USA) and the former Soviet Union. Non-alignment was a logical extension of India's nationalism, serving as an effective vehicle for promoting its national interests. It also signified India's determination to support anti-racist, anti-colonial and anti-imperialist struggles. In essence, through the policy of non-alignment, India achieved the freedom to express itself in international relations, thereby making its independence truly meaningful.

Non-alignment, both as a policy and a strategy, eventually became a subsystem in international relations after the Non-Aligned Movement (NAM) was formally established at the Belgrade Conference in 1961. During its initial phase of almost two decades, India's non-alignment, and the NAM in general, primarily focused on bringing up themes and issues that carried greater political significance (Harshé 1990).

Non-Alignment and its Political Significance

The political significance of non-alignment became evident at the dawn of India's independence. Committed to Pan-Asian solidarity, India took a major initiative in organising the Asian Relations Conference in New Delhi in March–April 1947, even before its independence. As a matter of policy, India, along with other Asian countries, opposed European imperialism. India extended support to countries like Indonesia, which was in the final stages of its struggle against Dutch imperialism. As far as Africa is concerned, India unequivocally opposed colonialism, racism and later, neocolonialism. Sadly, colonialism and racism have often been inextricably intertwined.

Owing to the existence of a sizable Indian population in the Republic of South Africa, India's attention was naturally drawn there. From 1910 to 1948, South Africa was initiating measures that promoted racial discrimination. However, with the victory of the National Party (NP) in 1948, the country formally adopted racism/apartheid as an official policy. South Africa divided its population along racial lines, i.e., Whites, Coloureds, Indians and Blacks.

Indeed, the Black population, which made up nearly three-fourths of the country, always constituted an overwhelmingly large proportion, followed by racial groups such as the Whites at roughly 10 per cent, Coloureds at roughly 9 per cent, and Indians at roughly 2.5 per cent. Racial inequalities and discrimination were legally justified in South Africa, and the Blacks who were at the bottom of the racial pyramid were the most obvious victims.

It is also worth noting that South Africa is the country where Gandhi first tried out his techniques of passive resistance, like the Satyagraha, during the late 19th and early 20th centuries. After perfecting these methods on South African soil, he applied them in the glorious non-violent freedom struggle of India in the last century. In light of this history, India was the first country to raise the issue of racial discrimination in the General Assembly of the United Nations (UNGA) in 1946. Following its independence, it also severed diplomatic relations with South Africa. India used every available international forum to condemn racism and apartheid in South Africa.

At the 1955 Bandung Conference of Afro-Asian countries, India stoutly supported the termination of racism in South Africa. In the aftermath of the infamous Sharpeville massacre of 1960, where 69 non-violent protesters were killed, India took the lead in ousting South Africa from the British Commonwealth of Nations in 1961.

During the Bandung Conference, India staunchly supported the liberation of Algeria, Tunisia and Morocco from French colonialism. Moreover, in the late 1950s, the Algerian War of Independence had taken an unusually violent turn, and in the midst of the conflict, the Front of National Liberation of Algeria (FLN) had established a Provisional Government in Algeria (GPRA). India, however, dithered over offering *de jure* recognition to GPRA and pleaded for the resolution of the Algerian issue through negotiations between the parties concerned (Harshé 2019, p. 179).

In fact, 1960 was termed the "Year of Africa" when 16 African states achieved formal sovereign statehood. Nevertheless, during the first Belgrade summit of the NAM, senior NAM leaders such as Jawaharlal Nehru were more concerned about promoting détente between the

USA and the former Soviet Union, as well as addressing disarmament issues. In contrast, Indonesia and several newly born African states and their leaders, such as Kwame Nkrumah, were more focused on promoting the agenda of decolonisation. This divergence of priorities left India somewhat isolated within the NAM during that period.

However, almost a decade later, under the leadership of Mrs Indira Gandhi, India took the bold decision of offering *de jure* recognition to the Provisional Government established by the African Party for the Independence of Guinea–Bissau and Cape Verde (PAIGC) in 1974. This decision was made against the backdrop of the Lusaka (Zambia) summit of the NAM in 1970.

Shifting Emphasis on Economic Factors

I consider the Lusaka summit of the NAM as the second important milestone in Indo–African ties (Harshé 1990). Just as issues related to decolonisation and self-determination were progressively resolved with the formal political independence of African states, India and these states turned their attention to making their independence economically meaningful. The Lusaka summit brought economic issues to the foreground, and consequently, the NAM as a policy and a movement had started gradually shifting its emphasis to economic concerns.

At Lusaka, the NAM states were particularly keen on rectifying the structural imbalances in the world economy. For instance, the constantly fluctuating prices of primary commodities produced by developing countries, coupled with the mounting prices of finished products manufactured by developed industrial economies, had aggravated the deterioration in terms of trade between developing and developed countries, placing the former at a disadvantage. As a result, the developing countries had to fight for the stabilisation of primary commodity prices. Similarly, they expected the developed world to share its technologies and lend financial credit to the former colonies to pursue their developmental objectives. Thus, the NAM countries were heading towards evolving a New International Economic Order (NIEO) through North–South dialogue as well as South–South cooperation.

The Group of 77 that was established in 1964 became a critical vehicle for pushing the demands of developing countries more assertively. By the 1970s and 1980s, the NAM had acquired a distinct economic emphasis, though it continued to address residual political problems as well.

In the 1970s, armed liberation struggles in the Portuguese colonies had come to the foreground. India categorically supported the liberation struggles in Angola, Mozambique and Guinea–Bissau. During the Angolan Civil War, among the three contesting liberation movements that were making a bid to capture power, India, the Soviet Union and Cuba had supported the Popular Movement for the Liberation of Angola (MPLA) which eventually came to the saddle of power after Angolan independence in 1976 (Harshé 2019, p. 180). By the mid-1970s, the former Portuguese colonies in Africa were set free. However, the focus of liberation struggles shifted towards White minority regimes in Southern Africa, such as those in South Rhodesia (Zimbabwe), Namibia and South Africa. India had always supported anti-colonial and anti-racist struggles through the liberation committee of the Organisation of African Unity (OAU), which was established in 1963.

South Africa was in its own right a powerful state in Southern Africa, bolstered by its geostrategic location in both the Indian Ocean and the South Atlantic Ocean. Besides, South Africa obtained economic, technological and military support from Western powers such as the USA, Britain, Germany and France. South Africa was an integral part of the Western alliance during the Cold War, owing to its geopolitical location as well as the investments of Western countries in South/Southern Africa. Liquidating racism and apartheid in Southern Africa was an uphill task.

India, for its part, had not recognised the Unilateral Declaration of Independence (UDI) by Southern Rhodesia under Ian Smith in 1965. Instead, India continued to offer moral support to the armed liberation struggle launched under the aegis of the Patriotic Front (PF), which eventually took power in 1980 when Robert Mugabe became the first President of Zimbabwe (formerly South Rhodesia).

At the 1986 Harare summit of the NAM, India took on the role of Chairman of the Action for Resistance to Invasion, Colonialism and Apartheid (AFRICA) Fund (Maitra 1987). This fund was designed to reduce the dependence of the frontline states of Southern Africa on South Africa as far as infrastructure, investments and markets were concerned. India handled a sum of US$40 million from the funds to pursue this objective. The prominent frontline states fighting apartheid South Africa were Angola, Mozambique, Tanzania, Zambia and Zimbabwe.

India and the NAM also supported the anti-racism struggles launched by the South West Africa People's Organisation (SWAPO) in Namibia and the African National Congress (ANC) in South Africa. Due to ongoing internal pressures from the anti-racial liberation movements and external pressures from left-liberal lobbies in the UK and the USA, the former Soviet Union, its East European allies, and Cuba, as well as the NAM, a referendum was held according to Resolution No. 435 (1978) of the UN Security Council (UNSC) in Namibia in 1990. Namibia became free in 1990. Subsequently, South Africa also transitioned to a post-apartheid state in 1994.

India under Liberalisation

The third major milestone in Indo–African ties was reached when India embraced liberalisation in the post-Soviet and post-Cold War world that emerged after 1991. With the end of the Cold War, India's non-alignment lost much of its erstwhile significance. India opted for the course of economic reforms more out of compulsion than by conviction. By 1991, India's economy was in dire straits. India was left with barely US$ 1 billion in foreign exchange reserves to cover its import needs. Besides, mounting inflation, to the tune of 17 per cent, declining growth rates and a struggling GDP in the malfunctioning economy of India, had necessitated reforms if India was to obtain a loan from the International Monetary Fund (IMF) to come out of severe economic crises (Harshé 2000).

Reforms were intended to roll back the state's participation in business, shut down sick public sector units, and cut back on government expenditure, including salaries and subsidies. Till 1991, India had witnessed a phase of some form of autarchy owing to its policy of self-reliance and emphasis on import substitution. India was also heavily dependent on the former Soviet Union both as a market and trading partner. With economic reforms, India had decided to undertake a difficult transition from selective participation in the world economy to the integration of its economy within the parameters of the world economy. Indeed, the path of reforms that it chose led to sustained growth of India's economy at an annual average of 6 to 7 per cent for almost 25 years. The gradual dismantling of the licence-quota raj liberalised the economy, allowing sectors like telecom and IT to flourish.

In the post-reform phase, India was concerned with security as well as economy-related issues in Africa. India's participation in UN peacekeeping missions in countries such as Somalia, the Democratic Republic of Congo (DRC), Mozambique, Rwanda, Liberia, Angola, Sierra Leone, Sudan and Namibia had built a bridge of understanding between India and Africa (Harshé 2010, p. 352). Besides, cooperation to boost maritime security as well as for the exploitation of the seabed resources in the Indian Ocean Region (IOR) has been an important objective of India and most of the southern, eastern and northeast African states. In view of the nefarious activities of pirates on the Somalian coast, India was particularly anxious about maritime security since its trade passes through the Gulf of Aden and the Red Sea.

However, in the post-reform period, India's rapidly growing economy became most concerned with energy security. African countries can meet India's energy requirements to a certain extent. For instance, countries such as South Africa and Niger have substantial uranium deposits, while countries like Angola, Nigeria, Algeria, Egypt, Equatorial Guinea, Sudan and South Sudan, Congo, Libya, and Gabon are rich in oil reserves. Even though India has depended heavily on Persian Gulf countries for oil, owing to the political instability in the West Asian region, it chose to diversify its sources of energy supplies by befriending countries such as Angola, Nigeria and Sudan. India's Oil and Natural Gas Videsh Limited (OVL) initially invested US$750 million in Sudan in 2003 and collaborated with Chinese, Malaysian and Sudanese state-owned oil companies to extract oil in Sudan. India also boosted its economic and trade ties with powerful countries in Africa, such as Nigeria and South Africa. India launched its Focus Africa programme in 2002, with the objective of expanding ties with African countries through export-promoting councils. Initially, seven Anglophone countries were part of it: Nigeria, South Africa, Mauritius, Tanzania, Kenya, Ghana and Ethiopia. Gradually, Lusophone countries such as Angola and Mozambique, as well as Francophone countries, such as Côte D'Ivoire, Madagascar, Senegal and Seychelles also joined the programme, as did Botswana, Uganda, Namibia, Zambia and Zimbabwe. Similarly, North African/Arab countries such as Egypt, Libya, Tunisia, Sudan, Morocco and Algeria became part of it. The trade between India and African countries increased substantially from US$967 million in 1991 to US$25 billion in 2007 (Harshé 2010, p. 355).

Institutionalisation of Indo-African Ties

The fourth milestone in India–Africa ties was reached when the India–Africa Forum Summit (IAFS) institutionalised Indo-African ties in 2008. So far, three IAFS have been held: in New Delhi (2008), Addis Ababa (2011) and New Delhi (2015). The fourth summit, scheduled to take place in New Delhi in September 2020, was postponed due to the COVID-19 pandemic. Since the IAFS has provided a framework for strengthening both multilateral and bilateral cooperation between India and African states, it has enhanced development cooperation, trade, investment and aid to African countries as far as India is concerned.

The third IAFS, held in 2015, was attended by 54 states (Ministry of External Affairs 2015). In addition to the US$7.4 billion concessional credit pledged in 2008, India decided to offer African countries US$10 billion for an additional five years. Further, grant assistance totalling US$600 million, including US$100 million in funds for development and 50,000 scholarships for African students wishing to study in India, were announced. Out of these scholarships, 40,000 have been utilised. Similarly, from 2015 to 2020, India undertook 34 visits to

African countries at the levels of President, Vice President and Prime Minister. In 2018, India also decided to open 18 embassies in Africa.

India has held three meetings with Regional African Communities (RACs), and by 2019, its trade with Africa reached US$69 billion, registering 12 per cent growth from the previous year (Shringla 2020). India maintains a sound network of business interests in Africa, with not only public sector enterprises but also private business giants like Reliance, Godrej, Apollo Tyres, Essar Group, Tatas, Mahindra, Kirloskar and Mittal actively engaged in Africa. The Mittal-run Airtel has captured a considerable share of the African market. The Tatas generally view their outward expansion as a fresh way of contributing to the process of nation-building in India (Taylor 2012, p. 790).

Security-related issues have continued to play a significant role in Indo-African ties. India has been training military personnel at institutions in Ethiopia, Nigeria and Tanzania. Besides, it has defence agreements with countries such as Zambia, Nigeria, Ghana, Ethiopia, Botswana, Uganda, Namibia and Mozambique. India and African countries are committed to wiping out terrorism. There are transnational terrorist organisations such as Al-Shabaab and Boko Haram in eastern and western Africa, respectively. Both these organisations, in turn, are connected with the multinational terrorist organisation, Al-Qaeda. India also has to deal with cross-border terrorist outfits such as Lashkar-e-Taiba (LeT), Jama'at-ud-Da'wa (JuD) and Jaish-e-Mohammad (JeM), which have bases in Pakistan. These outfits, too, are linked to Al-Qaeda.

India needs African cooperation in the Indo-Pacific region. The Indo-Pacific region extends from the eastern coast of Africa to the Western Pacific Ocean. Prime Minister Narendra Modi's visits to key strategic countries in the Southwest Indian Ocean, including Seychelles, Mauritius (2015), Mozambique, Kenya and Tanzania (2016), and Rwanda and South Africa (2018) are cases in point. In 2015, India declared that it stands for Security and Growth for All in the Region (SAGAR). It has constantly been working towards building naval ties with the coastal states of Africa located in the western Indian Ocean region.

In the educational and cultural domains too, India–Africa partnerships have made headway. India is promoting IT cooperation with Africa through a Pan-African e-network. Similarly, the establishment of educational institutions such as the India–Africa Institute of Foreign Trade (IAIFT), India–Africa Diamond Institute (IADI), and India–Africa Institute for Educational Planning and Administration (IAIEPA) demonstrates India's efforts to promote cooperation with African countries in higher education. India has also started vocational training centres in countries such as Ethiopia, Rwanda, Burundi, Burkina Faso, the Gambia, Zimbabwe and Egypt. In fact, both in India and in African states, more than half the population is in the younger age bracket, a much larger proportion than in other parts of the world. This can open up further areas of cooperation.

During the last decade, India has emerged as a rising power, with a presence in major international groupings including G20, and transcontinental organisations such as Brazil, Russia, India, China, and South Africa (BRICS). India is working to obtain a permanent seat at the UNSC and certainly needs backing from African states to attain this objective. To conclude, the four defining moments analysed above have evolved over the past seven decades, and have widened, broadened and deepened Indo-African ties.

References

Harshé, Rajen. "India's Non-Alignment: An Attempt at Conceptual Reconstruction", *Economic and Political Weekly* vol. 25, nos. 7 & 8 (1990): pp. 399–405.

———. "Reconstructing the Links between the Domestic and Foreign Policy of India", *Indian Social Science Review* vol. 2, no. 1 (2000): pp. 147–64.

———. "India and Africa in the Post–Cold War World: An Overview", *International Studies* vol. 47, nos. 2 & 4 (2010): pp. 347–61.

———. *Africa in World Affairs: Politics of Imperialism, the Cold War and Globalisation*. New York: Routledge, 2019.

Maitra, Susan. "Non-Aligned Leaders Launch AFRICA Fund", *Executive Intelligence Review* vol. 14, no. 6 (1987): pp. 44–45.

Modi, Narendra. Available online: Speech at the Inaugural Ceremony of the Third India–Africa Forum Summit in New Delhi (29 October 2015) (accessed on 27 July 2025).

Shringla, Harsh. "Why the India–Africa bond matters", *Hindustan Times*, 13 February 2020.

Taylor, Ian. "India's Rise in Africa", *International Affairs* vol. 88, no. 4 (2012): pp. 779–98.

Chapter 5

Indian Presence in Africa and African Presence in India: Historical Precursors to Contemporary India–Africa Relations

Sanjukta Bhattacharya

Geographically, India–Africa connections go back millions of years. According to the continental drift theory,[1] the Indo-Australian tectonic plate broke away from the supercontinent Pangea, from the eastern part of what is today Africa, about 100 million years ago. The Indian plate detached from the Australian plate more than three million years thereafter and collided with the Eurasian plate conceivably 55 million years ago. Recent plate reconstruction models, based on geological and geomagnetic data, have demonstrated how the Indian subcontinent separated from the supercontinent, more specifically from around the Horn of Africa (Yoshida and Hamano 2015). The Gondwana region resembles the Ethiopian countryside and has similar agricultural products like

1 The continental drift theory was proposed by German geophysicist Alfred Lothar Wegener in his 1915 book, *The Origin of Continents and Oceans*, where he called an original supercontinent "Pangea". At the time, the theory was met with scepticism because Wegener could not explain how plates moved, but modern science has since made progress in resolving this problem.

cotton. Minerals and precious stones found in Africa, including gold and diamonds, are also mined here.

Historically, studies on migration often mention the "Out of Africa" theory whereby early Homo sapiens moved to large parts of the world from Africa. Tools found at Jwalapuram, a 74,000-year-old site in southern India, match those used in Africa from the same period (Petraglia et al. 2007). In his book, *Sapiens: A Brief History of Humankind*, Yuval Noah Harari details the various out-migrations of ancient Africans to India and beyond (Harari 2015). This chapter will trace these migrations in more recent historical times, focusing on the creation of respective diasporas in India and Africa.

In any study of diasporas, the importance of historical context must be emphasised because broad trends in world political and economics are often the drivers of migration. Trade connections between India, Aden and Egypt possibly go back almost 5,000 years; this flourished further under the Roman Empire. India–Africa trade was perhaps a by-product of the commerce between India's west coast and the ancient civilisations along the Red Sea. Trade goes hand in hand with interaction and sometimes the relocation of people and cultures. Keeping world history and economy as a backdrop, the early origins of the Indian diaspora in Africa and the less-talked-about history of African-origin people in India will be traced in this chapter.

What is interesting is that both of these migrations were largely involuntary, mostly forced, although many Indians in the 19th century went to Africa of their own volition. What is also interesting is that, over time, both groups were able to overcome initial obstructions to freedom and were able to flourish. However, what also needs to be noted is that while Indians in Africa are distinctly identifiable even today, physically and culturally, very few Africans who came to India over the centuries are still recognisable as being African origin—although many Indians bear some African features—and little remains of their languages and cultures. Perhaps this disparity is because Africans who were brought as slaves in medieval times were single with no African partners; they intermarried and often blended into the population. In contrast, Indian men and women who migrated to Africa as indentured labourers often brought their families, so there was less intermarriage, though genome studies may reveal interrelations on a larger scale.

Pre-history can only be conjectured about in the absence of proof; therefore, this chapter will focus on recorded history to demonstrate the antiquity of India–Africa relations. But a moot point arises: what exactly is a diaspora? Or, more pertinent, who is a diaspora? The term is widely used in contemporary times, especially by the developing world, as an identification, perhaps again for political and economic reasons. It is interesting to note that people of English origin in the United States or Australia are not called an "English diaspora" by either the British, Americans or Australians, even though their antecedents are easily traceable. The same applies to French, Dutch, German or any other European immigrants to these countries. Yet, Indians speak of an "Indian diaspora" in the US, just as the Chinese do. Similarly, Indians who went to Africa six generations ago are being wooed by India as part of its Indian diaspora, while the Siddis in India are being researched as the African diaspora in India.

This actually raises a serious question because I think we have followed Western methodologies in academics and research for too long. The search for a global diaspora, and not just "roots", proves that the so-called Global South may have a different way of thinking, cultural identification, sociological orientation, etc., which could also give us new openings in bilateral and multilateral relations. Definitions of diaspora often mention a yearning to return; however, people of Indian origin in Africa, who have lived there for several generations, have no such longing, although they do take pride in their country of origin. Similarly, people of African origin have no desire to return, and, in fact, there is almost no trace of their country of origin. Perhaps the idea of "diaspora" needs to be redefined from a non-Western point of view.

I

The migration of Indians to Africa and their integration into the countries of their choice will be discussed first, followed by an examination of people of African origin in India. The earliest accounts of Indian presence on the eastern coast of Africa are found in *Periplus of the Erythraean Sea*, written in the first century CE by an anonymous author.[2] From this and other writings, it is evident that Indian merchants had been plying their trade through the Indian Ocean since Babylonian times and had even established trading posts along the East African coast.

Archaeologies of the coast appear to position the inhabitants as part of a well-attested network of trade and exchange from around the seventh century CE, which united regions along the Indian Ocean rim from early times, with contacts becoming denser and better documented from around the 13th century (Hawkes and Wynne-Jones 2015). Archaeological digs at the stone town of Shanga (in today's Kenya) on the East African coast have revealed some interesting items that reflect early contacts dating back to 1100 CE. For instance, an enigmatic figure of a bronze lion, typical of similar figurines found in the Deccan Plateau, was discovered. This figure uses technology available in India but depicts an African lion with a wild mane, not the trimmed mane of its Indian counterpart, possibly hinting at the presence of Indian craftsmen in Africa.

Interestingly, its metal content is similar to that of contemporary Chinese coins, suggesting that it may have been cast from melted Chinese coins, as part of a wider practice of metal recycling in the Indian Ocean world (Horton and Blurton 1988). This single find opens up the possibilities of the movement of people, materials, technologies, ideas and styles across oceans in the early medieval period. Another such find is a 13th-century wooden, gold-plated, one-horned rhinoceros, with gold locally sourced from Mapungubwe in southern Africa. The single horn suggests an Indian model (Fouché 1937). There are also sizable collections of Indian goods—mainly coins, carnelian beads and red-polished and burnished ceramics—found in Shanga and Tumbatu.

Apart from archaeology, the relative absence of written history means a reliance on oral traditions. A series of allusions in Swahili oral traditions hint at early connections, particularly with Sindh, mentioning the *waDebuli*, or *waDiba*, ethnonyms associated with a

---

2 The *Periplus Maris Erythraei* is the most important source of information about Rome's maritime trade in the Indian Ocean region from the first century CE. There is a good translation available (Casson 1989).

range of historical events and periods in different parts of the Swahili coast. Historical analysts associate the *waDebuli* stories with the port of Daybul at the mouth of the Indus, based on similarities in the name and the prominence of that site from the eighth century right into the 13th century (Walsh 2010). This could have been a point of origin of immigrants, although there is nothing more substantial than the stories to prove this. But it may be useful to remember that Sindh was the easternmost point of the Abbasid Empire and had direct contact with the Swahili coast. Coins also provide a hint about these contacts. The coins of Shanga and Sindh both have texts running from the obverse to the reverse and use dies with pegs, indicating strong similarities in technique (Hawkes and Wynne-Jones 2015).

Coming to recorded history, Vasco da Gama encountered Indian merchants in East Africa in the late 15th century. In Malindi, he obtained the services of a Gujarati-speaking sailor to navigate his ships across the Indian Ocean to Calicut (Herzig 2006, pp. 10–1).[3] The Portuguese soon dominated the Indian Ocean trade, displacing the Arabs, and Indians were their accountants and bankers, just as they had been for the Arabs (ibid.). In the early 19th century, Indian merchants began settling across the trading posts of East Africa. Their interests were enhanced when Said bin Sultan of Oman and Muscat, whose court shifted to Zanzibar in 1840, adopted a series of favourable policies towards Indians in the region, in response to emerging British naval supremacy in the Indian Ocean and British political support for Indian merchants along the East African coast (ibid.). In 1888, the British East Africa Association, founded in 1887 and headquartered in Bombay, was given a royal charter and became the Imperial British East Africa Company, moving its base to Mombasa. The company continued to have a strong Indian orientation, employing guards, police officers, clerks and accountants from Bombay. Significant Indian migration to modern-day Kenya began following the creation of the East Africa Protectorate in 1895. The rupee became the currency of the Protectorate, and the legal system was structured as an extension

3 See also https://en.wikipedia.org/wiki/Indians_in_Kenya

of Indian law. The vast majority of administrative roles were filled by Konkani Goans, Parsis and Gujaratis, while the British-officered police and army mainly consisted of Punjabis (Herzig 2006, p. 13).

This was the prelude to the advent of large numbers of Indians brought as labourers or indentured servants by the British, who were colonial masters on both sides of the Indian Ocean. For the Uganda railway, a total of 35,729 coolies and artisans were recruited, mostly from villages in Punjab, along with 1,082 subordinate officers, totalling 36,811 persons between 1896 and 1901. Nearly 2,500 coolies died due to various reasons, including being killed by the man-eaters of Tsavo. Most of the survivors returned to India, but 6,724 opted to remain, forming a community of Indians in East Africa. The railway opened up the interior regions of eastern Africa, and many Indian traders, mainly from Gujarat, followed. They set up shops and became *dukawallahs,* a term obviously derived from *dukandar*s or shopkeepers.[4]

The other well-known route of people of Indian origin to Africa was through the indenture system, following the abolition of slavery in 1834. This system involved the recruitment of labour through agents to serve on British (and some French) colonial plantations for a fixed period of time, when they were not free, but received some wages through which they could pay off the indenture at the end of their service and become free. Indian indentured labour was taken to Mauritius as early as the 1830s, mainly from Madras Province, modern Bihar and Uttar Pradesh; emigration to Natal in South Africa began in 1860. The system was rife with malpractices, and, faced with complaints, indenture to Natal was terminated in 1911 and to Mauritius in 1910. Interestingly, a large number of women also went as indentured labour, with the colonial rationale being that families were more likely to remain and cause fewer problems. Once free, or

---

4 It may be interesting to explore the illustrated memoirs of Kesi Rustomji, a Parsi born in Uganda, who grew up in Tanganyika, finished his schooling in Kenya and later moved to Australia. His memoirs include many photographs from his childhood, and, having grown up around Indian shops, he has re-created the picture of a "duka" in his poem, "Ode to the Indian Dukawala on East African Plains." See http://www.kersi.50webs.com/, accessed on January 28, 2020.

when the indenture system was finally banned in 1917, many were successful in bringing their families across.

But it should be noted that, apart from indentured labourers—many of whom chose to emigrate because of the push effects of impoverishment in India—there were other so-called passenger or unindentured Indians who migrated under the normal immigration laws of the British Empire. These individuals set up shops and trading centres in east and South Africa. They were largely Gujarati-speaking Muslims, mainly Khojas and Memons, as well as Hindus of different caste groups, such as the *Sonis* (goldsmiths), *Dhobis* (laundrymen) and *Mochis* (shoemakers), many of whom continued their professions in their new homes (Hiralal 2008, p. 28). In Natal, they faced discrimination from the British and restrictive legislation against fresh Indian immigration and trade. Nevertheless, the passenger Indians laid the foundations of the Indian commercial class in South Africa and also challenged the colonial economic system, which was based on racial prejudice.

Significant Indian migration also occurred in Kenya after 1895, with many people coming from Punjab, the Konkan, Gujarat and Goa. Many emigrants arrived with their families or caste members. One of the most significant early pioneers was A.M. Jeevanjee. His company, A.M. Jeevanjee of Karachi, was awarded the contract to supply labour for the building of the Uganda Railway in 1890, which helped him establish himself as the pre-eminent Asian businessman in Kenya. He established Kenya's first newspaper, now known as *The Standard*, in 1901 and became the first non-White to be elected to the Legislative Council in 1910 (Patel 2002, p. 13).

In Kenya, too, there were racial hostilities, but since Indians had greater economic power than Black Africans, they had better bargaining power with the British and made some political gains. Indians could be found in all professions, including the bureaucracy and the police, in addition to commerce, where their skills contributed to the economic development of Kenya and other parts of East Africa.[5] Many of them were also at the forefront of the fight for equal rights. For instance, Pio Gama Pinto was the founder of the Kenya African

5 See https://en.wikipedia.org/wiki/Indians_in_Kenya

National Union (KANU) newspaper, *Sauti Ya KANU;* Makhan Singh is regarded as laying the foundations of Kenyan trade unionism; and A.R. Kapila and Fitz de Souza are known in the legal profession for representing those accused of links to the Mau Mau movement.[6] It is a pity that today they are largely invisible in the local histories of Kenya, Tanzania or Uganda, where there is hardly any mention of their contributions to the national histories of these countries. This may be due to their business successes in non-agricultural sectors, but their presence is overtly visible in these sectors even today, which is a testimony to their role in the economic development of these countries.

It has already been mentioned that migration should not be taken in isolation from global economic and political trends. Here, it is important to emphasise that British colonisation on both sides of the Indian Ocean acted as a facilitator to the migration of Indians to Africa on a much larger scale and more systematic manner than before. The British and French colonial need for plantation labour acted as a pull factor, while impoverishment and man-made famines—resulting from British policies, such as the initial British pursuit of the opium trade and its promotion in the mid-Gangetic plains as well as the impoverishment caused by its later abandonment—was a push factor for indebted villagers from that region. The lure of new trade, especially among Indians who had migrated to Africa earlier, was also a pull factor. Without the demands of the colonial economy, this migration may never have taken place.

II

On the other hand, many Africans came to India, but their history has hardly been researched. The origin of the Siddis in India is lost in folklore, legends and historical speculations, but it is widely believed that the first Africans arrived on the Konkani coast around the first century CE. According to one theory, the kings and rulers along the west coast of India bought African slaves from Arab traders, who brought them from Africa (Pinto 2006, pp. 384–5). After the advent of Islam and especially after India came under the rule of the Turko–

6 Ibid.

Afghans and later the Mughals, there was a further influx of African slaves into the country. However, since Islam promotes equality and brotherhood among men, it is not surprising that many Africans rose to prominent positions, including that of rulers, during these years.

One feature that needs to be mentioned is that most of the Africans who came during this time were males, leading to intermarriage and racial mixing. Recent genome surveys using autosomal markers, Y-chromosomal and mitochondrial DNA indicate that while the Siddis trace their ancestry back to Bantu speakers of sub-Saharan Africa, they also have Indian and possibly European (that is, Portuguese) ancestry (Shah et al. 2011). However, the specific African group to which the Siddis trace their ancestry remains unknown.[7]

Another term used for the early Africans is *Habshi*, a corruption of *Habash*, the Arabic name for Abyssinia. This term is believed to have originated from Habashat, which the Arabs used to refer to the kingdom of Aksum, its people Habash and their Amhara-Tigrean successors (Ahmed 2013, p. 400). Siddi is a corruption of the Arabic Sayyid or master, but it later became a term of reproach or insult rather than distinction. Since many early African slaves converted to Islam and changed their names, it is impossible to trace their origins. However, it is known that they began to arrive in India in significant numbers from the 13th century, although some were already part of earlier armies and entourages like that of Mahmud of Ghazni.

Ibn Battuta, who travelled widely in India during the 14th century, speaks of the presence of Abyssinian soldiers on a ship at what he calls "Gandhar" on the western coast, 400 slaves who were the descendants of "Hindu chiefs and Abyssinians" in Gujarat and Abyssinians with javelins, drums and swords in Calicut. He also mentions that the governor of Alapur, north of Delhi, was a *Habshi*, as was Malik Sarwar, the governor of Jaunpur (Pankhurst 2003, p. 192). Thus, unlike Africans who were victims of the trans-Atlantic slave trade, slaves brought by the Muslim rulers of India were able to rise to positions of power, sometimes to kingship.

---

7 Attempts are now being made through scientific genome studies to find the African places of origin of the Siddis. See Das and Upadhyai 2017.

Given the constraints of space, only two such *Habshi/Siddi* kingdoms—Bengal and Janjira—will be outlined here. In Bengal, the *Habshi* commander of the palace guards under Jalal-ud-din Fateh Shah of the Ilyas Shahi dynasty seized power and became Sultan Ghiyas-ud-din Firuz Shah in 1487. He was succeeded by two other *Habshi* sultans, after which the throne was seized by the Husaini dynasty. The last of the *Habshi* sultans was reportedly cruel, which led to anti-*Habshi* agitation and ultimately the expulsion of the *Habshis* from Bengal (Roychowdhury 2016).

In contrast, the Siddi *nawabs* of Janjira, an island off the Bombay coast, were more successful. In 1489, this island was taken over by a Siddi employed by the Ahmadnagar Sultanate, possibly through deceit. The Siddi sultanate was able to hold on to it till India gained independence in 1947 (Ali 1996, pp. 157–92). Ottoman records mention that a combined force from the Ottomans and Janjira routed a Portuguese fleet in Yemen in 1587, and thenceforward, the Siddis played an important role in resisting the Portuguese in the region. In 1733, Peshwa Baji Rao of the Marathas launched a campaign against Janjira but was unable to capture the fort. Following this, the Marathas signed a treaty granting them indirect control over Siddi lands, which had earlier been under the overlordship of the Bijapur Sultanate. After British rule was established in the Konkan, Janjira State was administered as part of the Deccan States Agency of the Bombay Presidency, founded in 1799. Initially, the Janjira rulers called themselves *wazirs*, but from 1803, the British recognised them as *nawabs* entitled to an 11-gun salute (ibid., p. 187).

There were many significant Siddis who rose to high positions, with two of the most well-known being Jamal-ud-din Yaqut, a confidante of Razia Sultana, and later Malik Ambar. A first-generation slave sold by his parents, Malik Ambar served in the Bijapur state but rose to great heights as the regent of the Nizamshahi dynasty of Ahmadnagar between 1607 and 1627. During this time, he raised an army of 10,000 *Habshis* and 40,000 Deccanis, which successfully thwarted Emperor Jahangir's attempts to defeat Ahmadnagar. Malik Ambar also reportedly helped Shah Jahan to wrest power from his stepmother Nur Jahan, though he was later defeated by him. One of his daughters, from a Siddi wife, was married to an Ahmadnagar prince who, with Malik Ambar's support, was later crowned Sultan Murtaza Shah II (Ali 2016).

Many Siddis, aside from being soldiers, bodyguards, naval commanders and nobles, had skills that are still visible in the Portuguese churches of Goa, where slaves brought by the Portuguese served as artisans and even architects. The Siddi Sayyid Mosque in Gujarat, with its unparalleled *jali* work (stone lattice windows in the Islamic "tree of life" pattern), built in the 16th century, stands as a masterpiece of the African architectural legacy in India. This mosque was built with the fortune amassed by Siddi Sayyid himself. Malik Ambar is also known to have designed the city of Aurangabad.[8]

Although their contribution to the history of medieval India is little known and not included in modern textbooks, in the same way as the economic and political contributions of Indians to building certain states in eastern and southern Africa is bypassed, the influence of the Siddis in military, political and artistic fields was considerable. Today, they are scattered in locations in Goa,

---

8 Recently, the Schomburg Centre for Research in Black Culture at the New York Public Library curated the exhibition 'Africans in India: From Slaves to Generals and Rulers' in collaboration with the United Nations' Remembering Slavery programme. Co-curated by Sylviane Diouf and Kenneth X. Robbins, the exhibition showcased the rich history of Africans in India, featuring paintings of Siddi rulers, queens, noblemen in royal courts, and more. The exhibition text noted, 'As rulers, city planners, and architects, the Africans have left an impressive historical and architectural legacy that attest to their determination, skills, and intellectual, cultural, military, and political savvy'. India is still home to forts, mosques and mausoleums built by Africans over 500 years ago. The exhibition was brought to India by the Indira Gandhi National Centre for the Arts in collaboration with the Schomburg Centre in 2016, and it travelled to several cities. Some of the fascinating paintings can be viewed in Mridula Chari, 'Rare images document the centuries-long history of Africans in India', *Scroll* 8 October 2014, available at https://scroll.in/article/682635/rare-images-document-the-centuries-long-history-of-africans-in-india, accessed on 1 August 2020, and Lavina Melwani, 'Africans in India: From Slaves to Sultans', Khabar, August 2017, available at http://www.khabar.com/magazine/cover-story/africans-in-india-from-slaves-to-sultans, accessed on 1 August 2020. The online exhibition hosted by the New York Public Library is archived.

Diu, Daman, Karnataka, Maharashtra, Andhra and Gujarat, but have largely integrated into the complex cobweb of cultures that is peculiar to India. Yet, some still retain their strong cultural traditions of music and dance, sometimes known as *dhamaal*, which is derived from *ngoma* drumming and traditional dance forms of central, eastern and southern Africa (Samuel 2020). Ngoma drumming and dance are derived from the *Kiswahili* word *ngoma,* which means 'drums', and troops perform in India and abroad. In modern times, Indian percussionists are experimenting with these instruments and techniques.

III

Contacts between India and Africa go far beyond trade mostly non-voluntarily, over the last thousand years, with more Africans adopting India as their homeland during the early and late medieval periods, and Indians voluntarily migrating to Africa as what could be called partially bonded labour but also as free traders and merchants during colonial times. Both migrations were shaped by broad global historical, economic and political push and pull factors, relevant to the times, without which such large-scale migration would never have occurred.

If we look at the commonalities in both cases, many of those who were transported non-voluntarily, or their descendants, rose to economic and political power and contributed to shaping the histories of the regions to which they were brought. And here, we can draw a stark contrast between Africans and Indians who were sent across the Atlantic Ocean as slaves and indentured servants. It is only now that they are coming into their own, despite their significant contributions to the economic growth of their host countries.

However, it may be pointed out that while the people of Indian origin in African countries continue to keep a separate cultural identity although they have no desire to return to India, people of African origin in India have contributed to the highly mixed Indian gene pool and have largely adopted the languages and cultures of their localities. In some places where they once ruled, like Bengal, they are no longer traceable, having merged into the general population.

The British gave the Siddis, who still kept their identity, a separate tribal status under the MacDonald Award, and this was continued in independent India. In January 2003, the Indian government granted Scheduled Tribe status to the Siddis, but due to bureaucratic oversight, some districts were excluded from this designation, leading the Siddis there to miss out on benefits. Activists are currently fighting for the inclusion of all Siddis. In fact, the Union government has placed them under the "Particularly Vulnerable Tribal Groups" section, acknowledging that in current times, the Siddis are a fragile community in need of affirmative action.[9]

In conclusion, I would like to recommend that the history of migration and the contributions of these largely non-voluntary settlers in Africa and India, along with their struggles and how they adapted to their peculiar circumstances and overcame the effects of forced migration, should be highlighted in the countries concerned and in bilateral relations. Highlighting these narratives will help to strengthening both bilateral and multilateral Africa–India bonds.

References

Ahmed, El Amin Abdel Karim. "Habasha, Abyssinia and Ethiopia: Some Notes Concerning a Country's Names and Images", Annual Conference of Postgraduate Studies and Scientific Research, Humanities and Educational Studies, University of Khartoum, Conference Proceedings, Volume I. February: pp. 399–415, 2013. Available at http://khartoumspace.uofk.edu/bitstream/handle/123456789/9461/Habasha_Abyssinia_and_Ethiopia.pdf?sequence=1&isAllowed=y (accessed on 24 July 2010).

Ali, Omar A. *Malik Ambar: Power and Slavery across the Indian Ocean*. Oxford: Oxford University Press, 2016.

Ali, Shanti Sadiq. *The African Dispersal in the Deccan: From Medieval to Modern Times*. Bombay: Orient Longman, 1996.

9 In July 2020, Shantaram Budna Siddi was nominated to Karnataka's Legislative Council by the state government, marking a significant milestone as he became the first Siddi to hold such a governing post since medieval times (Sankaran 2020).

Casson, Lionel (trans.). *The Periplus Maris Erythraei: Text with Introduction, Translation & Commentary*. Princeton: Princeton University Press, 1989.

Das, Ranajit and Priyanka Upadhyai. "Unraveling the Population History of Indian Siddis", *Genome Biology and Evolution* vol. 9, no. 6 (2017): pp. 1385–92.

Fouché, Leo. *Mapungubwe: Ancient Bantu Civilization on the Limpopo: Reports on Excavations at Mapungubwe (Northern Transvaal) from February 1933 to June 1935*. Cambridge: Cambridge University Press, 1937.

Harari, Yuval Noah. *Sapiens: A Brief History of Humankind*. London: Penguin Random House, 2015.

Hawkes, Jason D., and Stephanie Wynne-Jones. "India and Africa: Trade Goods and Connections of the Late First Millennium", *Afriques* vol. 6 (2015). DOI: https://doi.org/10.4000/afriques.1752.

Herzig, Pascale. *South Asians in Kenya: Gender, Generation and Changing Identities in Diaspora*. Munster: LIT Verlag, 2006.

Hiralal, Kalpana. "Indian Family Businesses in Natal, 1870–1950". *Natalia*, 38 (2008): pp. 27–37.

Horton, M., and T. Blurton. "'Indian' metalwork in East Africa: The bronze lion statuette from Shanga", *Antiquity* vol. 62, no. 234 (1988): pp. 11–23. DOI:10.1017/S0003598X00073452

Pankhurst, Richard. "The Ethiopian Diaspora to India: The Role of Habshis and Sidis from Medieval Times to the End of the Eighteenth Century", in *The African Diaspora in the Indian Ocean*, eds. Shihan de S. Jayasuriya and Richard Pankhurst, pp. 189–222. Trenton, NJ: Africa World Press, 2003.

Patel, Zarina. *Alibhai Mullah Jeevanjee*. Nairobi: East African Publishers, 2002.

Petraglia, Michael, Ravi Korisettar, Nicole Boivin, Christopher Clarkson, Peter Ditchfield, Sacha Jones, Jinu Koshy, Marta Mirazón Lahr, Clive Oppenheimer, David Pyle, Richard Roberts, Jean-Luc Schwenninger, Lee Arnold, Kevin White. 2007. "Middle Paleolithic Assemblages from the Indian Subcontinent before and After the Toba Super-Eruption", *Science* vol. 317, no. 5834 (6 July 2007): pp. 114–6. DOI: 10.1126/science.1141564.

Pinto, Jeanette. "The African Native in Indiaspora", *African and Asian Studies* vol. 5, nos. 3-4 (2006): pp. 383–97.

Roychowdhury, Adrija. "African Rulers of India: That part of Our History We Choose to Forget", *The Indian Express*, 5 June 2016. Available online:

https://indianexpress.com/article/research/african-rulers-of-india-that-part-of-our-history-we-choose-to-forget/#:~:text=Barbak%20Shahzada%20laid%20the%20foundation,best%20of%20the%20Habshi%20rulers (accessed on 30 January 2020).

Samuel, Richard. "How the Siddi community has been thriving through music and dance", *The Hindu*, 20 January 2020. Available online: https://www.thehindu.com/society/history-and-culture/tunes-and-sounds-from-the-woods/article30607717.ece (accessed on 28 January 2020).

Sankaran, Sanjeev. "Shantaram Siddi, Karnataka's new MLC, is a link to India's African connection", *The Times of India*, 23 July 2020. Available online: https://timesofindiaindiatimes.com/blogs/cash-flow/shantaram-siddi-karnatakas-new-mlc-is-a-link-to-indias-african-connection/ (accessed on 8 August 2020).

Shah, Anish M., Rakesh Tamang, Priya Moorjani, Deepa Selvi Rani, Periyasamy Govindaraj, Gururaj Kulkarni, Tanmoy Bhattacharya, Mohammed S. Mustak, L.V.K.S. Bhaskar, Alla G. Reddy, Dharmendra Gadhvi, Pramod B. Gai, Gyaneshwer Chaubey, Nick Patterson, DavidReich, Chris Tyler-Smith, Lalji Singh, and Kumarasamy Thangaraj. "Indian Siddis: African Descendants with Indian Admixture". *American Journal of Human Genetics* vol. 89, no. 1 (15 July 2011): pp. 154–61. DOI: 10.1016/j.ajhg.2011.05.030

Walsh, Martin. "Deep Memories or Symbolic Statements? The Diba, Debuli and Related Traditions of the East African Coast", in *Civilisations des mondes insulaires (Madagascar, îles du canal de Mozambique, Mascareignes, Polynésie, Guyanes): Mélanges en l'honneur du Professeur Claude Allibert*, eds. Chantal Radimilahy, Narivelo Rajaonarimanana, pp. 453–76. Paris: Karthala, 2010. Available online: https://www.researchgate.net/publication/272202234_Deep_memories_or_symbolic_statements_The_Diba_Debuli_and_related_traditions_of_the_East_African_coast (accessed on 20 January 2020).

Wegener, Alfred. *Die Entstehung der Kontinente und Ozeane* ("The Origin of Continents and Oceans"). Braunschweig: Vieweg & Sohn, 1915.

Yoshida, Masaki, and Yozo Hamano. "Pangea Breakup and Northward Drift of the Indian Subcontinent reproduced by a Numerical Model of Mantle Convection", *Scientific Reports* 5 (2015): p. 8407. DOI:10.1038/srep08407

PART 2
Knowledge Systems

Chapter 6

Endogenous Innovation and Development in Comparative Perspective: Towards a Model for Africa–India Cooperation

Ogundiran Soumonni

Introduction

The dominant discourses on globalisation and international trade that emerged in the 1990s, whether advocative or critical, often mask the fact that the very history of humanity is one of migration, exchange and interpenetration in all facets of life. Furthermore, the prevailing institutional apparatus designed to foster "development" in most of the world is economistic in its orientation and tends to downplay the plurality of values that provide people with a higher sense of meaning and purpose. Thus, the task of formerly colonised nations in Africa, Asia and elsewhere must be not only to problematise these extremely influential policy positions but also to offer alternative pathways for a more just global order.

As a contribution to such a dual exercise, this chapter is anchored in the underpinnings of endogenous knowledge, which views collective self-knowledge as the first step on the long journey to autonomous or internally-directed development. It is nourished by critical research, training and practical action, and remains committed to intense, though selective, exchanges with others (Ki-Zerbo 1992). In contradistinction to the framing of Africa that was inherited from its arbitrary partition—an earlier manifestation of globalisation—however, the preferred understanding that grounds the chapter is that which was defined by the pre-eminent Beninese linguist, cultural theorist and diplomat Olabiyi Yaï as "the sum total of African cultures as sedimented for millennia in philosophies, wisdoms, ways of being and doing things, as well as ways of relating to otherness" (Yaï 2008).

In addition to the premise above, it is well established that Africa was fundamental to the very emergence of industrial modernity (Inikori 2002), and overwhelmingly at the expense of its own development (Rodney 1981). Analogous studies have similarly documented India's overwhelming contribution to England's industrialisation as having been underpinned by "tribute from conquest" and the destruction of the former's textile industry (Habib 1975), resulting in extreme impoverishment, several famines, as well as the entrenchment and creation of new forms of human subjugation (Bagchi 2010).

Parenthetically, it is worth noting the explicit acknowledgement by Bagchi (2015) of Inikori's theorisation of the link between the Industrial Revolution in England and its original motivation of replacing Indian textiles with British products, which Inikori deems more compelling than interpretations that privilege internal social and political dynamics for large-scale technological change. Nonetheless, a consistent theme across the works of these African and Indian economic historians is that the two dialectically related phenomena—development and underdevelopment—are rooted in exploitative power relations that have continuing implications for the asymmetry in human well-being between the Global North and the South. In this context, innovation, understood as the deliberate acquisition of domestic technological capabilities in order to satisfy a given society's needs, is central to sustained socio-economic development in the South.

Over and above the centrality of technological innovation for closing the gap in well-being with the North, it is also critical for the restoration of civilisational diversity, in contrast to excessive cultural homogenisation within the contemporary digitalised world. This is particularly relevant, given the outstanding scientific and courageous grassroots contributions made by various Global South communities during the COVID-19 pandemic (Soumonni and Muchie 2023). Thus, according to the late pre-eminent historian from Burkina Faso, Joseph Ki-Zerbo, there is a constant dialectic between the locally grounded and the global, and between the past and the present, that represents the living substance of development—a phenomenon that he termed "endogenous development" (Ki-Zerbo 1992). The subset of this broader developmental process that emphasises a society's interactions with its scientific and technological activities is what we refer to as "endogenous innovation" in this chapter. It subsumes the narrow, economically-oriented use of the term, but more significantly, embeds innovation in wider and deeper societal aspirations for human dignity. First penned in 1955 by the great Martinican poet and statesman, Aimé Césaire, the words below elegantly capture the concept of endogenous innovation in a dialogical perspective across space and time:

> Once again, I systematically defend our old Negro civilizations: they were courteous civilizations. So the real problem, you say, is to return to them. No, I repeat. We are not men for whom it is a question of 'either-or'. For us, the problem is not to make a utopian and sterile attempt to repeat the past, but to go beyond. It is not a dead society that we want to reviverevive ... . It is a new society that we must create... a society rich with all the productive power of modern times, warm with all the fraternity of olden days (Césaire 2000, pp. 51–52).

Césaire's perspective encompasses a concept of Africa (or the African world) that also informs this chapter. Temporally, it goes beyond its modern societies to include its ancient civilisations, and spatially, it includes both the people of the continent and their descendants in its diaspora, many of whom were forcibly displaced in order to enrich other climes. Therefore, the notion of a "Global Africa", which is endorsed by the International Scientific Committee of Volume IX of UNESCO's *General History of Africa* series, frames this chapter conceptually. It should be noted, however, that these spatial and temporal dimensions are also the loci of interaction between Africans and diverse peoples from other regions of the world.

According to Nigerian philosopher Sophie Oluwole, among the Yoruba of West Africa, a society is understood to be made up of four categories of people who are to be consciously included in the conduct of its affairs: the youth, women, men, and "foreigners", or, more accurately, "guests" (*àlejò*) (Oluwole 1998). While the emphasis of the above formulation is on inclusive political rights within a town or country (*ìlú*),[1] the worldview extends itself to the idea of nationhood as well. The nation (*orílẹ̀*), although referring to an original territory or land (*ilẹ̀*), is ultimately trans-territorial, being more fundamentally rooted in a shared consciousness (*orí*) and common values associated with an ancestral home (Yaï 2001). This view of nationality, therefore, necessarily implies a recognition of interwoven identities (and indeed, multiple nationalities) that still reverberates among several African diasporic communities in the Americas, thus preserving cultural and linguistic continuity in a manner that Yaï (2001) has characterised as "a reflection of Africans' conceptual and experiential retention and invention". For analytical reasons, and more importantly, as a reflection of lived realities, we extend the concept of Global Africa in a propositional manner to the Indian Oceanic world, which would include the Indian subcontinent and its diasporas, in the ensuing discussion on endogenous innovation.

Endogenous Innovation: A Historico-Cultural Basis

Given the high human cost associated with the advent of industrial capitalism, it is not surprising that the structural imbalances imposed during that period remain extremely challenging to overcome. This provides a root causal explanation (though not a sufficient one) for why the African economic landscape, for instance, is broadly characterised by "growth without development" and "growth without innovation". And although the Indian economy has demonstrated strong innovation performance in certain sectors, it is likewise

1 *Ìlú* can literally be explained as "a place of mixing" of people from various locales (personal communication with Olabiyi Yaï, New Delhi, February 2020).

characterised by relatively slow growth and income inequality. However, what is insufficiently appreciated by many observers of global affairs is that scientific and technological development neither began *ex nihilo* in the "West", nor have they been exclusive to those regions of the world and their ruling classes at any time in history. In fact, the term "creative destruction" (widely attributed to Austrian economist Joseph Schumpeter), which is used to suggest that capitalist economies grow through a cyclical, disruptive innovation process wherein new industries render old ones extinct, has been traced through Friedrich Nietzsche to Shiva, the Hindu deity of creation and destruction (Agarwal 2018). Thus, in the poem entitled "Brahma, Visnu, Shiva" by Rabindranath Tagore, we find the following lines that capture the idea of creative destruction in aesthetic form (Tagore 2005):

> Age after age after age is slave to a mighty rhythm—
> At last the world-frame
> Tires in its body,
> Sleep in its eyes
> Slackens its structure,
> Diffuses its energy.
> From the heart of all matter
> Comes the anguished cry—
> Wake, wake, great Shiva,
> Our body grows weary
> Of its law-fixed path,
> Give us new form.
> Sing our destruction,
> That we gain new life.

Furthermore, Africa's contribution to geometry, astronomy, medicine, architecture and metallurgy in antiquity has been demonstrated through a critical analysis of original texts by Senegalese scientist and historian Cheikh Anta Diop, showing that these contributions had a theoretical dimension originally developed in African languages (Diop 1991). This endogenous production of scientific and technological knowledge was not limited to Nile Valley Civilisations but has continued through to modern times throughout Africa, as well as in its diaspora (Van Sertima 2007). Beyond those cognitive and related edificial achievements, however, texts from as early as the third millennium BCE, such as *The Maxims of Ptahhotep*, underscored the principle that the quest for knowledge and skill was expected to be grounded in humility and moral rectitude (Obenga 2004).

On the other hand, the much later application of the nomenclature of evolutionary biology and palaeontology to the social character of human beings reflects the materialistic ethos that dominated Western accounts of the First Industrial Revolution. While the scientific terms, *Homo habilis* (the handy or skilful human), *Homo erectus* (the upright human), and *Homo sapiens sapiens* (the doubly wise human) can be understood to reflect increasing cognitive ability, analogous terms in literary and social science disciplines like Homo faber (the maker of instruments), Homo loquens (the speaking human), and Homo economicus (the self-interested human) do not capture any ethical dimension. In contrast, the very terms for the human being, as conceived in Bantu languages (e.g. *muntu*, *umuntu*, *motho*), are premised on the African philosophy of ubuntu, which, according to Ramose (2005), posits that a person's well-being is interdependent with that of other people and with that of the natural environment. Having observed that similar perspectives exist in other socio-linguistic communities across Africa, Oluwole (2014) goes on to recommend "binary complementarity" as a scientific and rational ethical framework that can simultaneously spur technological development and promote truly just societies.

The two mutually constitutive dimensions of the binary complementarity conceptual framework briefly introduced above include knowledge of matter and knowledge of the immaterial (both in the form of ideas and in their various social manifestations), and have been laudably integrated into different civilisations, including that of the Yoruba, at various times (Oluwole 2014). One historical African (Yoruba) figure cited by Oluwole as embodying such an outlook is the classical philosopher Ọ̀rúnmìlà (later canonised as a "saint" or *òrìṣà*), who asserted that a person should possess the strength of Ògún (the *òrìṣà* of technology) and the wisdom of himself (the *òrìṣà* of wisdom, who recognised that no one has a monopoly on knowledge and had even gained some of his expertise from his own child, *amósùn*). With respect to this delicate balance between technology and society in the Global South, Ki-Zerbo (1993) lamented that in the name of universality, many societies have uncritically embraced the adoption of modern technologies at the expense of transcendental values and their sense of community.

A profound illustration of this necessity for critical engagement has been provided by Yaï (1999) in his discussion of the concept of "tradition" (*àṣà*) in relation to artists in Yoruba Civilisation. He defines *àṣà* as "a set of customs, deeds and habits after they have been subjected to a historical process of deliberate choice" and reiterates the emphasis on its openness to new influences (Yaï 1999, p. 34). In fact, he underscores the seemingly paradoxical statement by many Yoruba artists that their tradition is "very modern"! Thus, *àṣà* is better understood as "tradition-innovation" (Yaï 1999, p. 35). Furthermore, Olabiyi Yaï offers a hermeneutical interpretation of a Yoruba proverb, which states that after the work of the sculptor (*gbẹnàgbẹnà*) is completed, that of the critic (*gbẹnugbẹnu*) begins. The critic must provide commentary in poetic language that speaks to the sculpture, its relevance for admirers, the background of the artist, and generally situates these in a wider cultural discourse (ibid.).

Our understanding of the process of "tradition-innovation" (or innovation within a tradition), as described above, reflects a complementary dialectical approach that could offer valuable insights into how science and society co-evolve, particularly in the context of the Global South. With respect to socio-economic development, Padgaonkar (1993) emphasised that intellectuals in the South should strive to balance the relationship between economic progress, science, technology and the efficient organisation of resources (that is, innovation), on the one hand, and the respect for human rights, the environment and cultural identity, on the other. However, an earlier, more critically focused analysis by Alam (1978) identified the mechanistic, nominally "'value-free" philosophical stance of science that emerged in 17th-century Europe as being monistic (rather than pluralistic) in its view of nature. Such a conception of science not only advanced the goals of colonial conquest and exploitation but also initiated the ongoing, arbitrary denigration of all other forms of carefully accumulated knowledge and know-how as being "unscientific" (ibid.).

A much more in-depth investigation of this "defeated" knowledge led to the concept of "alternative science", as articulated by the anthropologist of science and technology, Shiv Visvanathan. This term refers to various critical Indian engagements with the hegemony of "modern" science, subsequently associated with the early 20th-century Swadeshi (self-sufficiency) movement in Bengal (Visvanathan 2006). These critiques came from traditionalists, neo-vitalists, theosophists, Nehruvians, Gandhians, Leninist technocrats and Swadeshi nationalists themselves (ibid.). It is also important to note that the early Appropriate Technology movement (typically attributed to British-German economist E.F. Schumacher) was largely inspired by Indian economist J.C. Kumarappa and Sri Lankan geologist and scholar of Indian culture Ananda Kentish Coomaraswamy, both of whom contributed to the Swadeshi movement (Coomaraswamy, 2010).

In a not-so-dissimilar vein, Bobb (2005) argues that in formerly enslaved and colonised Caribbean nations, innovation has a dual role: that of promoting economic competitiveness, and a simultaneous commitment to liberation, understood as restoring domestic control over domestic resources. But even more profoundly, Bobb views the task of innovation for liberation as that of reconstituting a positive cultural relationship with technology. This view was brilliantly summed up by esteemed Kenyan innovation scholar, Calestous Juma, who wrote that "... issues of science and technology are so crucial to survival that they should be placed on the agenda of those items necessary for maintaining and enhancing national sovereignty" (Juma and Ojwang 1989, p. 1). Similarly, Mammo Muchie (2003) has emphasised the need for a cross-cutting supra-national innovation system, one that not only seeks to re-position Africa in the world economy but does so in part by leveraging its own knowledge traditions. One example he offers is tapping into the genetic wealth of its cereal heritage to address chronic food crises in certain regions. Therefore, far from being essentialist or nativist, these perspectives provide a broader set of insights for integrating diverse knowledge forms, while remaining true to "endogeneity" as a referential yet self-critical and evolving matrix.

Towards a Model of Africa–India Cooperation

The considerations highlighted above make evident the multiform and overlapping imperatives of endogenous innovation in India and Africa. Given the world's entry into the big data-driven digital revolution, the need to deepen technological and related governance capabilities required to attain equitable outcomes becomes ever more pressing. However, while there is a justified impetus to "catch up" with the North, Ki-Zerbo (1993, p. 19) reminds us that "It's all very well to move fast as long as you know where you're going." Ensuring that such a direction remains desirable requires constant alertness to the potential excesses of state officials by the repressed and their allies.

This tradition of civic resistance in Africa goes back as far as the "Tale of the Eloquent Peasant", a successful protest against the unlawful expropriation of property and injustice by state officials in Ancient Egypt (Third Millennium BCE) (Obenga 2004). This continued insistence on free speech in the face of attempts to deny it in the Late Songhay Empire in the sixteenth century (that of the Askia Dynasty as opposed to the founding Sonni Ali Dynasty, see Ki-Zerbo 1986). We also cite the innovative strategies employed by the Tofinu people in modern-day Republic of Benin—such as building stilted homes on Lake Noukoué—to resist capture by the similarly Gbe-speaking Dahomean army during the period of transatlantic enslavement.[2] According to the highly respected Beninese historian,

2 The Fongbe language of the Dahomean "nation-state" is closely related to the Tofingbe language of the Tofinu people, both being part of the Aja-Fon family (Soumonni 2003, 7), itself a sub-set of the Gbe family of languages. However, the word, *Tò*, which is used to refer to a country in Fongbe, etymologically means "order" (a cognate term in Yoruba as well). It is simultaneously used to refer to both the nation and the state, which reflects the militaristic outlook of

Elisée Soumonni (2003, 6), any substantive reconstruction of the emergence of the Noukoué lacustrine complex must be conceptualised by accounting for this defensive imperative, which explains why the Tofinu named their main village Ganvié, meaning "safe at last".

Thus, this dimension of vigilance in the face of an oppressive order—whether foreign, domestic or collusive—is crucial for societies in the Global South to forge equitable and just futures. In this regard, the perennial resistance to Dahomey's expansionism by its Yoruba-speaking neighbours, namely, the Ìdàíṣà, Kétu, Ṣábẹ, and most notably, the successful simultaneous resistance to French colonial conquest by the smaller Ọhọri-Ije polity, are very instructive (Soumonni 1991).

From the vantage point of ecological consciousness at the planetary level, for instance, scholar-activists such as Sunita Narain of India and Wangari Maathai of Kenya have offered cutting-edge critiques and alternatives to some of the dominant environmental discourses and practices. In Narain's co-authored book entitled *Global Warming in an Unequal World: A Case of Environmental Colonialism*, the authors severely critiqued the methodology and goals of a highly influential 1990 report that aimed to "prove" that greenhouse gas emissions in the Global South were only slightly lower than those in the North. Agarwal and Narain (1991) brought worldwide attention to the fact that it was unethical to establish equivalence between the methane emitted from rice fields and draught animals of subsistence farmers in densely-populated territories like Thailand or West Bengal, and carbon-intensive emissions from automobiles in the West. They argued that a more balanced method would allocate emissions on a per capita basis per country and establish systems to make large energy users more efficient while investing in off-grid renewable technologies for the impoverished (Narain 2010).

the Kingdom of Dahomey. This is in contrast to the Yoruba language, in which a clear distinction is made between the nation (*orílẹ̀*), and the state or government (*ìjọba*). The former is understood metaphorically as being constitutive of a familial or ancestral relationship (*ẹbí*), with a common consciousness of identity, while the latter is viewed more instrumentally as an administrative apparatus (personal communication with Olabiyị Yaï, New Delhi, February, 2020).

For her part, Maathai (2009) revisited her life's work with the Green Belt Movement (a civic organisation that helped communities plant trees) from the perspective of her roles as a government official, university professor, and in international organisations. She was insistent in her view that the environmental ecosystem should be central to development, urging Africans to come together for the purpose of restoring themselves and their communities.

At the level of individual states, while the focus on the internally-directed shaping of technology in relation to society is often considered axiomatic in the Global North, there have also been a few laudable attempts to define innovation and development independently in the South. In this regard, the innovation systems framework, which has been employed for comparative studies on Africa and Asia (Oyelaran-Oyeyinka and Rasiah 2009), offers valuable insights that predominantly provide strategies for acquiring technological capabilities from external sources and then upgrading them for the purpose of economic development.

Another approach within this systemic perspective emphasises low-cost, grassroots and socially-inclusive innovation (Muchie et al. 2017). While the upgrading approach is justifiably focused on productivity gains, increased wages and advancement within global high-tech value chains, the grassroots innovation outlook suggests that such improvements in productivity can be informed by non-commercial values. These values include inquisitiveness in learning, the need to democratise technology access, improved physical and mental health, and, as demonstrated by some highly innovative pashmina wool makers in Kashmir, simply the need for much more time to rest (Sheikh and Bhaduri 2020).

A preference for either of these approaches with respect to innovation-based development can also be observed in the policies championed by various political leaders—that is, one emphasising the ability of "big science" to address socially relevant challenges, and the other leaning towards community-driven solutions that obviate the excesses of contemporary science. The late Tanzanian President, Mwalimu Julius Nyerere, for instance, was widely known for his advocacy of *Ujamaa* (a communally-based development model). In contrast, the late Indian Prime Minister, Jawaharlal Nehru, focused on investing in world-class technological education, believing it would ultimately alleviate human suffering. Nevertheless, both leaders were committed to national self-reliance, South–South solidarity and, as Chakrabarty (2005) observed in a comparative analysis of their speeches, shared a pedagogical leadership style that sought to instil in their people confidence about their position of equality among the world's nations.

From the vantage point of connecting ideas to practice, we underscore the significance of three illustrative cases related to non-governmental organisations that offer innovative models and services in an "endogenous" manner. The first is the Songhaï Centre, based in Benin but operating in 17 sites across Sub-Saharan Africa. This innovation-award-winning centre focuses on applied research, training and social entrepreneurship in sustainable agro-ecology. It was founded by Godfrey Nzamujo, an electrical engineer, biological scientist and priest who was influenced in part by the Appropriate Technology movement. However, the centre has expanded upon AT and now promotes the concept of "authentic technology", which combines contemporary technologies with time-tested popular knowledge to promote innovation based on biomimicry rather than bio-arrogance (Nzamujo 2016). The centre works closely with the UN's South–South Global Access and Technology Exchange (SS-GATE) platform, where India is also actively involved.

The second organisation is the Mauritius-based Global Rainbow Foundation (GRF), founded by Armoogum Parsuramen, a former Minister of Education and UNESCO Director. The GRF's mission is to provide prosthetic limbs to those who have lost theirs, offer associated therapy, and ultimately restore their dignity as fully functioning members of society. In collaboration with Jaipur Foot, a non-profit scientific research, development and service organisation, the GRF now moulds and assembles prosthetic limbs and provides a full range of diagnostic and therapeutic services to the differently-abled, including telemedicine consultations with specialist doctors in India (GRF 2021).

A third example is the non-profit Aravind Eye Care System in South India, which has been studied extensively by African American science, technology and society scholar Logan D.A. Williams. Her work underscores its significantly impactful "Robin Hood" social entrepreneurship model for financing the eradication of cataract-linked blindness among the rural poor. This model is based on the principles of *swaraj* (self-rule) and *swadeshi* (self-sufficiency). Additionally, she provides detailed descriptions of community-based ophthalmological organisations that have adopted the model, in Kathmandu, Mexico City, Nairobi and even in New Haven, Connecticut (Williams 2018, 333–52). From a technological perspective, the author addresses the possible tension between Schumpeterian innovation needed to scale up ophthalmological solutions through advanced manufacturing on the one hand, and appropriate technology-based ophthalmological solutions developed by the health cooperative, on the other. This can be resolved by emphasising the need to decentralise organisational structures and promote community ownership that are characteristic of the Robin Hood model. Indeed, this case demonstrates that there is ample room to critically re-appropriate the Indian roots of the "creative destruction" metaphor, and reconcile it with the objectives of the Swadeshi self-help movement.

In terms of human sensibility, the GRF and Aravind cases both give life to Tagore's touching short story, "Subha", which describes a non-speaking girl coming into womanhood (Tagore 1918). Similarly, they animate the insights of literary scholar Anurima Chanda, who in a critical review of Indian books for children calls for normalising the experiences of differently abled children as that of "children first" (Chanda 2024).

Conclusion

In this chapter, we have elucidated a basis for endogenous innovation in the Global South that draws on some of the historical, cultural experiential and ethical dimensions of the developmental imperative in that part of the world. Our approach consists first of a historically informed critique of globally dominant economistic paradigms. We nevertheless underscore the continuing relevance of millennial values, as expressed in literary traditions and cultural metaphors, in shaping contemporary innovative activities. Second, the notion of "tradition-innovation" can enable us to critically select from a diversity of technological solutions, ranging from grassroots to scientifically advanced ones, that could bring forth an era of ecologically sustainable industrialisation. Third, we highlight novel organisational, service-driven, and financing models that are being brought to bear to propel societal transformation in more inclusive ways. These three dimensions provide a foundation for reflecting on a mutually-reinforcing model for South–South cooperation, in general, and for Africa–India cooperation, in particular. Finally, endogenous innovation, as a component of the broader pursuit of endogenous development, offers avenues for scholars, state officials, community-based organisations, business firms and concerned individuals alike, to work out concrete plans for future engagement towards creating a more just and equitable planet. For in the words of Wangari Maathai (2004):

> We are called to assist the Earth to heal her wounds and in the process heal our own—indeed to embrace the whole of creation in all its diversity, beauty and wonder. This will happen if we see the need to revive our sense of belonging to a larger family of life, with which we have shared our evolutionary process (Maathai 2004).

References

Agarwal, Anil, and Sunita Narain. *Global Warming in an Unequal World: A Case of Environmental Colonialism*. New Delhi: Centre for Science and Environment, 1991.

Agarwal, M. *Enslavement, Persisting through our Political Economy*. Newcastle-upon-Tyne: Cambridge Scholars Publishing, 2018.

Alam, M.A. "Science and Imperialism: What is Science", *Race & Class* vol. 19, no. 3 (1978): pp. 239–51. https://doi.org/10.1177/030639687801900302

Bagchi, A.K. *Colonialism and Indian Economy*. New Delhi: Oxford University Press, 2010.

———. "On Colonialism and the Indian Economy", *Review of Agrarian Studies* vol. 5, no. 2 (2015): pp. 95–109.

Bobb, K.I. "The Duality of Innovation: Liberation and Economic Competitiveness", Doctoral Dissertation, Georgia Institute of Technology, 2005. Available online: https://citeseerx.ist.psu.edu/document?repid=rep1&type=pdf&doi=1444a7a1a51fa35cad0132e5ec46d532f737ce7b (accessed on 23 December 2024).

Césaire, Aimé. *Discourse on Colonialism* (trans. Joan Pinkham). New York: Monthly Review Press, 2000.

Chakrabarty, Dipesh. "Legacies of Bandung: Decolonisation and the Politics of Culture", *Economic and Political Weekly* vol. 40, no. 46 (2005): pp. 4812–8.

Chanda, Anurima. "Children First, Disabled or Not: A Study of Inclusivity in Twenty-first-century Indian English Children's Literature", in *Articulating Childhood Trauma: In the Context of War, Sexual Abuse and Disability*, edited by Kamayani Kumar, 180–192. New Delhi: Routledge India, 2024.

Coomaraswamy, Ananda K. *Art and Swadeshi*. Madras: Ganesh and Co. Publishers, 1910.

Diop, Cheikh Anta. *Civilization or Barbarism: An Authentic Anthropology* (trans. Yaa Lengi Meema Ngemi, edited by Harold J. Salemson and Marjolijn de Jager). New York: Lawrence Hill Books, 1991.

GRF. Global Rainbow Foundation (GRF): "Empowering, Educating, Enabling". Available online: https://grftrust.org/ (accessed on 2 January 2021).

Habib, Irfan. "Colonialization of the Indian Economy, 1757–1900", *Social Scientist* vol. 3, no. 8 (1975): pp. 23–53. Available online: https://doi.org/10.2307/3516224 (accessed on 23 December 2024).

Inikori, J.E. *Africans and the Industrial Revolution in England: A Study in International Trade and Economic Development*. Cambridge: Cambridge University Press, 2002.

Juma, C., and J.B. Ojwang. "Innovation and Sovereignty", in *Innovation and Sovereignty: The Patent Debate in African Development*, ed. C. Juma, pp. 7–27. Nairobi: African Centre for Technology Studies, 1989.

Ki-Zerbo, J. "Le développement clés en tête", in *La natte des autres: Pour un développement endogène en Afrique*, ed. J. Ki-Zerbo, pp. 1–71. Dakar: CODESRIA, 1992.

———. "The universal and the particular", UNESCO *Courier* vol. 46, no. 12 (1993): pp. 18–20.

———. "Africa: Silent Continent?" *Index on Censorship* vol. 15, no. 2: pp. 16–18. Available online: https://doi.org/10.1080/03064228608534038 (accessed on 23 December 2024).

Maathai, Wangari. Nobel Lecture. NobelPrize.org. Nobel Prize Outreach 2025. Available online: https://www.nobelprize.org/prizes/peace/2004/maathai/lecture/ (accessed on 3 Aug 2025).

——— . *The Challenge for Africa.* New York: Pantheon Books, 2009.

Muchie, M. "Re-thinking Africa's Development through the National Innovation System", in *Putting Africa First: The Making of African Innovation Systems*, edited by M. Muchie, P. Gammeltoft, and B.Å. Lundvall, pp. 43–62. Aalborg: Aalborg University Press, 2003.

Muchie, M., S. Bhaduri, A. Baskaran, and F.A. Sheikh. *Informal Sector Innovations: Insights from the Global South.* London and New York: Taylor & Francis, 2017.

Narain, Sunita. "A 'Just' Climate Agreement: The Framework for an Effective Global Deal", in *Global Sustainability: A Nobel Cause,* edited by H.J. Schellnhuber, M. Molina, N. Stern, V. Huber, & S. Kadner. Cambridge: Cambridge University Press, 2010.

Nzamujo, G. Songhaï: *l'Afrique maintenant!* Paris: Editions du Cerf, 2016.

Obenga, T. *African Philosophy: The Pharaonic Period, 2780–330 BC.* Popenguine: Per Ankh, 2004.

Oluwole, S.B. "The Labyrinth Conception of Time as Basis of Yoruba View of Development", in *Temps et Développement Dans la Pensée de L'Afrique Subsaharienne*, edited by S.B. Diagne and H. Kimmerle, pp. 139–49. Amsterdam: Rodopi, 1998.

———. *Socrates and Ọ̀rúnmìlà: Two Patron Saints of Classical Philosophy.* Lagos: Ark Publishers, 2014.

Oyelaran-Oyeyinka, O., and R. Rasiah. *Uneven Paths of Development: Innovation and Learning in Asia and Africa.* Cheltenham: Edward Elgar Publishing, 2009.

Padgaonkar, D. "Asking the Right Questions", *UNESCO Courier* vol. 46, no. 12 (1993): pp. 32–35.

Ramose, M.B. *African Philosophy through Ubuntu.* Harare: Mond Books Publishers, 2005.

Rodney, W. *How Europe Underdeveloped Africa.* Washington, D.C.: Howard University Press, 1981.

Sheikh, F.A., and S. Bhaduri. "Grassroots Innovations in the Informal Economy: Insights from Value Theory", *Oxford Development Studies* vol. 48, no. 1 (2020): pp. 85–99. https://doi.org/10.1080/13600818.2020.1717453

Soumonni, E. "Lacustrine Villages in South Benin as Refuges from the Slave Trade", in *Fighting the Slave Trade: West African Strategies,* ed. S.A. Diouf, pp. 3–14. Athens: Ohio University Press, 2003.

———. "Dahomean Yorubaland", in *Yoruba Historiography,* edited by Toyin Falola, 65–74. Madison: African Studies Program, University of Wisconsin-Madison, 1991.

Soumonni, Ogundiran, and Thema Monroe-White. "Endogenous Innovation and Digital Inclusion: A Global African Perspective", Tayarisha Centre for Digital Governance Working Paper Series, Wits School of Governance, Johannesburg, 2023. Available online: https://wiredspace.wits.ac.za/items/97552d64-1c87-4a04-9da4-0b219b0c6f60 (accessed on 3 August 2025).

Soumonni, Ogundiran, and Mammo Muchie. "Endogenous Knowledge and Secondary Innovation in the Age of COVID-19: A Global South Civilisational Dialogue", *Science, Technology and Society* vol. 28, no. 3 (2023): pp. 387–406. https://doi: /10.1177/09717218231178241

Tagore, Rabindranath. "Subha", in *Stories from Tagore,* 101–12. New York: Macmillan, 1918.

———. *Selected Poems,* trans. and ed. William Radice. London; New York: Penguin Classics, 2005.

Van Sertima, Ivan. (ed.). *Blacks in Science: Ancient and Modern.* New Brunswick; London: Transaction Publishers, 2007 [1983].

Visvanathan, Shiv. "Alternative Science", *Theory, Culture and Society* vol. 23, nos. 2–3 (2006): pp. 164–9.

Williams, L.D.A. *Eradicating Blindness: Global Health Innovation from South Asia.* Singapore: Springer Nature, 2018.

Yaï, Olabiyi B. "African Diasporan Concepts and Practice of the Nation and their Implications in the Modern World", in *African Roots/American*

Cultures: Africa in the Creation of the Americas, ed. S.S. Walker, pp. 244–55. Lanham: Rowman and Littlefield, 2001.

———. *Africa, African Diaspora and the Prospect of Global Cultural Dialogue*. New Delhi: India International Centre, 2008.

——. "Tradition and the Yoruba Artist", *African Arts* vol. 32, no.1: pp. 32–93. Available online: https://doi.org/10.2307/3337535 (accessed on 23 December 2021)

Inikori, J.E. Africans and the Industrial Revolution in England: A Study in International Trade and Economic Development. Cambridge: Cambridge University Press, 2002.

Chapter 7
African Culture and Traditions as Sources of Knowledge

Mamoudou Djibo

Introduction

Despite being endowed with innumerable natural resources, sub-Saharan Africa is grappling with the problem of undevelopment, a situation aggravated in the early 21st century by a host of challenges such as security, food production, industrialisation, environmental issues and education. Africa's youth, the driving force of development, does not see a place for itself in this world, which it finds for the most part incomprehensible. Lacking points of reference and unable to find appropriate answers to current concerns, these young people wonder what the future holds. This situation poses a grave concern for the survival of African societies, as, on the one hand, crises are multiplying and becoming more complex, and, on the other, development thinking is failing. School education introduced and enforced by European colonialism, and presented thus far as the panacea for development and for comprehending the world, does not appear to provide meaningful help. What, then, do African societies retain that can serve as sources of knowledge and contribute to an understanding of this world, and help in finding a place within the universal?

In order to understand this very complex, inaccessible and inhibiting world—and to be able to tackle the problems it presents—

one must first understand oneself and one's physical and non-material environment. In other words, since sub-Saharan Africa, despite its apparent physical unity, has a diverse ethnic composition, each group owes it to itself to get to know its past and the societal mechanisms that make community life possible and enable the preservation of the capital of positive experiences, disseminate these, and warn against—or find solutions to—the problems that arise. This body of knowledge, products and experiences, collectively shared and perpetuated by each society, constitutes the traditions that express the culture of a people to the point of creating its distinct identity.

Sub-Saharan Africa is a region rich in traditions. Developed and transmitted over centuries by each society, these traditions have come to constitute a body of knowledge specific to a given social group or a section of this group. At times, elements of this body of knowledge transcend ethnic borders and extend to larger geographical areas and more diverse human communities. It is through this endogenous knowledge that, in societies without writing, the youth are educated, trained and exposed to the universal.

To facilitate analysis, the approach proposed here is based on the traditional knowledge of Songhai societies,[1] in order to draw attention to what is perhaps common to several African societies.

General Overview of the Culture[2]

Culture can be understood as the set of social structures, along with the artistic, religious and intellectual expressions that define a community or society as distinct from others. This refers to all the creations, beliefs and practices developed over centuries of shared communal living by a group of people, which give the society its specific character and distinct identity. Tradition is the "vehicle" for the values of a culture, passed down to posterity, and it constitutes the social reference points for virtues, norms, interdictions, and more.

---

1 These societies, successors of the ancient Songhai (Soŋey) Empire, are dispersed across the borders of Niger, Mali, Burkina Faso, northern Benin and north-western Nigeria.

2 This section and the conclusion are inspired by Léger 1988.

Handed down from generation to generation, traditions perpetuate the way of being, acting or thinking of the social group in question. It is through these traditions that the group teaches its past and builds its own explanatory system for real-life situations, as well as those of its immediate neighbours, its activities (artistic, political or economic), and the behaviour of its members (mentality, religion, community life, etc.), thereby populating its identity with models and reference points. This is the school of social life in Africa.

Essentially oral, traditions include the whole gamut of products and cultural creations that a community has developed over time and space, over the course of its existence, to explain its circumstances, educate and socialise its members, identify its enemies, deride neighbouring rival or dissident groups, or simply explain facts and situations related to its own history. Tradition thus appears as "the repository and vector of the capital of sociocultural creations accumulated by 'preliterate communities': a true living museum" (J. Ki-Zerbo, quoted in Moutari 2020, p. 28), in which each social group sees itself and builds its own identity around the legacy of the past shared by its members. This process nurtures and reinforces their sense of belonging to the same human community and fosters, in each one, the will to make sacrifices, the obligation of solidarity, the duty to succeed and the desire to live together—important requirements for social cohesion and progress. It is thus, cardinal values are taught, such as patience, humility, a sense of honour, reason, solidarity, courage, honesty, the virtues of work, love, altruism, the obligation to move ahead and giving of oneself for the sake of the group.

Interpreted in this manner, culture and the traditions through which it is passed on are crucial in the life of a human group, particularly in societies without writing. Songhai society, inheritors of a rich past, gave birth to social and political organisations that have had a lasting impact on the history of Central and Western Sudan.[3]

---

3 In this way, from Gungia (Kukia, Bentiya or Lentia), the Songhai State of the Za (from which comes Zarma) captured Gao (around 1009) and, under the impetus of dynasts like Sonni Ali Ber and later Askia Mohamed, extended its political control to Timbuktu and well beyond, right up to Aïr, to the Hausa States (Gobir, Zamfara and Kabi), Borgou and elsewhere.

Its political and administrative influence led to the intermingling of populations and languages, resulting in unprecedented cultural development.

Unfortunately, here, as in other societies, the youth, who need benchmarks and references, have only an approximate, if not uncertain, knowledge of this past and the practices, values and references upon which their society was built. The young people have only a vague and remote idea of the great figures from their community's past. However, the heroic deeds of the great men who influenced their era represent endogenous models that should be a matter of individual and collective pride and, more importantly, provide a certain confidence with which to face the trials of everyday life. Descendants of Sonni Ali Ber, Askia Mohamed, Mali Béro, and more recent figures like Issa Korombé, Babatou, Zarmakoy Aouta, Alpha Seybou and Morou Karma, could thus instil the aspiration and boldness needed to contemplate the future with calm and face the challenges of the modern world.

In any human society, young people must have recollections of the past. These recollections refresh the memory and stimulate the individual and collective consciousness. Vitalised and enriched with fresh inputs, these memories can help avoid repeating the same mistakes, suffering the same constraints and rehearsing the same failures. The path to progress and the basis for all development require drawing from culture the elements that enrich life and give it meaning—in other words, the practical, intellectual and moral experiences of the past. Shedding light on culture should offer young people the ability to discover their origins and the legitimate feeling of belonging to a human community that has lived, achieved important things for the benefit of all, collectively faced and overcome ordeals to survive, and visualised solutions for every problem faced.

Rather than trying merely to fire the imagination of the young, this "... sum of theorised or codified past and present epistemological experiences of a people" (Kouma 2013, p. 3) must broaden their intellectual horizons, stimulate their societal commitment and strengthen their sense of belonging. These "learnings from gnoseological, inventive and technological experiences ..." (Badogo

2009, p. 62) must reinforce certainties and solidarities in each one and educate and edify each generation so that it can build on the past in order to progress, through rationalised moral principles that are to be shared and perhaps even made into models.

At times, endogenous knowledge, specific to particular spheres and transmitted exclusively within them, is taught by groups representing different trades, clans or faiths. Thus, for example, the secret of fire and metal is known only to blacksmiths who are initiated and experienced in blacksmithing; that of the bush is known only to hunters and other practitioners (such as healers), among whom it is formally maintained and taught. Similarly, the secrets of water (the river) are known only to the Sorko, Kara and Do.[4] In the same way, only a weaver's son, through daily practice under the guidance of his master, can successfully learn the complex process of making different fabrics and the distinct motifs that adorn them. These esoteric skills confer specific powers, which are transmitted endogenously, exclusively and secretly, through family or community worship and rites that mark the life of these groups. This is the case of the *Sonyanké,* who, it is believed (Djibo 2015, 2019; Rouch 1960, 1989; Konare Bâ 1977; Hama 1967) were capable, like the vulture—their fetish bird—of penetrating "the secret of God", to the point of being able to transcend space and time to "save", heal or punish: this deemed power gave them the status of protector of the social group.

It is through the spoken word that knowledge and power are transmitted, that is to say, that which can ward off bad luck, heal from evil and protect. It is through the word that the invisible "weapon" is carried, one that kills, punishes and annihilates the misdeeds of others. It is through the spoken word that we ask for and strengthen good fortune. The spoken word is then associated with "saliva"—which carries it and gives it another dimension:[5] as the bearer of the

4 The Sorko, Kara and Do are Songhai sub-groups mainly characterised by their relationship with water, and the Niger River of which they are said to be the "masters".

5 Sometimes, one speaks without distinction of saliva (*yollo*), mouth (*me*) and tongue (*dene*), while at other times, one combines "saliva" and "mouth" (*me-yollo*) or "tongue" and "word" (*dene-senni*).

mystical and esoteric word, active and formative, it is no longer just the liquid that moistens the mouth! Indeed, it is through the "spoken word" that the zima (priests of the Holley faith, mediums of genies that possess humans) act, just as the *Sonyanké* and even the witch-doctors, masters of Koranic science, do: every invocation is always followed by bouts of saliva on open hands, as if to spread on them the power of chanted "words".

Some Constituent Elements of the Traditions and their Functions

As sub-Saharan Africa does not have a tradition of writing, it is through oral traditions that cultural values and "historical" information about each group and its neighbouring human groups are passed on. For centuries, these traditions have conveyed a wealth of information that has served to train young people. This overall social experience of the group, a "potential driver of African cultures" (Kouma 2011, p. 2), is passed down through myths, tales, legends, epics, cosmogonies, genealogies, proverbs, rituals, invocations, and more.

A myth is a type of fictional story that serves to impart knowledge relating to the creation of the world, the arrival of human beings, the origin of their links with nature in general, the constitution or differentiation of the elements that make up the group, the appearance of different types of inequalities, the origin of life, death and illnesses, the definition of the relationships with the supernatural world, etc. By teaching how something is born, myths endeavour to establish a connection between (perceptible) historical time and (imperceptible) primordial time, using present narrations on origins as paradigms (models) for the youth: their purpose is to explain, justify, strengthen and codify beliefs and practices that constitute the driving forces of social organisation.

A tale is a story in which human beings, animals, genies, and at times even plants play roles. A purely literary invention, its principal function is to teach, through a depiction of society, virtues such as humility, respect for others, courage, loyalty, work, merit and particularly honesty—non-observance of which is necessarily punished.

A legend is a type of story characterised by the marvellous, where facts, sometimes real, are distorted by popular imagination to embellish the narrative. It refers to a common ancestor of the group, which might not have existed but for the sacrifice made for the community.[6]

An epic revolves around a real historical event or an individual who influenced his era or social group, and whose memory is worthy of mention as a model, reference, or benchmark for all members of the group.[7]

A cosmogony is an all-encompassing story that explains the creation of the universe, establishing a link between nature and humans, as well as between the founding ancestor and the environmental factors that favoured or hindered his settlement. One of its functions is to teach respect for nature and what it offers humanity.

Proverbs and sayings allow us, through the construction of phrases, combinations of words and other stylistic effects, to reflect on a problem or situation, understand for ourselves what is fitting, convey a coded message, publicly receive a secret and challenge others in rhetoric: it is the "material" that enables us to master a language in depth, along with all its subtleties.

Rituals—whether family or community ones[8]—are a preparation for group dynamics and the sharing of experiences, joy and/or moments of suffering for the social group in question. When rituals are initiatory and individual, they enable the transmission, in secrecy, of the codes that ensure the survival of the family or group that holds them, perpetuating the power derived from those codes.

---

6 This is the case of Mali Béro for the Zarma whose legend is peppered with both bravery and magic which makes everything possible and gives a particular bearing and status to the existence of the ancestor and his unique adventure in the history of the group. It is in this way that the Baoule (Côte d'Ivoire) explain their relationship with the crocodile from the time of queen Pokou.

7 Boubacar Louloudjo, Babatou, Issa Korombé (Niger) thus really existed even if they were not exactly the same as their portrayal in the stories that developed around their lives, as in the case of Sundiata Keita, vanquisher of Soumaoro Kanté and founder of the Mali Empire.

8 Like circumcision (*gosi*), "consultation" ceremonies (*yenandi*, *hari ŋwarey*, etc.).

When rituals are collective, they encourage solidarity, reciprocity and duties for each age group, forged in hardship and sealed by inviolable secrets: the "sets of participants" (*wade-wadda*) owe each other respect and support, which contributes in large measure to pacifying social relations and facilitating intracommunity and intercommunity generational dialogue.

The Transmission Channels for Endogenous Knowledge

There are several channels through which this knowledge is transmitted. The primary channel of education is the family. Education that begins in the family is complemented in the neighbourhood, through contact with, and by the actions of, the various members of the social group: all elders, whether parents or not, are duty-bound to intervene when it comes to the children of the neighbourhood or village, with no risk of protest from any quarter. Education can also be imparted specifically by those "initiated" whose role is precisely to train young people.

Chiefs (of neighbourhoods, villages, cantons, lands, bush, rivers, etc.) also play a role in the chain of transmission of cultural values through their positions as regulators and administrators of collective activities (rituals, incantations, sacrifices, etc.). These group activities (collective work, hunting beats, fishing, traditional festivals, etc.) provide education in solidarity and social cohesion, teaching that together, everything is possible and easier to achieve: each member of the group discovers through this that division weakens and exposes one to failure.

The griots and troubadours (African storytellers and minstrels) "... use extreme language and stinging criticism as a pedagogic tool to educate the public, sing praises ... express their admiration or their sympathy" (Niang 2012, p. 123), denounce the lazy and the miserly by mocking them, or celebrate noble deeds, exploits and prowess, as well as the virtue of work and the generosity that sustains them.

The genealogist griots recall the lofty deeds of each lineage, denounce the cowardice of some people and the betrayals by others, warning how harmful these actions are to the group. By evoking events from the past, they impart knowledge of the ties that bind families and groups, serving as reminders of the pacts concluded between ancestors and the risks incurred by those who disrespect or violate them: "The griot is the memory or the testimony of ancestral pacts between communities ..." (Talibi 2012, p. 68). By teaching family genealogies, they highlight the relations and reciprocal obligations between members of the group. Their knowledge of the group's past and the various social connections, their eloquence and their verve are effective weapons for resolving difficult situations: this knowledge invests the griot with the moral audacity to speak the truth to any other member of the social group, including the king!

In the Songhai nation, there are "guardians" of morality and social norms, known as the *sasale*. Like sentinels of societal morals, this group ensures the observance of good moral standards. Their function is the public denunuciation of social aberrations (indecency, immodesty, incest, theft, rape, etc.), which can constitute a crippling social punishment. The fear the *sasale* inspire reminds all members of the group, on a daily basis, of their place in society, their obligation to exercise restraint, and their duties of uprightness. The "policemen" of society, this group constitutes an essential link in securing moral values through vigilance and social censorship.[9]

Beyond the emblematic image of the palaver tree, in the Songhai nation, there are other settings for confabulation and training. The courtyards of mosques (where the faithful rest between prayer sessions), public places (such as *bitinga* or *ci ni ibayi*[10]), marketplaces and ceremonial sites provide opportunities to discuss various issues. These informal settings for free discussion are where problems are dealt with "in the first instance", and it is here that inquiries can be made, points of view shared and crisis-prone situations defused and prevented from escalating.[11] They allow each one the opportunity to "get things off his chest" without being bothered by anyone, to ask questions in order to understand better, to react in order to inform

9 On the "*sasale*", see Sardan 1976 and particularly his film *Sassalé*, 1971.

10 "*ci ni ibayi*" literally means "*speak freely and say what you wish to, without restrictions or fear*".

11 Thus one would reprimand someone for having committed adultery, theft or any other bad social practices, even before the political chief is informed of it.

or let off steam. These settings make it possible to decompress the social atmosphere, provide initial advice and sound the alarm on potentially contentious situations.

Religions (both adopted and indigenous) have succeeded in inculcating values, practices and attitudes that play a part in the development of humanity and the maintenance of social peace. For example, each one has learnt that violating the *amana*[12] is never forgiven and that good is always well rewarded (*gomni ga hin zaari*), while evil always attracts evil. Each person has internalised in his subconscious the fear of the afterlife or punishment by the "invisible" in the face of injustice, malice, cheating, slander, betrayal and other forms of deception or misconduct. Such certainties help cement the foundations of a peaceful society.

Even though Islam and Christianity have finally established themselves as factors of cohesion, tolerance and social solidarity, the indigenous religions (*Soŋencetarey*, *Holley*) continue, in the background, to offer immediate answers to concerns: the punishments being sometimes immediate and radical (such as the ire of *Dongo* or *Harakoy*, etc.),[13] they inspire more fear than those that "propose" justice in the afterlife.

Conclusion

African societies have produced an inexhaustible mine of knowledge in the form of social values through which communities perpetuate their memories, teach their history, organise their daily life and envisage the future. It is thanks to this knowledge, which neither the advent of modern schooling nor the standardising induced by globalisation have been able to wipe out, that these societies continue to organise their existence and teach the past, geography, sociology, the environment, psychology, rhetoric, philosophy and moral science, it is through this endogenous knowledge that they provide training for life in society.

---

12 A "word given", a pact of honour between individuals, sub-groups and with other ethnic groups.

13 *Dongo* = god of lightning; *Harakoy* = the goddess of water.

The school of traditions is neither formal nor closed: education is imparted in all circumstances, without dedicated staff, without a formalised curriculum and without "standardised" official instructions or directives. The transmission of knowledge is continuous, through life and through events. As this school corresponds with the social horizons of the group, it socialises through its pragmatic dimension, with society and the daily routine being, at the same time, objects of study and fields of reference and practice.

It is through this education that citizens are trained—people who will go on to hold positions of responsibility (husbands, wives or leaders). It is this education that prepares young people to learn what is universal, in other words, what others are and how they got to this point, thus widening their social horizons.

When put to good use, this knowledge can serve as a vector of peace, non-violence, peaceful coexistence and social advancement that can strengthen the will and desire to live together. It can reduce the stench of mistrust and rejection of others, ban aggressive or intolerant behaviour and make up for the shortcomings of the current education system, which is often unsuitable and badly managed.

This approach necessarily requires the rehabilitation of this knowledge, which has been neglected and is "fossilising". However, rather than a rehabilitation that remains "prisoner of its difference" (Dibi 1981), the enhancement of cultural heritage should be open to new inflows, through its adaptation and integration with school curricula after identifying host subjects. It is all the more important, as opening up to the world requires an intellectual and moral equilibrium that makes each member of society fully aware of their affiliation to the group. Armed mentally with self-confidence, each one is well-equipped to contemplate their future, contribute to the general development of their country and participate in global development in a responsible way.

In order to contribute to the emergence of "new universal knowledge", traditional African knowledge must be stripped of prejudices regarding the Other, naïve contemplation of the past and individual fantasies of self-promotion. Once these traditional African learnings are enhanced and structured, it is possible to "... show their rationality" (Kouma 2013, p. 5), and help young people serenely "board" the train of globalisation, and contribute to an endogenous, well-rounded and sustainable development of Africa.

References

Badogo, Obarè. "Savoirs endogènes et défis de la modernité scientifique: réflexions d'un archéologue", in *L'ancien et le nouveau. La production du savoir dans l'Afrique d'aujourd'hui*. Cotonou: Centre africain des Hautes études, 2009.

Dibi, Augustin Kouadio. *L'Afrique et son autre, la différence libérée*. Abidjan: Stratéca Diffusion, 1981.

Djibo, Mamoudou. *Karma: du Siciya au canton (1640–1960)*. Cotonou: Editions du Flamboyant, 2015.

———. "The Sonyanké in Songhai society", *Colloque Semaine Soŋey de Ouagadougou*, Ouagadougou, 2019.

Konare Ba, Adam. *Sonni Ali Ber*. Niamey Institut de Recherches en Sciences humaines, Études nigériennes, no. 40, 1977.

Kouma, Youssouf. "Des savoirs endogènes au développement endogène: le pari de l'intégration africaine", *Lettres d'Ivoire, Revue scientifique de Littératures, Langues et Sciences humaines*, no. 012, special issue (2011): pp. 129–40.

Hama, Boubou. *Histoire traditionnelle d'un peuple: les Zarma-Songhay*, publication of the Republic of Niger. Paris: Présence africaine, 1967.

Léger, Jean-Marc. "Histoire et progress", *Le Devoir* (Montreal), vol. 79, no. 188 (1988).

Moutari, Abdou. "Un parcours d'accommodation: colonisés et colonisateurs dans le Gobir et le Katsina nigériens, 1898 à 1946". Thesis for Doctorate (History), Abdou Moumouni University 2020.

Moussavou, Raymonde. "Savoirs endogènes en classe des sciences: points de vue d'enseignants et d'enseignantes en formation au Gabon", *Education relative à l'environnement*, vol. 11 (2014), Available online: http://journalsopenedition.org/ere/823 (accessed on 4 February 2020).

Niang, Ibrahim Abdou Salam. "Excès de langage et critiques acerbes comme expression voilée de la sympathie vis-à-vis d'autrui", *Etudes sahéliennes,*

Revue scientifique de la Faculté des Lettres et Sciences humaines (Sciences de l'Homme et de la Société), special issue (2012): pp. 123–49.

———. *Sassalé*. Paris: Comité du Film ethnographique, 1971.

Olivier de Sardan, Jean-Pierre (trans. and ed). *Quand nos pères étaient captifs … Récits paysans du Niger*. Paris: Nubia, 1976.

Rouch, Jean. *Religion et magie songhay*. Paris: P.U.F., 1960.

———. *La religion et la magie songhay*, 2nd edition, revised and expanded. Brussels: Editions de l'Université de Bruxelles, 1989.

Talibi, Moussa Hamidou. "Porter à l'universel les valeurs et principes pertinents des traditions des sociétés ouest-africaines pour une culture mondiale de la paix", *Etudes sahéliennes, Revue scientifique de la Faculté des Lettres et Sciences humaines (Sciences de l'Homme et de la Société)*, special issue (2012): pp. 63–77.

Chapter 8

Traditional Knowledge Heritage and Inter-generational Continuities

Ajeet N. Mathur

Introduction

It is remarkable that negotiations being conducted since 2001 by the WIPO Intergovernmental Committee (IGC) on Intellectual Property and Genetic Resources, Traditional Knowledge and Folklore have been unable to reach a conclusion to date (WIPO 2020). Doubts have been expressed as to whether it would ever be possible to develop an international system to protect traditional knowledge, and also whether it is even necessary or desirable to have such a system.

In this chapter, I will first provide an overview of the controversial question of whether the rights to use traditional knowledge (TK) should fall within international intellectual property rights (IPR) regimes or remain outside them, with a view to bringing conceptual clarity to a topic that arouses passions but is often poorly understood. Secondly, I present the complexities and contradictions inherent in the underlying policy choices aimed at formulating *sui generis* systems to bridge the knowledge gap between holders of TK and its commercial prospectors through appropriate forms of new institutionalities and enforceable contracts involving access and benefit-sharing arrangements.

TK constitutes a valuable heritage of intergenerational continuities everywhere in the world. Yet, in a world dominated by market economies, the market for TK is not well developed, and it is often exploited and underpriced. In developing countries of Africa, Asia and South America, TK is a particularly underutilised treasure trove, at risk of loss and shrinkage, and vulnerable to misappropriation. TK is transmitted largely through oral traditions and customary practices that embody values, norms, beliefs and attitudes collectively appreciated as culture. It is often bundled with the way genetic resources are spread and with how folklore manifests in cultural expressions of various kinds.

There is an African proverb, "When an old person dies, it is like losing a whole library in a fire." The task of formulating policies, designing systems, developing structures and nurturing institutional processes for heritage conservation and the use of TK in intergenerational continuities becomes mired in questions of title, precedence, authority and responsibility for use, as well as transmission of knowledge through learning inspired by groups and communities, whether they are communities of habitat or communities of practice.

The Problematique

The question of who owns TK assumes significance because TK, genetic resources and cultural expressions constitute a trine. TK consists of information in the public domain as well as trade secrets. The novelty thresholds of patent laws vary greatly across countries and are notoriously low in those where the pharmaceutical industry is strongest. Moreover, patentability under Trade-Related Aspects of Intellectual Property Rights (TRIPS) does not require Prior Informed Consent from the countries or communities from which organic and informational resources are procured. As a result, traditional medicine, which could be one of the easiest forms of TK to bring into the market economy, has emerged only gradually. In India, AYUSH, a publicly supported initiative, is little over two decades old.

The recognition of TK, genetic resources and folklore as important sources of heritage and contemporary knowledge poses profound moral, legal, social and political problems. Several skills or forms of tacit knowing are not limited to definable or articulable sets of knowable elements. Yet, intergenerational equity can be irreversibly impacted depending on the way access and benefit-sharing solutions are structured, particularly in terms of vesting ownership or use rights, because the availability and use of resources are interconnected.

In the contexts of trade and issues concerning environmental commons, TRIPS and the Convention on Biological Diversity (CBD) respectively required the creation of new economic rights and obligations to complement the IPR system under WIPO (World Intellectual Property Organization). Matters concerning TK, hitherto pursued only in the form of cultural rights or heritage issues at the UN, UNESCO and WIPO, are also relevant to development rights for which UNCTAD was created, and economic rights for which UN-ECOSOC and WTO were mandated. The debates at WIPO, UNCTAD, CBD conferences, and WTO have focused on understanding the complex set of issues rather than on developing international norms. Much of the recent discussion at WIPO in the IGC was hijacked from substantive issues to procedural ones of who should participate in the discussions and how the participation of Indigenous communities could be financed.

Does TK require National or International Protection?

Countries opposed to internationally binding instruments on the protection of TK maintain that international norms may be difficult to create with any degree of certainty before national systems and norms have been developed and there is some experience to draw upon. Yet, instruments like the CBD, TRIPS and the Cartagena Protocol were developed internationally long before countries legislated on these issues and created national systems. If one solution cannot suit all countries, a range of policy choices harmonisable with international regimes may need to be envisaged. The TRIPS agreement is the most important development in international intellectual property law because it was made as an Annex to the WTO Agreement, bringing intellectual property under the rubric of trade for the first time. TRIPS subsumed the international IPR regime created in the 1880s based on the Berne and Paris Conventions by providing for administrative and judicial enforcement of IPRs and border control of trade in infringements.

This development was regarded as necessary because of the perceived toothlessness of the Paris and Berne Conventions and the inability of WIPO to modify the Paris Convention. The protection of TK, its ownership and use are among the most contentious issues discussed in international negotiations at WIPO, UNESCO and WTO negotiations, and the issues and challenges posed have remained unresolved. This was acknowledged in Paragraph 19 of the Doha WTO Ministerial Declaration (Document WT/MIN(01)/DEC/1), which called for the TRIPS Council to examine the issue.

UNESCO was left with no role in intellectual property matters after the US left UNESCO to join the Berne Convention. The Model Conventions of UNESCO left no working legacy. Moreover, Article 9 of TRIPS refers to the Berne Convention administered by WIPO and redefines it by excluding moral rights under Article 6*bis* of the Berne Convention from TRIPS. Further, under Article 10.2 of TRIPS, copyright protection accorded to databases as compilations of data does not extend to the data or material itself. Thus, registration and recording of TK in databases are worthless from the perspective of being rewarded for drawing attention to prior art unless it constitutes a disclosure as part of a registerable claim. The silence of the TRIPS Agreement on any specific scheme of protection for appellations of origin—after considerable discussion on whether to incorporate the scheme provided for in the Lisbon Agreement—suggests that the TRIPS regime has also superseded the protection contained in these earlier instruments.

UNCTAD, founded as an organ of the UN General Assembly in 1964, remained focused on the transfer of technology issues and developed a voting pattern based on blocs: Group A, comprising developing countries of the Afro-Asian region and Yugoslavia; Group B, consisting of Western industrialised countries; Group C, composed of Latin American countries; and Group D, made up of socialist countries. This bloc pattern of working carried over to WIPO, but of these groupings, only Group B retains its coherence. The creation of WTO as a specialised agency of the UN, armed with adjudicating authority, marginalised the role of UNCTAD, although the establishment of an organisation such as WTO formed no part of the Ministerial Declaration at Punta del Este, which launched the

Uruguay Round of Trade Negotiations in 1986. TRIPS endorses the catalogue of prohibitions on restrictive trade practices identified by UNCTAD in its Transfer of Technology Code. It was left to Articles 7 and 8 of TRIPS to be interpreted by dispute panels on questions of compulsory licensing, parallel imports and national or international exhaustion of IPRs.

An important policy question in this context concerns whether the aims would be better fulfilled through systems that confer on people in general and communities in particular certain rights over their traditional knowledge, or whether the creation of parastatal monopolies over such knowledge would be a better alternative to ensure intergovernmental coordination. This issue is not easily resolved because non-contemporary traditional knowledge comprises unarticulated and unrecorded intangibles, and there is an investment or cost involved in documenting it for databases that can be privately owned. Also, exhaustible plant genetic resources have implications for biodiversity in certain categories of traditional knowledge like traditional medicine, besides subserving public health objectives under WHO's Traditional Medicine Strategy. Moreover, TK is valued not because of its antiquity (an argument that would limit its scope merely to the protection of cultural expressions and museum artefacts), but because much of it is transmitted orally as part of the knowledge necessary to sustain lives and livelihoods, and it has an economic value, which is variable. The Barton Commission (DFID 2002) noted that a multiplicity of measures—only some of which relate to intellectual property rights—would be necessary to protect, preserve and promote traditional knowledge.

To hail TK as *sui generis* is inadequate without a system of use rights and obligations that can be created and operated at least at the national level. It is doubtful that international *sui generis* protection can be organised without first establishing national *sui generis* systems, although it would be useful if international guidelines could be agreed upon so that, at some stage, the national systems created may be harmonised. With China having opted to bring TK under IPR ownership, the main initiatives for *sui generis* protection appear to emanate from Peru, Egypt, Ethiopia, Tanzania, Kenya, Brazil and India. The question of who is entitled to seek protection for which forms of TK, and who may confer recognition and status on holders of TK in a *sui generis* modality, raises a number of policy questions about the role of communities and the functions of communally held knowledge in traditions that are part of heritage and culture, as well as in living traditions of habitat preservation and human interaction. Policy questions also arise regarding the structuring of economic incentives, and about rights and obligations that are anchored in responses and behaviour rather than in resources.

How is the Worth of TK to be Valuated?

Questions of valuation are vital to the sharing of value-added benefits and to the role of private and public investors organised as nationally networked or globally networked bio-conservationists and bio-collectors. Mere digitalisation of published or codified information to ease the work of patent examiners cannot resolve the question of how holders of traditional knowledge should be rewarded for their care and feeding of ideas. The attention accorded to traditional medicine could serve as a way to identify characteristics that also apply to other forms of traditional knowledge and folklore, particularly those concerning living communities at risk of being dislocated from their past traditions, their present habitats and their future, in terms of intergenerational continuity of life itself. Consider the following taxonomy (Mathur 2003) with an illustration of "neem", which has been in the news for being misappropriated.

Figure 1. Taxonomy of Traditional Knowledge

Traditional Knowledge	Contemporary	Non-Contemporary
Tangible	-1	-2
	Neem packaged as tooth paste	Neem twig for dental care
Intangible	-3	-4
	Neem for calcium absorption in mammalian bone tissue	Neem as antiseptic

Source: Mathur 2003, p. 4473.

The neem tree (*Azadirachta indica*) has over 153 patents worldwide. Inventions described in virtually all neem-related patents used public domain traditional knowledge as the starting point. Neem-related traditional knowledge is cited to distinguish categories of TK. In Figure 1, knowledge of neem in categories (3) and (4) could constitute a trade secret or be disclosed for taking a patent. Thus, category (3) has been patented, but category (4), being part of prior art in the public domain, remains unpatented until someone succeeds in adding an inventive step or some other ingredient and claims a new use. Category (1) can only be protected by trademark, unless neem is synthesised which could make it patentable. Category (2) knowledge is in the public domain. In this example, the diffusion of TK delimited this knowledge from being confined to a local Indigenous group or community.

The value of Category 4 TK depends on:

i. How much of such knowledge is known outside the close-knit bonding of a family, clan, tribe or community
ii. The degree to which such knowledge is replicable
iii. The extent of measures taken to guard the secrecy of the information
iv. The value of the information within the community, both to its holders and to their competitors, if any
v. The effort or expense required to care for and keep developing such knowledge
vi. The ease or difficulty with which the information could be acquired or discovered by others

As far as the informational value of Category 4 TK is concerned, unless the cost of fostering the knowledge and the difficulty of acquiring it are prohibitively high, such knowledge is hardly likely to remain secret and is in the nature of a public good—it can be promoted in a non-rivalrous and non-excludable manner through proactive, supportive policies. However, the experience of the exploitation of agro-climatic zones associated with principal crop varieties, as demarcated by N.I. Vavilov, suggests that once such resources are geographically mapped by bioprospectors, the prices of organic components tend to rise steadily until they are eventually synthesised in *ex situ* collections.

Consider the relationship between organic resources and informational resources. Informational resources are neither rivalrous in consumption nor exhaustible, but they can be made excludable if locked up as a trade secret or under an intellectual property right. Organic resources, on the other hand, are both rivalrous in consumption and exhaustible. For example, when the value of *sarpagandha* (*Rauwolfia Serpentina*) became known as a source of reserpine, *sarpagandha* growing in the Himalayan *terai* was plucked to extinction and is now grown only on commercial farms supplying the pharmaceuticals industry.

Where knowledge cannot be divorced from the natural habitat, excludability to real property changes the status of Type 3 TK and Type 4 TK from being non-rivalrous and non-excludable to becoming rivalrous, excludable, and more importantly, *exhaustible*—significantly affecting the valuation of its economic worth. In some cases, the value may be bid up to the notion of a market price, and in others, the value may be eroded in the absence of a suitable pricing mechanism. For example, May apple (*Podophyllum peltatum*), used by Indigenous communities for centuries to ameliorate skin warts, ulcers and cancerous growths, is the source of *Etoposide* used for the treatment of cancerous growths with a US$500 million global market value. Vinca alkaloids, originating from the traditional medicinal use of periwinkle, have led to blockbuster drugs Vincristine and Vinblastine, with estimated global sales of US$600 million. Oil of evening primrose (*Oenthera*), used by Indigenous populations for skin problems, is now marketed for eczema and pre-menstrual issues, with an estimated market value of over US$400 million. The natural resource curse that impoverishes Indigenous populations in areas where minerals are mined also applies to forests where tribal communities have traditionally lived.

Feasibility of Traditional Resource Rights

There have been attempts to propose traditional resource rights (TRRs) to solve problems of access to plant genetic resources.

Due to the inability of statutory and contractual laws to recognise communal property, the problem of vesting authority to contract—by structuring roles and responsibilities into custodianship concepts of customary traditions—remains unsolved. For this reason, it is difficult for marginalised Indigenous local communities to influence policy planning and implementation on these issues of vital significance to them unless they are able to participate.

This has led to the suggestion that *sui generis* protection systems be instituted to place a higher value on respect for life, biological diversity, developmental rights, human rights, community rights and cultural heritage than on individual property rights. The classification of biological knowledge into "life sciences" and "ethnobiological knowledge" is itself questionable. Biological knowledge within its own habitat can hardly be "ethnobiological" just because the ethnicity of the traditional knowledge holders differs from the mainstream ethnicity of researchers in the so-called "life sciences". The time and energy required, as well as the delay before some part of folklore is adopted as a finding of fact, distance and disconnect the Indigenous communities from whom organic and informational resources are sourced. Most Indigenous people live in transition or developing countries, which possess the largest part of rainforests and wetlands. The areas of greatest biodiversity are also areas of the most linguistic and ethnic diversity. Tropical rainforests, which account for only 7 per cent of the planet's surface, are home to at least 1,400 distinct Indigenous and traditional peoples. These ecosystems contain between 50 and 90 per cent of the world's known species. Considering the abundance of known and unknown life forms in nature, the expense and time saved by using traditional knowledge are obvious.

Numerous groups of Indigenous peoples from all across the world have made countervailing moves to assert their right to discover and make what they consider appropriate use of new knowledge derived from their habitats. Three main planks of new laws to promote biological resource innovations, which could equitably balance Indigenous community interests, can be identified:

1. Heritage legislation could recognise biological and cultural heritage as inextricably linked and provide authorities and incentives for self-managed community initiatives.
2. Biodiversity conservation and national biodiversity registers can be linked to global registers with a transparent system for the transfer of biotechnology, organic and informational resources. This can be done under different permissible arrangements with Prior Informed Consent and participation of Indigenous communities, enabling them to choose from different structurable economic incentives.
3. The institution of plant varieties protection and farmers' rights under a *sui generis* system, after reviewing the accessibility of *ex situ* collections in gene banks and germplasm banks for food and agriculture, could be normed. The model, *mutatis mutandis,* can then be extended to community control of *in situ* and *ex situ* collections, including decisions of what is allowed to be preserved *ex situ* and under what conditions.

Conclusion

Traditional knowledge evolves within communities as a living tradition but storing it in *ex situ* collections temporarily fixes it as information, and its value as information depreciates rapidly unless it is updated. Secondly, knowledge holders and their communities, if divorced from their heritage, would perish—just as knowledge without holders to practise it can be lost. It is also pertinent to pay attention to how toxicity around TK is expressed, repressed, suppressed or oppressed in containment or spillovers (Mathur 2020). Thirdly, it is unethical to document traditional knowledge without Prior Informed Consent of its holders, who are often treated as "informants" by "experts" who create retrievable databases. Fourthly, it is irresponsible to engage in actions that might reduce the world's flow of knowledge, even if they temporarily increase digitalised information stored as zeros and ones (Mathur 2000).

It is noteworthy that representatives of Indigenous peoples attending the Workshop on Traditional Knowledge and Biodiversity, organised by the Secretariat of the Convention on Biodiversity in November 1997, demanded a moratorium on the registering of traditional knowledge. A pertinent question that deserves further research is how recording or registering traditional knowledge affects the market for innovation and particular rights to income or property. Developing countries could then establish conventions and protocols for access and benefit-sharing arrangements, if the toxicity surrounding the exploitation of TK could be mitigated.

References

DFID. "Integrating Intellectual Property Rights and Development Policy", *DFID Commission on Intellectual Property Rights*. London, 2002.

Hayek, F. "Use of Knowledge in Society", *American Economic Review* vol. 35 (1945): pp 519–30.

Mathur, Ajeet N. *What Knowledge is of Most Worth?* Tampere: Tampere University Press, 2000.

———. "Who Owns Traditional Knowledge", *Economic and Political Weekly* vol. 38, no. 42 (2003): pp. 4471–81.

———. "Psychological Containment of Organisational Toxicity and its Spillovers", *Organisational & Social Dynamics* vol. 20, no. 1 (2020): pp. 60–78. Available online: doi:10.33212/osd.v20n1.2020.60 (accessed on 20 August 2020).

WIPO. Report of the 40th Session of the Intergovernmental Committee on Intellectual Property and Genetic Resources, Traditional Knowledge and Folklore. Geneva, 16–20 March 2019.

———. Draft International Legal Instrument Relating to Intellectual Property, Genetic Resources and Traditional Knowledge associated with Genetic Resources. Geneva, 14 January 2020.

Chapter 9

India–Africa Knowledge and Skill Transfer

Nivedita Ray

Africa stands at a crossroads: on the one hand, it is striving to reclaim and rebuild its traditional knowledge systems to develop sustainable solutions tailored to local needs; on the other hand, it is forging partnerships to acquire the knowledge and skills necessary to build a modern knowledge economy. In this context, India's partnership with Africa assumes immense significance, not only in addressing Africa's development priorities but also in bridging the knowledge deficit that exists between the two regions.

The chapter examines the role that India is playing in addressing Africa's needs with regard to capacity building and human resource development, and analyses how far these efforts have led to promoting mutual knowledge and cross-cultural understanding. Before discussing engagements in the field of knowledge and skill development, it is imperative to understand Africa's developmental priorities.

Africa's Priorities

Today, advancing education and skill development remains the core development agenda for various African countries. The African Union's "Agenda 2063: The Africa We Want" clearly spells out the need for an education and skills revolution. It emphasises the need to "actively promote science, technology, research and innovation, to build knowledge, human capital, capabilities and skills to drive innovations for the African century" (African Union 2015, p. 14). Beyond Agenda 2063, the significance of education and skill development is also expressed in the Common African Position (CAP) on the Post-2015 Development Agenda. The CAP specifies that in order to improve education and skill development, Africa must achieve excellence in human resources capacity development through an improvement in the quality of education and training by investing in learning infrastructure, increasing the use of information and communications technology (ICT), ensuring higher completion rates, promoting pre-schooling, integrated adult education and tertiary education, and improving the quality and conditions of service of educators and trainers (AU 2014). In this context, the experiences of Southern countries are highly relevant for African countries looking to improve education and skill development. African countries are entering into partnerships with various developing countries within the South–South framework to benefit from the exchange of knowledge skills, resources and technical know-how.

Modalities of Skill and Knowledge Transfer to Africa

Vazquez (2015, pp. 28–30) provides an overview of India's contribution to locally relevant approaches for advancing education and skill development in African countries. The share of education and skill development in India's development cooperation with Africa was estimated at 30 per cent in 2011. Most of this is related to information technology, rural development, management, finance, environment, renewable energy, business administration, international business, tourism, computer science, and medical disciplines. The majority of projects are implemented through the Indian Technical and Economic Cooperation Programme (ITEC), the Special Commonwealth Assistance for Africa Programme (SCAAP), and the Pan African E-Network Project (PAENP).

ITEC was instituted in 1964 to assist developing countries with capacity building. Nearly half of its slots are allotted to Africa, amounting to about 4,300 annually. In 2015, at the Third India–Africa Forum Summit, an additional 50,000 slots over the next five years were announced (Vazquez 2015, p. 28). Under ITEC, about 47 institutions offer over 280 courses on IT, textile design, foreign affairs, commerce, science and media. These include the Indian Institute of Technology (IIT), the National Institute of Training and Standardization, The Energy and Resources Institute (TERI) and the Centre for Development of Advanced Computing (CDAC) (Vazquez 2015, p. 30).

PAENP was launched in 2009 through the public sector company, Telecommunications Consultants India Limited (TCIL), and provides education and medical support to African countries via satellite technology. It links universities like the Amity Institute of Higher Education, the Indira Gandhi National Open University, the University of Delhi, and others with dozens of learning centres across various African countries via a satellite hub station in Senegal, delivering distance education programmes to thousands of African students. In addition, it connects African medical facilities with speciality hospitals in India, enabling Indian doctors to review digitised medical records in Africa and provide live teleconsultations.

Knowledge and Cross-cultural Connections

India also offers up to 900 scholarships for African students to pursue undergraduate, postgraduate and higher studies programmes at institutions in India. It is observed that these scholarships have not only empowered students with life-sustaining skills but also exposed them to the multicultural and pluralistic ethos of India, leading them to seek a lifelong association with India (Vazquez 2016, p. 31). Many ITEC students have risen to top positions, including over 24 per cent of senior government officials in Tanzania and members of the defence establishment in Botswana (Vazquez 2016, p. 31).

On the Indian side, the ITEC association has given a distinct brand identity to Indian Public Sector Undertakings in Africa, such as National Small Industries Corporation, Hindustan Machine Tools International Ltd. (HMT), Water and Power Consultancy Services Ltd., and Rail India Technical & Economic Services (Vazquez 2016, p. 31).

India as a Destination for Higher Education

Besides these skills development initiatives undertaken by the Indian Government, which have led to the flow of students and professionals from Africa, there are other new opportunities emerging in the Indian education sector that attract students from the African region. Of late, India's popularity as a higher education provider has been growing, shifting from an undergraduate education pivot to a hub for postgraduate and doctoral studies, thereby opening immense opportunities for fostering ties in the higher education sector.

Waruru (2013) observes that India has been a destination for education, particularly for East Africans, since the time of British colonial rule in the 1940s, and this trend continued after India attained independence and began granting scholarships to support liberation movements in the region. The trend continued into the 1960s, when East Africa had only two universities—Makerere in Uganda and Dar es Salam in Tanzania—primarily intended to educate civil servants and staff for corporations in the newly independent states (Waruru 2013). The demand for higher education abroad began to decrease as East African countries started building more public universities, and in the 2000s, it fell further when private higher education began to flourish, led by Uganda and Kenya. This trend continues, but as student demand soars, local institutions struggle to find enough places. India remains the top non-African developing country destination for African students because of its quality and affordable education, as well as the professional and technical courses it offers.

UNESCO data on higher education, however, shows that the percentage of African students among foreign students enrolled in India has declined over time; in 2000, students from sub-Saharan Africa in India outnumbered those from South and West Asia. By 2014, as per geographically disaggregated data from UNESCO, students from South Asia outnumbered those from the Arab states and Africa put together (*Huffington Post*, 2017). In terms of absolute numbers, the African student population in India rose from 2,239 in 2000 to 25,000 in 2024. This growth is largely attributed to India's initiatives such as ICCR scholarships for African students, the Study in India Initiative, commitments made under the India-Africa Forum

Summit, the Pan-African e-Network Project and the e-Vidya Bharati platform, all of which have expanded access to higher education for African students, particularly in public sector universities.

Apart from the public sector, private universities attracting students from Africa include Manipal University, OP Jindal Global University, Sharda University, Amity University, RK Degree College, SRM University, Patkar College and the University of Punjab (Waruru 2013). Tanzania sends the highest numbers, followed by Ethiopia, Mauritius, Kenya, Zambia and Sudan. According to Waruru, what attracts students are the lower fees, wide choice of courses, and lower cut-off marks for admission compared to those in their respective countries. To facilitate travel, Indian institutions also arrange for visas for admitted students, making it easier for parents. Courses being marketed include bachelor's degrees in commerce, engineering, information technology, and health sciences (including nursing) and law (Waruru 2013).

Kenya has over 1,655 students studying across India, with some enrolled in state universities through scholarships offered by Indian government institutions or the Commonwealth, while others pursue education through self-financing schemes. Uganda has approximately 800 students in India, primarily based in Delhi, whereas Tanzania has around 3,600 students, most of whom are studying in the Hyderabad region. In response to the growing number of Ugandans seeking education in India, the Ugandan government has been in talks with Indian authorities to streamline visa processes and facilitate the issuance of temporary work permits for students (Waruru 2013).

Primary/ Secondary Education and Indian Teachers in Africa

While much of the focus on education collaboration between India and Africa has been on higher education and skill development, with the goal of creating a skilled, employable workforce, it is also necessary to pay adequate attention to cooperation in building the primary and secondary education sectors. India's education collaboration in the area of elementary and secondary education with African countries goes back to times when Indian teachers went in bulk to these countries. They were invited to teach in elementary and secondary schools. Thousands of Indian schoolteachers taught in Eastern and Southern African countries, including Uganda, Ethiopia and South Africa, until changes in governmental policies and xenophobic outbreaks in some countries forced them to leave. For instance, in the 1950s and 1960s, when Ethiopia was set to expand its education system, India provided support by sending teachers to Ethiopian schools. The Indian teachers remained in high demand. Students took them more seriously, and the schools also paid them handsomely. The Indian teachers, in turn, benefited, as teaching in Ethiopia was lucrative enough for them to save money and return home with a distinct advantage (Kasturi 2015). This led to the development of a strong bond between the two countries, which, in present times, seems to be slowly fading, as Indian teachers no longer find it attractive to adopt the migrant path.

Between 1960 and 2012, it is estimated that more than 200,000 Indians taught in Ethiopia. During the 1960s and 1970s, more than 6,000 Indians were teaching in the country at any given time. Some came and left within weeks, while others stayed for years. By the late 1990s, when India's economic liberalisation led to salaries too low to match teachers' ambitions, over 10,000 Indian teachers could be found teaching in Ethiopia at any given time. This continued through the first decade of the 21st century. After that, there was a shift in teacher recruitment to various Eastern and Southern African countries. As India moved up into the global upper-middle class, its teachers began to receive better pay, and Eastern and Southern African countries were no longer in a position to compete with the lucrative offers from India.

Why Indian Teachers were in Demand

India's colonial experience under imperial Britain, unlike Ethiopia's under the Italian rule, created an odd irony. India's long colonial experience under the British rule left the nation with a high-quality English education system. So, when African countries attempted to expand their educational system in the post-colonial period in the middle of the 20th century, they could not afford American or European teachers, and the void was filled by Indians (Kasturi 2015).

According to the Ethiopian Ambassador to India, Gennet Zewide, Ethiopia offered up to US$1,500 a month for foreign university professors and between US$600 and US$800 to schoolteachers. But after India implemented a 70 per cent pay hike for its university and school teachers beginning in 2013, it became difficult for Ethiopia's budget to stretch further.

However, through these teachers, many Ethiopians came to know India. The students and Indian schoolteachers were able to build a cultural connection, lifelong friendship and strong bonds. The teachers travelled to the remotest parts of the country, instilled values and ideals in young minds and dedicated their lives to the cause of teaching. By contributing to building an educated workforce in these countries, they helped improve the socio-economic infrastructure, which, in turn, generated goodwill for India and its people.

After independence, India has taken various policy initiatives to foster education cooperation, as discussed above. This cooperation is grounded in the recognition on both sides that people are fundamental resources and that capable and skilled human resources are the foundation of socio-economic development. At present, educational cooperation between the two countries has further diversified. Not only do EAC and SADC countries take teachers from India but they also send students to India. Besides, they have been offering scholarships to train their future professors and instructors at universities in India (MEA, GOI).

Conclusion

India's strengths and experiences in education, knowledge and skills are well-suited to Africa's needs. The connections created are meaningful not only in enhancing knowledge and skills but also in fostering wider cross-cultural and social connections, leading to a better understanding of each other. However, the collaboration today is still relatively one-sided. Africa has a lot to offer to India in terms of knowledge and skills, whether it is in the field of traditional medicine, the environment, sports or wildlife conservation. There is a need to create opportunities for Indian students to benefit from Africa's knowledge systems.

References

African Union. *Common African Position on the Post-2015 Development Agenda*, 2014. Available online: https://au.int/sites/default/files/documents/32848-doc-common_african_position.pdf (accessed on 26 December 2024).

———. "Agenda 2063: The Africa we Want", 2015. Available online: https://au.int/sites/default/files/documents/36204-doc-agenda2063_popular_version_en.pdf (accessed on 30 April 2025).

Mullen, Rani, and S. Jain, H. Shivakumar, K. Prasad, S. Haribhakti. "IDCR Report: The State of Indian Development Cooperation", 2014, p. 5. Available online: https://cprindia.org/wp-content/uploads/2021/12/Spring_2014_IDCR_Report_the_State_of_Indian_Development_Cooperation.pdf (accessed on 26 December 2024).

Economic Times, "Benefits for Africa as India expands the ITEC programme", 30 November 2015. Available online: https://timesofindia.indiatimes.com/business/india-business/benefits-for-africa-as-india-expands-itec-programme/articleshow/49983707.cms (accessed on 26 December 2024).

Rukmini S. "In the Developing World, India is a Major Hub for Foreign Students", *Huffington Post*, 13 March 2017. Available online: https://www.huffingtonpost.in/2017/03/31/in-the-developing-world-india-is-a-major-hub-for-foreign-studen_a_22020122/ (accessed on 26 December 2024).

Chand, Manish. "Skill Development: The ITEC Way", in *India Africa Shared Future,* 2012. Available online: http://indiafrica.in/FViewsManishChand.html (accessed on 26 December 2024).

Kasturi, Charu Sudan. "Pay Rise in India hits Ethiopia", *The Telegraph*, 8 March 2015. Available online: https://www.telegraphindia.com/india/pay-rise-in-india-hits-ethiopia/cid/1474292 (viewed on 4 January 2025).

Ministry of External Affairs, *Indian Technical and Economic Program*, Available online: http://mea.gov.in/Uploads/PublicationDocs/24148_REVISED_50_yrs_of_ ITEC_brochure.pdf_(accessed on 26 December 2024).

MEA, GoI, "Ethiopia once again looks to Indian teachers", 7 April 2014. Available online: http://mea.gov.in/articles-in-foreign-media.htm?

dtl/23179/Ethiopia + once + again + looks + to + Indian + teachers (accessed on 26 December 2024).

MEA, GoI, 2018. Available online: http://mea.gov.in/images/attach/NRIs-and-PIOs_1.pdf (accessed on 26 December 2024).

Mullen, Rani. "India's Development Assistance: Will it change the Global Development Finance Paradigm?" Prepared for the *Workshop on Innovation in Governance of Development Finance: Causes, Consequences & the Role of Law Conference,* 8–9 April 2013, Giesen and New York University School of Law.

NIIT. "Assistance for Africa Programme (SCAAP) and TCS of Colombo Plan at NIIT", 2016. Available online: http://www.indianembassy.hu/embassy/wp-content/uploads/2012/05/Brochure-NIIT-2015-16.pdf (accessed on 26 December 2024).

Ray, Nivedita. *India's Engagement with East Africa: Opportunities and Challenges,* New Delhi, 2013.

UNESCO. *BRICS, building education for the future. Priorities for National Development and International Cooperation*, Paris: UNESCO, 2014.

Vazquez, Karin Costa. "Advancing South-South Cooperation in Education and Skills Development: Lessons from the Field", New York: UNDP, 2016. Available online: https://pure.jgu.edu.in/id/eprint/3405/1/Advancing%20South-South%20Cooperation%20in%20Education.pdf (accessed on 26 December 2024).

Waruru, Maina. "India back in East Africa to recruit students", University World News: Africa Edition, 20 July 2013. Available online: http://www.universityworldnews.com/article.php?story = 20130719173344434 (accessed on 26 December 2024).

PART 3
Languages and Literatures of Africa

Chapter 10

Ancestry, Heritage, Legacy: Languages and Literatures of Africa

Kofi Anyidoho

This chapter makes a case for transforming the rich ancestral heritage of African languages and literature into a powerful legacy capable of sustaining a vibrant and articulate future for African peoples in the global community.

The phenomenon of contemporary African literature written in colonial heritage languages is a serious anomaly that has been normalised by the furious logic of European imperial and colonial history. African literature in English, French, Portuguese or Spanish represents a reversal of what is considered normal in the traditions of literature across the globe. Greek literature is written in Greek, Italian literature in Italian, German literature in German, Swedish literature in Swedish, Russian literature in Russian, and so on. Yet, somehow, "African literature" written in English, French, Portuguese, or Spanish is regarded as "normal".

However, let us consider the possibility of English literature being written in Yoruba, Twi, Hausa, or French literature in Fulfulde, Bambara, Hausa or Kiswahili. That sounds unthinkable, doesn't it? Of course, we acknowledge that African literature written in English has led to some truly amazing achievements, such as the Nobel Prize awarded to Nigerian writer Wole Soyinka for works written in English. We must, however, not forget that the first Indian writer to win the Nobel Prize, Rabindranath Tagore, received it for literature primarily written in Bengali.

To understand how the course of Africa's literary tradition has been diverted, we must first turn to the more fundamental issue of colonial language policy and practice. In other works, I have described European imperial and colonial history as a period in world history during which Europe voyaged around the globe, discovering people and places, including oceans, seas, lakes, rivers, tributaries, waterfalls, mountains and valleys, and renaming each of them in her own image. We recognise this process of renaming as a foundational strategy for claiming ownership (Anyidoho 2005).

The fate of African languages and literature as victims of this imperial/colonial adventure must be seen in its proper historical perspective. As Chinweizu (1988, p. xviii) reminds us, "twentieth-century African literature is not a fledgling offspring of European literature; rather, it is a continuation (partly, but only partly) in European languages, of a 5,000-year-old Indigenous African tradition." It is important that we do not forget the essential dimensions of that 5,000-year-old history of Indigenous African literature produced in African languages.

Language and the Destiny of African Civilisations

In defence of African languages as primary vehicles of cultural renewal, Ngũgĩ wa Thiong'o argues that the European Renaissance would have been impossible without a major revolution against Latin as the dominant, and often the only vehicle for education and intellectual and cultural production:

> Erich Auerbach (1965: 319) describes the European Renaissance as 'the movement through which the literary languages of the various European peoples finally shook off Latin.' Before this, Latin had occupied a position not too dissimilar to that currently occupied by European languages in Africa: 'it was virtually the sole vehicle of intellectual and written communication ...a foreign language that had to be learned... cut off from the spoken language' (ibid 269) (Thiongo 2012, p. 1526).

Despite the clear advantages of mother-tongue education and intellectual production, as demonstrated by the experiences of many other peoples, African educators and cultural experts continue to debate its merits. Unfortunately, they often arrive at the same conclusion, favouring the continued use of the various languages of colonisation, dehumanisation and enslavement. Ngũgĩ admits that, given the multilingual nature of most African nations, promoting education and intellectual production in African languages is no easy task. However, he asserts that it is a necessary one.

Significantly, Ngũgĩ points to translation as a key tool in dealing with some of the challenges. We must take note of his own practice of ensuring that all his major works in Gikuyu are immediately translated into English. Through this, Ngũgĩ demonstrates that we cannot ignore the necessity of engaging with the language most widely used in the world today. His argument, however, is that it is suicidal to continue doing business in English (or French, Portuguese, Spanish, or even Chinese) to the near-total exclusion of the majority of our own people, who remain non-literate.

We must take a cue from the determination with which the enslavers and colonisers ensured the silencing of our mother tongues. Afro-Caribbean Canadian poet M. NourbeSe Philip reminds us of the ultimate punishment reserved for those enslaved Africans who insisted on speaking their mother tongues: an edict recommending "removal of the tongue… the offending organ should be hung on high so that all may see and tremble". Another edict recommends that, whenever possible, no slave owner should allow enslaved Africans who shared the same mother tongue to congregate: "If they cannot speak to each other, they cannot then foment rebellion and revolution" (Philip 1989, pp. 44, 46).

Another African diaspora writer reminds us that the loss of language is indeed the beginning of the loss of self:

> With the killing of language, the transfiguration of the African was complete and lasting... [F]ew things are as important as language, and for most, the quieting of the tongue, more than anything else, sealed their faith in the new world, for without language, one cannot express the indigenous self, and

> therefore, one has nothing to express other than the selves of others in their language (Madhubuti 1984, p. 123).

The Central Role of Language in Our Cultural Heritage

The centrality of language to our cultural heritage is difficult to overestimate. Culture, it has been suggested, is not only a force of creativity but also the utilisation of human intelligence for social development. But culture cannot achieve its creative and utilitarian potential without language. The fruits of human creativity and intelligence cannot be accumulated or disseminated without the vehicle of language. Yet, language both represents and misrepresents truth, fact, or experience.

During the history of African slavery and colonisation, the imposed languages of the enslavers and colonisers did a great deal to misrepresent the human experience, and contributed to the crisis of consciousness today. Until we forthrightly address the issues involved, until we formulate and execute bold, intelligent strategies for the creation of an effective language plan of action, our otherwise excellent blueprints for material development will largely remain at the talking stage. Somehow, in our globalised world, we speak with ease to the rest of the world but find it difficult to speak to and with our own people.

Some have argued that African languages are inherently inferior to our colonial heritage languages and that they lack the capacity to handle the full range of experiences associated with modernity. This, of course, is a lie, but it has been repeated so often that many are actually persuaded that it is the truth. Early German missionary scholar Jakob Spieth, in his monumental work, *The Ewe People* (1906), had the following commendation to make regarding the Ewe language:

> Such a rich language, which is capable of further enrichment, would be highly suitable as a language of culture, education and trade and the greatest crime that Europe can commit against that tribe would be to suppress their most valuable native inheritance under European languages or even as much as declaim against it. If we want the Ewes to retain their valuable intellectual individuality, then we must seriously ensure that this language remains, and

> that the up and coming youth of that country develops an insight into the beauty and worth of their mother tongue (Spieth 2011, p. 41).

Spieth, along with his Bremen missionary colleagues like Westermann, as well as Basel Missionaries such as Christaller, based in the Akuapem area, did their best to lay the foundations for the future development of our languages. Unfortunately, much of their pioneering work was followed by a series of disastrous language policies that have now left us with a generation that is neither fluent in their own languages nor proficient in the colonial languages. Even more seriously, those of us who claim the right to direct the affairs of our nation-states are unable to carry out any meaningful dialogue with the majority of the population we claim to represent. The blame largely lies with us: "There is only one primary crisis in the developing world. It is the crisis of transformation which is generated when and practically everywhere the political [and professional] elite try and reshape or re-invent their society and culture by imposing their [often alien and alienating] ideological blueprint on both" (Uchendu 1988, p. 17).

It is all very well for us to be impatient to move forward, maybe even to move ahead, but we are reminded again and again that "Our languages are our primary instruments [of development]. Without them, we cannot move forward ... In order to retrieve our cultures, particularly our languages, we need to harmonize their orthographies, modernize them and develop their terminological competencies" (Prah 2009, p. 30). This is just one recommendation among many, but it is one that is well founded on the experiences of others who share the retarding effects of colonialism. Malaysia and Japan have advanced, but only after they took up the challenges of modern education, fully grounded in the enabling capacity of their mother tongues as the primary vehicles of creative intelligence.

The Special Role of Stories in the Life of a Nation, a People

Every culture and every people define themselves by the stories they tell themselves and others about themselves. Among the most primary and enduring of these stories are myths of origin.

Every people, in their myths of origin, place themselves at the centre of the universe. According to the Yoruba, the world began at Ile Ife, and with the Yoruba people. The Gikuyu tell of how God created the earth and took care to place their ancestral Mother, Mumbi, and Father, Gikuyu, in charge. An Ewe elder, when asked about how the world began, insisted that when Mawu finished creating the earth, the very first people he created were the Ewe. Then He created the Akan. The last people He created were the Yevu or Whiteman, who, for some strange reason, sneaked out of the ancestral garden only half-baked. Of all the myths of origin I know, I consider that of the Fulani to be perhaps the most memorable, filled with complex scientific concepts and fundamental moral values: "At the beginning, there was a huge drop of milk" (Chinweizu 1988, p. 321).

Each of these origin stories once had its cultural, if not historical, validity—until one particular story of the origin of the world arrived, at the point of the sword, the cannon and on the authority of the Bible. Suddenly, everyone's story of origin faded into insignificance, and most of us became captive to the Western world's "old domineering monologue in the world" (Achebe 2001, p. 83).

The gifted Nigerian writer Chimamanda Ngozi Adichie has warned us against what she calls "The Danger of a Single Story":

> It is impossible to talk about the single story without talking about power. There is a word, an Igbo word, that I think about whenever I think about the power structures of the world, and it is 'nkali.' It's a noun that loosely translates to 'to be greater than another.' Like our economic and political worlds, stories too are defined by the principle of nkali. How they are told, who tells them, when they're told, how many stories are told, are really dependent on power. Power is the ability not just to tell the story of another person, but to make it the definitive story of that person (Adichie 2009).

The story of colonisation as told by Europe is one in which Africans and other colonised peoples came off with "a badly damaged sense of self" (Achebe 2001, p. 81), while the high seas were filled with heroic, almost mythic characters such as Ferdinand Magellan, Amerigo Vespucci, Vasco da Gama, and Christopher Columbus, and our continent was trampled upon by giants like Henry Stanley and "Dr Livingstone I presume". Together, they invented the dubious art of discovery and betrayed the actual intent of "civilisation" to be a series of thefts.

Indeed, if the story were properly retold, and for our particular benefit, these men should have been sent to the gallows as buccaneers and dangerous highwaymen. But of course, we were not the ones telling the story. So, they all went home to glory and to deification in history books written by their people for themselves and for our miseducation.

In his novel *Anthills of the Savannah*, Chinua Achebe offers us a compelling view of life as a struggle—a battle in fact—pointing out the relative importance of the role that each of us may play according to our talents and skills:

> The sounding of the battle-drum is important; the fierce waging of the war itself is important; and the telling of the story afterwards—each is important in its own way. I tell you there is not one of them we could do without. But if you ask me which of them takes the eagle-feather I will say boldly: the story. ... Why? Because it is only the story can continue beyond the war and the warrior. It is the story that outlives the sound of war-drums and the exploits of brave fighters. It is the story, not the others, that saves our progeny from blundering like blind beggars into the spikes of the cactus fence. The story is our escort; without it, we are blind (Achebe 1988, pp. 113–4).

Often, we may not like the story told by the artist who re-enacts it for us, but we need not blame the artist for the unpleasantness of the tale, especially if it happens to be the truth. Any people who turn away from the path of truth soon run into a dead end.

Nketia (1999, p. 13) reminds us that "creative writers and masters of verbal art bring to us an unusually intimate and perceptive understanding of society and the individual." He elaborates, "Literature, whether written or oral, printed or performed, is an art that forces us to think or reflect as it stimulates our imagination and excitement, awakens our sensibility as well as our aesthetic appreciation of language and its surrogates."

We must pay special homage to the poets as musicians and the musicians as poets in the ancestral traditions of African literature—those "masters in the art of eloquence", who are regarded as the "memory of mankind", as noted by master griot Mamoudou Kouyate of the Sundiata epic tradition (Niane 1965, p. 1). If the claim that life cannot be normal without the poet-musician seems somewhat exaggerated, perhaps we need only to contemplate a world without the sound of music, a world without poetry's peculiar ability to give rhythmic intensity to our joys, its ability to lift our minds and spirits above our many sorrows and transform our keenest misery into delicious pain. The poets' ultimate gift to the community is their unfailing ability to move even kings and queens into song and dance, though they themselves may be as handicapped as the ailing frog. It is also their ability, through the creative power of the human voice, to paint back onto a dying tree those green leaves and flowers that carry the promise of future fruits.

Ewe thought views life in the image of *Kodzogbe*, a wilderness of poverty and misery. The poets, through their songs, create those essential oases, without which all travellers on life's many paths are doomed to endless hallucinations and to eventual death by dehydration. Yet, it is often the fate of the poets to suffer neglect, and the lonely life of pilgrims who must keep vigil over other people's fortunes and misfortunes (Anyidoho 1995, p. 258).

Conclusion

It is estimated that Africa accounts for about half of the total number of languages spoken in the world. We agree with Prah that the notion of African languages as small units which are developmentally untenable is entirely false. On the contrary, a closer study reveals several clusters of language groups or families within which there are significant structural similarities and also mutual intelligibility. We also acknowledge Prah's demonstration of how various interventions, especially by missionaries, colonial administrators and colonial-heritage anthropologists and linguists, imposed fragmentation on what were once more or less homogeneous language groups across Africa.

We endorse Prah's proposals for what needs to be done to restore or construct a sense of closer relationships towards the re-constitution of larger communities of closely related language groups. This would be the foundation for transformational language policies and plans of action, and would expedite the achievement of widespread literacy, especially in African languages—a basic requirement for rapid development. The spread of literacy in African languages, facilitated by new harmonised orthographies, will inspire a new age of literary culture in Africa.[1]

African literature, nurtured in African languages and value systems, will grow rapidly alongside literature produced in colonial-heritage languages. Ultimately, African language literature will once more come into its own as a truly representative tradition, which rivals any literary tradition in the world. It will remind us of the glory that once belonged to Ancient Egyptian literature, whose legacy of models of excellence still dazzles the imagination with countless treasures of the mind, spirit and soul of a people who own their civilisation and are generous enough to share it with the rest of humankind.[2]

References

Achebe, Chinua. *Anthills of the Savannah.* Ibadan: Heinemann, 1988.

———. "Today, the Balance of Stories", in *Home and Exile*. New York: Anchor Books, 2001.

Adichie, Chimamanda Ngozi. "The Danger of a Single Story", 2009. Available online: https://www.ted.com/talks/chimamanda_ngozi_adichie_the_danger_of_a_single_story#t-1110036 (accessed on 17 August 2021).

Anyidoho, Kofi. "Beyond the Communal Warmth: The Poet as a Loner in Ewe Oral Tradition", in *Power, Marginality and African Oral Literature*,

1 See Prah 2009 for a detailed discussion of his arguments and proposals.

2 See Forster 1992 for an impressive selection and translation of representative genres of Ancient Egyptian literature.

eds. Graham Furniss and Liz Gunner. Cambridge: Cambridge University Press, 1995.

———. "Playing GOD with WORD: LANGUAGE and POWER of SELF-NAMING", Bashorun M.K.O. Abiola Distinguished Lecture. African Studies Association 47th Annual Meeting. New Orleans, Louisiana, 2004.

Auerbach, Erich. *Language and its Public in Late Latin Antiquity and in the Middle Ages*. Princeton University Press, 1965.

Chinweizu, *Voices from Twentieth-Century Africa: Griots and Towncriers*. London: Faber and Faber, 1988.

Forster, John L. *Echoes of Egyptian Voices: An Anthology of Ancient Egyptian Poetry*. Norman: University of Oklahoma Press, 1992.

Madhubuti, Haki. "Remembering the Middle Passage: Culture as Motion", in *Earthquake and Sunrise Missions: Poetry and Essays of Black Renewal 1973–1983*. Chicago: Third World Press, 1984.

Niane, D.T. *Sundiata: An Epic of Old Mali*. Essex: Longman, 1965.

Nketia. J.H. Kwabena. "Welcome Address", in *Beyond Survival: African Literature and the Search for New Life*, ed. K. Anyidoho et al. Trenton, NJ: Africa World Press, 1999.

Philip, Marlene NourbeSe. *She Tries Her Tongue, Her Silence Softly Breaks*. Charlottetown: Ragweed Press, 1989.

Prah, Kwesi Kwaa. *African Languages, African Development, and African Unity*. Lagos: CBAAC Occasional Monograph no. 14, 2009.

Spieth, Jacob. *The Ewe People: A Study of the Ewe People in German Togo*, translated by Marcellinus Edorh, Emmanuel Tsaku and Raphael Avornyo. Accra: Sub-Saharan Publishers, 2011 [1906].

Thiong'o, Ngũgĩ wa. "Remembering Africa: Memory, Restoration and African Renaissance", in *Reclaiming the Human Sciences and Humanities through African Perspectives*, eds. H. Lauer and K. Anyidoho, vol. 2. Accra: Sub-Saharan Publishers, 2012.

Uchendu, Victor C. "Towards a Strategic Concept of Culture: Implications for Continental Unity", in *African Unity: The Cultural Foundations*, eds. A.I. Asiwaju and B.O. Oloruntimehin. Lagos: CBAAC, 1988.

Chapter 11

The Traditional Sahelien Oral Epic in Niger

Ousmane Mahamane Tandina

Niger is a land of ancient civilisations (Séré de Rivières 1952; Clair 1965; Salifou 1991). Geographically, it is situated in the heart of Africa. The country is simultaneously part of the Maghreb, Central Africa and Western Africa. Historically, it has been at the crossroads of great empires from the fourth to the nineteenth centuries of the Common Era.

As far back as antiquity, Ghana is believed to have had relations with towns in North Africa. The Soninke Empire of Ghana, also known as Wagadou, encompassed countries extending from the Atlantic to Lake Debo and the Sahara. It reached the height of its glory in the 11th century CE. There was regular contact between Ghana and Nigerian cities such as Djenné-Djeno, from where, according to some historians, the Soninkes of Wanzarbé in Niger originated. The historical traditions of the ethnic groups in the Dosso region, compiled and transcribed by Diouldé Laya (Laya 1969), mention a figure named Magan Sunjatta, a matrilineal relative of Zarma, who is believed to have come to the court of Zarma Koy Sambo. The story follows the same lines as the Mandingo epic of Soundjata, alias Mari-Diata. In the 14th century, the Mali Empire reached its zenith under the reign of Mansa Kandou Moussa (1342–1360) and extended from Niamey (the current capital of Niger) to the Atlantic Ocean.

The foundations of the Gao Empire were laid before the 6th century CE by the Sorko in Kukia, located in the islands of Tillaberi-Ansongo. In 1464, the famous Songhai king of Gao, Sonni Ali Ber, rushed from the deep South (Dendi) to deliver Gao from the hands of the Tuaregs and re-establish the authority of his ancestors.

The kingdom of Ségou (or Sâ as per our epic texts), which flourished from 1712 to 1818, was a warrior state. War was an "inescapable vocation" for the kingdom, as it was the key source of its income. War enabled the kingdom to acquire slaves, who were sold and traded, especially for arms. The kingdom spanned all of Western Niger. The Macina Empire, a Muslim state on the outskirts of Ségou, grew so powerful that it became a force to contend with for the Bambara Empire. Under El Hadj Omar (1850–1864), the Fulani authority of Macina extended over the entire Niger Delta. The French conquest of the regions between Senegal and Niger took place between 1637 and 1890 and led to outbreaks of resistance.

Hence, we observe that Niger is a multicultural country that has been populated in different stages. After the Songhai-Sonianke and Gourmantché farmers, the pastoral and nomadic Fulani, followed by the Tuaregs and Arabs, came from the north to occupy the Sahelian and Saharan areas of Niger. The Fulani and the Songhai established quite powerful kingdoms, ruled by the Ardo and the Si, respectively.

This coexistence was not always peaceful; it led to conflicts and intermingling that witnessed the birth of great heroes and great griots. We can easily understand why Nigerian griots still sing today about Albouri Ndiaye (Senegal), Da Monzon, Soumaoro Kanté (French Sudan), and Bachar Dan Moussa (Daura, Nigeria)! The feudal society that produced this genre existed before the independence of African states and extended beyond French Sudan (Mali) and the current borders.

This mixing of cultures, thus, led to the development of a vast body of traditional oral literature, especially in the 19th century. The most popular genre in this literature is the epic, which accounts for several thousand verses. Epics in Niger can be categorised into several types: "feudal epics", "clan epics" and "corporate epics", according to the classification in Kesteloot and Dieng (1997), each with specific characteristics. They have certain distinctive features, unique to the different regions they are from. We will try to provide the essential content of these epics through summaries of the texts we have compiled and presented below, without making broad comments in this section. The primary objective is to highlight the range of epic narratives identified in Niger.

In addition to the flourishing epics of the West, where Fulani and Songhai-Zarma griots pitted their talents against each other with shifting success, and which include those of Djado Sékou, we can cite three epics whose variations are found in Nigeria, Burkina Faso, Mali and almost all across the Sahel.

Gama Gari Kanta

The story of Gama Gari Kanta by Amadou Toudou of Tahoua is the only true epic of a political nature that we have found in the Hausa regions of Niger, and we have translated it ourselves. It was published in its entirety in Kesteloot and Dieng in 1977.

Apart from the confrontation between Agadez (Air) and Tahoua (Ader), what is fascinating about this text is the element of fantasy. Agabba owes his ascent to cunning and deception: he overhears a conversation between his master and an eminent witch doctor, who recommends that, in order to be powerful, he (the master) should drink the first drops of milk from one of the cows in his herd that is about to give birth, which the witch doctor identifies. Agabba, being the herdsman of this flock, seizes the opportunity. When the cow gives birth, he drinks the milk, outwitting his master. In this way, he becomes a powerful man, a true warrior and the only one capable of confronting the chief of Agadez.

To defeat him, Agabba uses another strategy. He charms his daughter, his sole heir, the only one who knows the secret words her father uses to retrieve his fearsome magical spear from the lucky hole. Agabba seduces the girl, who reveals her father's Achilles' heel to him. He then takes hold of the spear and defeats the all-powerful Amenokal of Air. This sequence of the narrative reminds us of the "Open Sesame" used to access Ali Baba's cave in *One Thousand and One Nights*. The imaginary world takes over reality to such an extent that the text slides into fantasy.

Shago

The corporate epic of the Shago butchers, who practise Dambe, a brutal style of traditional boxing, is also a marvellous story in which Dan Anache sweeps his hero along from city to city, much like Ulysses, as he vanquishes his adversaries. Dambe is practised in Hausa communities as part of the festivities marking the grand annual gathering of butchers. There are several variants of Dambe practised in different geographical areas. For instance, there is "Damben Karfe" from the Gaya region, where the boxer wears a glove on one hand and equips the other with a square or circular metal piece to parry the blows of his opponent. Furthermore, in the southern part of Nigeria, another form of Dambe is practised, in which the boxer can use both his hands and his feet in combat. Dambe is a very dangerous sport. The rules differ from those of modern boxing, where there are strict controls on the gloves used. Attached to the bandage that serves as a glove are many "gris-gris" or small amulets that can stab and cut. Today, this game is prohibited because of its violent nature. However, a few years ago, Dambe was considered the national sport.

It is in this context that the griot Dan Anache recounts the exploits of Dan Abdou Shago, one of the heroes of his time. Shago is endowed with Herculean strength that places him above ordinary mortals and makes him comparable to a god. Dan Anache sings of the invincibility of his hero. Indeed, Shago had, in his time, brought misfortune to many traditional boxers who were renowned for their toughness. Many of them saw their star sink the moment they faced him. This is why Dan Anache begins his narrative by singing praises of "Dan Abdou, the destroyer of reputations".

Shago is a fearless boxer whose presence in the arena terrorises his adversaries with "his hyena-like howls which make hunting dogs tremble". No butcher can measure up to him because he is "the queller of lies". No one can boast in front of him, as "the hyena knows that the caiman sleeps under the stars, but who dares confront it?"

Dan Anache made an epic hero of Shago. Indeed, the griot exalts the hero from the beginning to the end of the story, praising the physical and intellectual qualities he displays in all the matches he participates in. These include matches against giants such as Dan

Dounawa, Kourama, and Harou Djallaba, whom boxing fans in Nigeria and East Niger know well. The figures of speech the author uses show the extent to which these boxers are feared. Thus, he names them *mayya* and *gouma goumay*, which mean "great" and "hefty pieces", respectively.

The versification of the narrative and its marvellous character add to the depiction of Shago as invincible. Expressions like "the chosen one of the gods has entered the scene" elevate the hero to the rank of superior beings. Indeed, the story says that if Shago remained undefeated during his entire boxing career, it is thanks to a genie (the Dogoua) who offers him his services whenever needed. In so doing, the genie gives him a giant hammer to knock out adversaries who refuse to fall, without anyone having a clue as to what happened. This fictional device conveys the power of the hero's blows. Still, it is said that when confronted by formidable opponents like Dan Dounawa, Shago sometimes falls KO'd (a boxing term for knocked out)! However, his genie veils the scene from the public eye, and no one notices anything. In addition, even if someone does realise what happened, they must refrain from speaking about it publicly, or risk losing their life instantly. In his song, the griot retains the spirit fostered by the myth of the Dogoua and urges the hero to take note of it and make the most of it.

Labdeedjo

Labdeedjo is a story of another texture. It was recorded by my colleague at the University of Niamey, Paulette Maïga Fanta. We integrated it into our study after translating it ourselves. The story depicts the feudalism of the Gourmantché, an ethnic group from Niger and Burkina Faso. The text is relatively recent, from the time of colonisation, and was rendered in the Zarma language by Tinguizi, who alternates between song, speech and music.

In both the development of the story and the conception of its characters, the griot emphasises elements that give his work the socio-political colour of the time. In fact, these structural and symbolic elements bear witness to a profound historical upheaval that has left a lasting mark on the popular consciousness.

Through its actions, the colonial administration challenges the principles of traditional society and undermines the social and political organisation by creating a conflict of which it does not understand the ramifications. Traditional Gourmantché society is rigorously organised and structured. The chief is single-minded in his determination to preserve these institutions, even if they appear outdated in the eyes of the coloniser.

The story is based on a heroic protagonist, Labdeedjo, and his arch-enemy, the Commander. The epic is grafted onto this social structure to highlight the sociological upheaval taking place. The griot presents Labdeedjo as a true nobleman, faithful to the ideals of dignity and honour. On these grounds, the chief and his lineage deserve respect and devotion from their subjects. Anyone who refuses to observe these rules, codified by society itself, is considered a rebel and deserves to be punished.

Armed with this sense of duty, Labdeedjo decides not to respond to the Commander's summons. This decision shows his determination not to ally with a structure that has been imposed upon them and that governs the territory through the might of cannons. This is why the wise men of the region, in a particular context symbolising a dislocated popular consciousness, get frightened and request Sipti, the king's beloved wife, to come to their aid in order to ward off the fury of the Commander, who is all set to intervene with force.

The griot shows the insidious penetration of the Whites (colonisers), beginning with scenes of recruitment and incorporation into the army based on physical fitness. These are followed by scenes of repression against all forms of resistance, which take centre stage. The character of Labdeedjo reclaims a glorious past. He enters a literature of refusal, a theme that will become more visible in the writings of intellectuals during the colonial period. Today, in our Gourma societies, Labdeedjo is a reference point. He is seen as a hero who rejected colonial hegemony. We come to understand Labdeedjo through the songs of his griots and his own songs about his ancestors, whose legacy he claims, but this does not seem to be enough for the griot. He confers on him great nobility in both his appearance and his gestures.

When the Commander decides to imprison Labdeedjo, the Chief becomes a character without a name, as the griot describes him: he is nothing but nobility. His attire signals all the distinctive marks of nobility: the coat, the pants—made from a single piece of cloth— and his armament, which distinguishes him from the other characters. Moreover, Labdeedjo adopts an attitude that is in keeping with the ethics of a warrior. He is a fully realised character: he declares that he is not a dog to be enticed with bones. If the Commander wants to kill him, he can find him in Koola, his village.

When his wife arrives by stealth to lead him to the Commander, Labdeedjo responds without hesitation to all his ironic remarks.

The Commander receives the Chief; his greeting is full of irony:

—“Welcome, Sir from the Government!”

—“Don’t call me that anymore, my Commander,” retorted the Chief vehemently.

—“Do not insult me!”

—“I do not find this dubious joke worthy of me.”

—“Even less so in front of my subjects.”

It is thus that the character of Labdeedjo influences the popular consciousness with his superb retorts that express his rejection of foreign ideology.

Later, dismissing Labdeedjo from his post, the Commander replaces him with his cousin and asks his victim for his opinion:

—“Have you understood?”

—“Yes!”

—“Does that reassure you?”

—“Very much so!”

—“Do you approve?”

—“That is another matter,” he replies.

—“The ears hear what they may not like.”

—“The eyes see what may not please them.”

In reality, his opinion does not matter! A new era is beginning, and the hero finds himself completely alone. What stands out even more is the betrayal by the cousin, which seems to sound the death knell of the previous era. The cousin abandons Labdeedjo in his time of need: this act signifies the breakdown of the social structure and is perceived by the hero as the end of stability. The quest for power will now be the business of the colonisers and will depend on how the chief behaves towards them. The future that awaits the people can only be tragic. The griot does not offer any prospects for the future; instead, he turns the character's gaze towards a bygone period, to which he wishes to link him.

This portrait essentially underscores the importance of staying true to oneself. The symbolic representation of loyalty to traditions is better understood through the depiction of the overbearing actions of the White man in this epic. Indeed, the prison plays an important role as the hero himself faces the threat of captivity. The Commander orders that he be stripped and made to wear the garb of a prisoner. What is even more humiliating is that this takes place in the presence of his wife and subjects. It is in this context that we must understand Labdeedjo's gesture of stabbing himself, presented as an act of refusal to go to prison. Labdeedjo prefers death to being imprisoned as a chief.

Sipti, his favourite wife, encourages him. She becomes the strong woman who represents the physical embodiment of the indomitable warrior. Does she not ask her husband to give her his pants if he agrees to have his stomach stitched up? Dressed as a man, she cannot be distinguished from the brave man of Gourma (a region to the north of Niger, whose inhabitants are called Gourmantchés).

Shortly after the death of her husband, she decides to imitate him:

She takes the knife
And plunges it between her breasts.
She stabs herself so hard
That the knife pierces right through her.
Then, using both hands,
She pulls the knife out from between her breasts
And plunges it back in below her navel.

She is no longer able to pull it out.

She collapses.

Before the horsemen can come to her rescue,

Her body is already tepid.

She is buried alongside her husband in a tomb in Koola.

Note here that the knife was planted in two symbolic places: the breast and the navel, which represent feminine attributes such as maternal nurturance and childbirth—the bedrock of an entire sociopolitical system. This act is truly revealing of a world collapsing, where the nobility, once the guarantor of the preservation of tradition, now itself accepts domination.

This text resembles a play. However, Tinguizi is one of the greatest griots of West Africa. It was from him that Christiane Seydou was able to collect several stories, including the famous epic of Silamaka and Poullori. Tinguizi is an exceptionally gifted, talented and powerful griot. He does not recount simple anecdotes—he himself says that he only sings of the great feats of kings and the political crises of his time. This is what leads us to characterise this narrative as an epic, despite its peculiarities.

Currently, African experts interested in this field are taking part in the systematic collection of epic stories from across the continent. The work done by African universities has enabled extensive theorisation on the subject of African epics and their relationships to ethnic groups, territories and history. This research is linked to the four types of epics defined in the classification by Kesteloot and Dieng (1997): the royal or dynastic epic, the corporate epic, the religious epic, and the mythological clan epic.

As in any first attempt, we can see that this typology of African epics is rigorous, with each narrative having underlying historical and political foundations. However, the research is far from complete, and the distinctions between the feudal epic and the clan epic are still not well defined. Many epic stories also don't find a place in this classification—particularly those in which the heroes experience romantic encounters and embark on marvellous adventures, such as the courtly or romantic epics we have discovered in the

Sahel, especially in Niger. Examples include *Sombo Soga, Mamudu Diawondo* and *Lobbo Django*, which we have compiled, transcribed and translated (Tandina 2004).

The epics mentioned above celebrate those who dedicate their valour to the conquest of a woman. The conflicts one comes across in such works are inherent to the feudal system itself—namely, a lack of propriety on the part of the chief, who seeks to abduct the beloved of one of his subjects, leading to strife. Unlike works that use memories of historical events, these stories have no specific historical backdrop. However, the hero's qualities and behaviour remain thoroughly epic. *Sombo Soga*, for example, pits the chief and Sombo against each other in an extraordinary adventure that lends the narration the structure of a tale where the hero is launched on a dangerous quest to reclaim his lost fiancée and exposed to a confrontation with the chief. Meanwhile, allies are placed in his path, the foremost being Baïdari, the chief's slave, who comes to Sombo's aid in winning back his beloved and securing justice for him.

References

Clair, A. *Niger, pays à découvrir*. Paris: Hachette, 1965.

Kesteloot, L. and B. Dieng. *Les Epopées d'Afrique noire*. Paris: Karthala, 1997.

Laya, Diouldé. *Histoire des songhay-zarma: traditions historiques des ethnies de la région de Dooso (Dosso)*. Niamey: CELHTO, 1969.

Salifou, A. 'Histoire du Niger', notre Librairie, vol. 107 (1991): pp. 6–10.

Séré de Rivières, Edmond, ed. *Niger: Pays Africains*. Paris: Société d'éditions géographiques, maritimes et coloniales, 1952.

Tandina, Ousmane. *Récits épiques du Niger*. Amiens: Presses du Centre d'études médiévales, Université de Picardie-Junes Verne, 2004.

Chapter 12

Of Chosen Exile and Ambivalent Homelands: An Indian Writer on Pre-Independence Kenya

Sukrita Paul Kumar

Salman Rushdie initiated a discussion on "imaginary homelands" nearly two decades ago, focusing on expatriate writers and those in exile—writers who are haunted by an acute loss of a sense of belonging. Unable to reclaim what is lost, these writers, he argues, create fictional homelands through their imagination. Migration to a different land, even when not forced, can also lead to such a predicament. Economic compulsions or the search for better professional prospects may prompt people to leave their countries. Nevertheless, the physical disconnect with one's homeland and culture necessitates a reconstruction of both identity as well as new imaginaries.

In this chapter, while I aim to take off from where Rushdie left, I also seek to trace the journey of a writer's existential need in calling the country to where he has migrated home. This is a personally witnessed and experienced story about an Indian writer, Joginder Paul, who left for Kenya as a Partition refugee. He was deeply conscious of his Indianness but was not able to align culturally and socially with the Asians living in colonial Kenya in the mid-20th century. As a result, he became more of a witness than a participant in social life there, bearing the ambivalent position of an insider who was also an outsider. While he carried his India in his mind, the process of "homing" in Kenya became equally compelling for him. His acute sensitivity and strong empathy for the Indigenous black people of the land evoked in him a fervent creative urge to connect with their predicament in colonial Kenya.

This occurred in the 1950s during the period when the Mau Mau Movement was at its peak in Kenya. While, on the one hand, there was a heightened consciousness and a strong will amongst the Indigenous African community to seek freedom from the British, on the other hand, there was a repressive silencing of the rebellious African voice by the administration. The constant threat of an outburst of violence loomed heavily on the minds of the Asians and Britishers in Nairobi and other urban centres, but apart from occasional rumours of violence, there was not much evidence of rebellion in the cities. The conscious erasure of the African face from public life had resulted in social distancing between the African and the Asian communities. What further alienated the Africans was the atmosphere of fear and suspicion towards them, generated by the politics of the time. British rule in Kenya had effectively pushed the people of the land to the periphery of urban life, as menial domestic help, peons in offices, and labourers, or relegated them to villages and forests away from the cities. It was in such a scenario that this young writer from India landed in Kenya after experiencing Partition in his own country. Having migrated from Sialkot, Pakistan, a few months earlier and still residing in the refugee camp in Ambala, in 1948, Joginder Paul—a 23-year-old young man struggling for survival and taking care of his old parents—married a girl from Kenya on the condition that he would go back with her to settle there. A refugee by circumstance, he migrated once again, this time to a country still under British rule, while, ironically, his own country had just won its hard-earned freedom.

Struck by the racial discrimination, social inequality and linguistic hierarchy that he witnessed there, Paul was unable to relate to the social environs there and felt like a complete outsider. However, the Asian community around him seemed to accept that social reality as a given fact and fully participated in its perpetuation. Completely blinded to the plight of the Africans, they lived as if in a bubble, managing their own insular world. Paul failed to relate to them and felt more "in exile" than he had in the refugee camp back in India, longing to return to his homeland from the very first year of his stay in Kenya. This writer happens to be my father. I remember acutely of how he desperately tried to create an "imaginary homeland" for us (his children)—week after week, month after month—hoping to train us in Indian languages and educate us about India as our home.

The turmoil within the mind of the writer was fanned by the simmering anger he discerned amongst the Kikuyus—the fighter African tribe in the forests—something not as visible in the cities, where discipline and full control were exercised by the white rulers. The Asians seemed smug and well-protected in these environs and kept a safe distance from the Africans socially. When Dedan Kimathi Waciuri, the most prominent leader of the Mau Mau Movement, was captured in 1956, they actually heaved sighs of relief and celebrated this as a triumph of the British Government's competence. Kimathi, the revolutionary who had mobilised the African freedom struggle, knew that he would be executed by the British to cripple the "liberation army". True enough, he was put to death in 1957 after a so-called trial. Except for a few murmurs from some Asians who saw the parallel between the Indian freedom struggle and the African liberation movement, most people took this as their own freedom from fear, fear of violence. They did not wish to align with the Africans and thus invite the rancour of the white people. The Asian community was mainly middle class, comprising mostly businessmen and professionals, which created a class divide between them and the Africans, who generally held blue-collar jobs or remained in the villages. Later, in 1964, Ngũgĩ wa Thiong'o, the well-known Kenyan writer, wrote his novel *Weep Not, Child,* and the play *The Trial of Dedan Kimathi* in 1976, recording the story of Kimathi and the Mau Mau revolt against the British colonial regime.

A little earlier, Paul had started writing short stories in Urdu, empathising with the Africans. While he did not focus on their freedom struggle, he was deeply affected by it.

His short stories emerged from his keen observation of Asian–African interactions and relationships, which were rooted in a complex structure bred by prejudice and oppression that came out of the colonial mindset. What the Asians received at the hands of the white-supremacist leaders was, in turn, meted out to the Africans, almost with a vengeance. Asian supremacy manifested itself in subtle ways, with an obvious exclusion of Africans from their society.

Paul's first collection of stories in Urdu, entitled *Dharti ka Kaal* (1962, translated into English as *Land Lust* in 2019), is a collection of 11 stories that capture the spirit and social ambience of Indians settled in colonised Kenya. These stories, much to the amazement of the Asians, included African characters. This was indeed a conscious choice by the author, wishing to acknowledge their presence and assert, in a manner, the dignity of the black people who were otherwise invisible in the urban social domain of the country. Paul used fiction to express, through these stories, his anguish and sensitive observations regarding the nature of the relationship—or rather, the nonrelationship—between Asians and Africans.

The Kenya of the 1950s was, in a pronounced way, a multiracial society where the British, Asians and Africans coexisted in a falsely enacted harmony, with a harshly xenophobic environment beneath the surface. It is in the story entitled "Multiracial" that the author exposes the hypocrisy of the white and Asian parliamentarians, who make loud proclamations in their speeches to advocate the healthy growth of a multiracial society.

> It is not a mere coincidence that our three races have come together on this Dark Continent. In fact, Nature wishes to test man's claim that his allegiance is to one race—that of humanity, and that his best virtues show up only when he extends his hand in friendship and lives amicably amongst any and all people of the world (*Land Lust*, 2019, p. 82).

The above words in the story are a part of Honourable Kumar's speech in Parliament in which he also declares how the Africans, Europeans and Asians are bound together, and that the word "race" needed to be redefined as they are united politically, socially and ideologically. His progressive proclamations win over the African members especially when he says, "We are here all Africans!" or when he professes the need to eliminate inequalities in society. While he is making such a laudatory speech, the African by the side of the Asian lady sneezes without using a handkerchief, and drops of water from his nose and mouth spray over her. "Idiot", thinks the Asian lady with contempt spreading over her face, "not an iota of good breeding in these barbarians" (Paul 2019, p. 84). These ironic asides in the story inserted consciously by the author betray the irony of the situation and reveal poignantly the racist orientations set in the mind of the Asian lady, no matter what might have been idealistically discussed about racial harmony and equality. Integration amongst the different races was too distant a dream!

The lived experiences of Paul fed effectively into the fictional world he was constructing in his stories during the 1950s and 1960s. Expression in art was like an exploration into the unacknowledged reality, unlocking his consciousness to the otherwise unrecognised bits of life in Kenya. There was indeed the "privilege of lies" to be conserved, maintaining the status quo comfortable for those in power. What Paul seemed to be doing was creating an aesthetics of resistance through his articulation of silences—silences that were available to him as the muted voice of the oppressed. While eminent folklorist Devendra Satyarthy, in his afterword to *Land Lust*, remarked on how these stories had built a bridge for him with Africa, a land thousands of miles away (Paul 2019, p. 137), I believe the author was actually in the process of connecting himself with the hearts of the people of the land he had made his own for this while. He did this by empathetically apprehending African lives under the exploitative colonial regime and understanding its fallout on their relationship with the Asian community. By aligning with the Africans, Paul was actually further alienating himself from his own society, which was emulating the British!

In another story, "Seeking Answers", one may wonder: *who is Makoji seeking answers from?* The narrator imagines the soul of his African friend, dressed in the robes of a barrister, standing before God to cross-examine Him on the unfairness of making him die before he could fulfil his dream of earning a degree from Lincoln's Inn.

In this story, the pain of the narrator is, in fact, the pain of the author over the injustices suffered by Africans due to class, race, and economic inequalities. The story accords a human face to Makoji, portraying him as someone who has spent his life pursuing a futile hope. Consumed by his dream, he ultimately appears like a lunatic, unable to accept reality or his destiny. The questions raised at the end can only be answered by God.

The lure of money, the "development project" of African cities, the beautiful weather and the "highlands" drew people from all over the world to Kenya. The stories in *Land Lust* unfold the author's sensitivity to the incipient racism and the operative colonial hierarchies, as well as the tussle between nature and the professed project of "development" in this country. "Jambo Rafiqui", one of Paul's much-acclaimed stories, deftly explores the naivety of the locals while also giving us a glimpse into the social pecking order, complicated by the presence of Asians, who occupy an uneasy position between the black and the white. Here and elsewhere, what quietly creeps up is the belief in the superiority of one's own race, which runs across the spectrum—it is a different matter that while the colonisers overtly declared themselves to be superior, others just emulated them and operated with similar consciousness.

To come back to the theme of "development" versus nature, in the story, "Jambo Rafiqui", nature appears as a character, the mountain is blasted with dynamite and its "body is split apart" for the railway line to be laid:

> When Nature witnessed her beloved mountain blasted to tiny fragments, her voice drowned in a flood of tears, 'Poor child of mine—this mountain had stood there with such pride for thousands of years ... Your hard-hearted cruel men have brutally murdered my precious child. I feel like tearing them all to pieces, and then strangle you' ... Nature's anger made the railway line tremble in fear (Paul 2019, p. 73).

Here is where the tussle between nature and development is articulated in no uncertain terms. In a sense, the mountain becomes a metaphor for the natives, while the metaphor for the British assertion of "development" is the dynamite, or something that can only blast and destroy, not bind or conserve. The story seems to question the very premise of the presence of the colonial masters, which was to rule over the Dark Continent, "civilise the natives" and develop the continent, country after country.

As the Asians projected their superior airs vis-à-vis the Africans, the dynamics amongst different cultural groups in the country assumed varied postures. Ruing the fact that there was no "life" in Kenya and no decent people to converse with, they became smug and made no bones about not wanting to socialise with the Africans. They vied to enter the clubs meant for the whites and then created their own exclusive social spaces where the Africans were relegated to menial roles. This is portrayed in the story, "Slump". Ironically, these "menials" do not know the meaning of the term "economic slump" being discussed at a table by the Asians in the club, but it is they who are actually suffering from it. They drink, eat and consume what is left over on the plates of the people they are serving.

Here, then, was an Indian writer who confronted this rather convoluted world, where racism did not manifest only in shades of white and black, but presented itself as a knotted web, with a liberal sprinkling of "brown". Subsequently, while the world has made strides in technological progress and there are loud claims about explorations in outer space, many dimensions of this sad phenomenon remain alive even today, quite clearly defying the notion of civilisational progress. The context of the stories is historical, but the themes remain as relevant today as they were then.[1] It is pertinent to take

1 The writer, Joginder Paul, and the stories in the chapter reflect on Afro–Asian relations socially within a specific period in Kenya's history—the 1950s and early 1960s. While there is no doubt that racism continues to expose its fangs world over, even several decades after Kenya's liberation from the colonial regime, the social dynamics in the country have changed. The Asians who remained in Kenya have tried to integrate with the African society much more. Many have actively participated in the professional, political as well as cultural domains in the country. In fact, a mention here must be made about the Asian African Heritage Trust set up in Kenya, conceptualised by Dr Sultan H. Somjee. The initiative is not only to recall and collect stories about the presence of Asians in East Africa but also to document their contributions to nation-building. This forum also tackles the important question of "identity" for the Asian community in Kenya, a community with a bi-continental cultural heritage.

the example of the Black Lives Matter movement and its worldwide spread in recent times, challenging the continuation of the deeply ingrained racist norms. Paul's stories provoke one's consciousness, making us aware of the different ways in which racist tendencies played out in everyday life in pre-Independence Kenya.

In one of the stories, entitled "Miracle", young African boys dive into a deadly lake for coins thrown in by an Asian family, just for their amusement. Lake Kikuyu is a body of water of great depth, but the miracle lies in the fact that there is a layer of earth over a large part of it. Walking over this layer is a memorable experience—one feels the earth tremble beneath one's feet. An old African in the story responds to the Asian:

> But what I consider a miracle is the fact that only the earth above the lake shakes under your feet, and not the whole of Africa! (Paul 2019, p. 27)

This remark comes from the bitter frustration of a black man reading a newspaper and perceiving the hopelessness of the wretched people of the continent, oppressed under the powerful weight of the imperialistic regime that also reflects in the Asian mindset. Even Jaroge, the well-meaning African employee with a cheerful demeanour in the story, "When Life Dies", becomes a victim of institutional racism and is unjustifiably fired by his boss, Mr Albert. This is the same Mr Albert whom Jaroge had always defended as a good-hearted person amongst his colleagues. Deeply humiliated by the sudden firing, Jaroge dies inside. Corpse-like, he is unable to respond to his mother, wife, child, or even his surroundings. Through the mapping of the African employee's attitudinal transformation, the writer effectively conveys the bitterness and anger of the subjugated victim. This story unravels the psyche of an African whose right to live has been snatched away. The narrative is created entirely from his point of view, which not only makes the African character visible but also gives him a voice. This was, in itself, something new happening in fiction by an Asian writer in East Africa.

Somjee himself defines his identity as "Asian African".

That Africa is not merely a land of green parrots and long-necked giraffes, nor a land of barbarians, is what needed to be pointedly and artfully communicated to the prejudiced minds of non-African citizens in this country. Joginder Paul underscores how people in Kenya were generally referred to not as Africans, but as *habshis* (a term for Africans who came to settle in India, deriving from the Arabic name for Abyssinia), indicating a biased mindset. Ugly stories about their "dangerous" character and personality were circulated and instilled into people's consciousness, creating a scare about *habshis* even in the minds of children. In that atmosphere of mistrust and fear of Africans, these stories were not only written but also broadcast in Urdu on Kenya Broadcasting Asian Service. This served to foster empathy for Africans among the Asian community and also helped to build bridges between the two communities. In the foreword to these stories, well-known Urdu fiction writer Krishan Chander wrote:

> What kind of people are the Africans? What kind of lives do they lead? How do they love? What kind of land do they live on? What has the so-called new civilization brought into their old jungles? ... Listen to it from Joginder Paul who has narrated it beautifully, artfully and aesthetically through this collection of short stories in a way that life in Africa comes alive ... (Chander 2019, p. 11).
>
> ... the African who breathes in his stories is very close despite being thousands of miles away (Satyarthy 2019, p. 118).

Both these senior Urdu writers from India acknowledged the young writer of *Dharti ka Kaal* for initiating a greater understanding of East Africa and its inhabitants for their readers. Joginder Paul had lived in Kenya for 14 years and often referred to this period as his *vanvaas* (exile). However, the way he had homed with the natives of the land is evident in the stories he wrote during this time. In the story, "Land Lust", he enters the mythopoeic imagination of the Africans, for whom Mount Kilimanjaro is Dada Kilumu, the one to whom all the land belonged, and who now sees it being taken over by the white man. They believed the white man had been entrusted by Dada Kilumu with the task of clearing the jungles. Why else would he remain silent when the white man cleared the forests and nearly reached the top of the mountain? This is how they explained the phenomenon to themselves, not realising that what they witnessed was really the imperialist's lust for their land.

In the story, "Jambo Rafiqui", the displaced African, who is now bewilderingly poor, meets his counterpart at Voi Railway Junction. Both greet each other, connecting as fellow Africans in their shared poverty and desperate search for work—both having been pulled away from their agricultural vocation and habitation.

That it is not the colour of one's skin that makes one a thief or a criminal, but poverty or hunger, is established in the story "Everywhere". The creative journey of the writer straddles the mindscape of racial prejudices and differences, asserting the need to at least recognise human dignity in various contexts of everyday living. Starting with an acute sense of alienation and a search for home, the writer kept weaving stories during his 14 years in Kenya, through which he experienced the African landscape and its people. This was his process of homing existentially; it was how he filled the sense of loss within himself while in exile. He realised the truth of the world he was living in by creating a fictional world, chaffing off the façade of lies on the surface, story by story.

References

Paul, Joginder. *Land Lust*, eds. Sukrita Paul Kumar and Vandana R. Singh. New Delhi: Niyogi Books, 2019.

Thiong'o, Ngũgĩ wa. *Penpoints, Gunpoints, and Dreams: Towards a Critical Theory of the Arts and the State in Africa*. New York: Oxford University Press, 1998.

Chapter 13

Hidden "Her-stories": A Socio-Literary Reconstruction of Gendered Experiences in the East African Asian Diaspora

Mala Pandurang

Emigration from the Indian subcontinent is generally categorised according to geographical location as well as historical period. Under the broad category of the "old" Indian diaspora, which took shape during the expansion of colonial capitalism from the mid-19th century onwards, we see the mass movement of Indian labour to far-flung colonies such as Fiji, Mauritius, Caribbean Islands and South Africa, mainly as indentured workers. In the case of East Africa, however, they arrived largely as passenger Indians who paid for their passage out of their free will. Unlike the indentured labourers sent to South Africa and Mauritius, women arrived in East Africa mostly as wives of petty traders known as *dukawallahs*. These traders played an important role in commercial activities along the east coast of Africa through periods of Arab, Portuguese, German and British control. The consolidation of trade and administrative controls by the British colonial enterprise from the 19th century onwards led to a significant influx of traders from the East Coast further inland.

The colonial authorities accorded the growing Asian community a "buffer" status, which allowed them to retain their unique social and cultural heritage. By and large, community members were comfortable within a colonial hierarchy of white/brown/black, which allowed privileges based on class and caste. This strong retention of group ties led to social exclusion from the host culture, which, in turn, hindered identification with the adopted society in terms of political loyalty and cultural affinity. Women, in particular, played a crucial role in retaining and transmitting spatial connectors such as religion, rituals, language, dress and food. They were entrusted with the responsibility of maintaining social networks, which formed the basis of the economic, social and cultural capital of their households. The non-assimilationist and endogamous nature of the diasporic community subsequently led to conflicts between black Africans and the Asian community following the independence of the East African territories in the 1960s. Post-independence nationalisation policies and the dire socio-political-economic circumstances of the newly independent East African nation-states of Kenya, Uganda and Tanzania compelled members of the community to relocate to countries like the United Kingdom, Canada and the United States from the late 1960s onwards.

The literature on the experiences of the Indian community in East Africa is a relatively unexplored area in terms of the larger body of writing available under the rubric of the Indian diaspora. However, in recent years, an emerging body of work has offered perspectives on the experiences of women within the community. This chapter provides an overview of select narratives, with a specific focus on how gendered identity is represented in the context of the East African Asian diasporic experience.

Nanji Kalidas Mehta's *Dream Half-Expressed* (1966) is an autobiographical account of a trader from Gujarat who displayed remarkable entrepreneurial spirit in establishing a vast cotton and sugar empire in Uganda, such that by the 1940s he had become one of Uganda's foremost industrialists. Mehta describes how two devastating famines of the 1890s in British India compelled his family to send him, at the age of 13, to Madagascar, where he worked as an apprentice to a petty trader before starting his own small venture in Uganda. Mehta was married in 1900 to a 12-year-old child bride, who joined him from India only 13 years later, at the age of 25. There are no references to his wife by name, and Mehta's description of his married life is limited to mentioning that his meals were now looked after, so he could be free from domestic worries. When his wife died during an influenza epidemic in Uganda in 1918, Mehta returned to India with his 3-year-old son and remarried a 16-year-old bride. He was 32 years old—the practice of second marriages among traders who had been widowed in Africa was not uncommon. Indian traders were initially not accompanied by their wives, but this changed after the First World War, when more women started to join their husbands to ensure the community retained its fundamentally endogamous character.

We can discern a similar pattern in *Tide of Fortune: A Family Tale* (2008), the biography of another prominent Ugandan business tycoon, Manubhai Madhvani. Madhvani's first wife, Gangaba Unadkut, was born in Africa in 1906 and raised in Mombasa. She was married to Madhvani at the age of 14 in 1920 and died six years later in Kampala, leaving behind two children—both under the age of five. In 1928, Madhvani remarried Parvatiben Kotecha from Saurashtra in Western India. There was a considerable age difference between the couple, and it is probable that the marriage took place partly because Madhvani needed assistance to take care of his two young children.

Similar to Mehta's autobiography, the account of Madhvani's life focuses primarily on the entrepreneurial skills and risk-taking attributes that contributed to his successful rise as a business tycoon. The role of the women in the Madhvani household, however, remains confined to the domestic space and they are commended only for playing a crucial role in preserving the home culture.

Zarina Patel offers a semi-autobiographical reconstruction of her grandfather's political career in *Challenge to Colonialism: The Struggle of Alibhai Mulla Jeevanjee for Equal Rights in Kenya* (1997). Jeevanjee, a semi-literate trader from the Bohra community, arrived in East Africa in search of trade opportunities after an exploratory stint in Australia. By 1891, Jeevanjee had established a branch of the Karachi-based AMJ and Co., a shipping firm that operated two steamship lines between Bombay, Mauritius and Jeddah. Jeevanjee is portrayed as a stalwart of early Indian nationalism in Africa, especially for his efforts to block the white settlers' bid for self-government in Kenya in the early 1920s. The book mentions his marriage to a widow but does not go into details. By the end of his life, Jeevanjee's businesses slid into bankruptcy, and he died in 1936, leaving his wife and children penniless.

The thought of the wealth of information we could have gained had we had access to the stories of these three wives of eminent entrepreneurs is echoed by Dana April Seidenberg in *Mercantile Adventurers: The World of East African Asians, 1750–1985*. In the section titled "The Forgotten Pioneers: Indian Women 1895–1985", she observes:

> No one therefore ever really can know the extent to which these forgotten pioneers were plagued by the break-up of their communities in India, the exacting conditions of East African colonial life, unfulfilled career expectations, unhappiness in marriage or even deadening, empty boredom (Seidenberg 1996, p. 94).

Women remain marginalised in the life histories of these celebrated male entrepreneurs, appearing only in the roles of wives and mothers of the male protagonists. Any recognition accorded to them of their labour is restricted to the domestic sphere (Pandurang and Modi 2017).

Moyez G. Vassanji, recognised as the first Tanzanian-Asian novelist, descends from Khoja-Ismailis who migrated from Gujarat, India, to East Africa. His creative writing reconstructs the multi-generational history of this predominantly trading community. Born in Kenya and raised in Tanzania, Vassanji migrated to Canada in 1978. His publications set in Africa include *The Gunny Sack* (1989), *Uhuru Street* (1991), *The Book of Secrets* (1994), *The In-Between World of Vikram Lall* (2003), and *The Magic of Saida* (2012).

Unlike the accounts of Mehta and Madhvani, Vassanji acknowledges the presence of women in the history of his community in East Africa. Through his fiction, we can glean fragmented accounts of the gendered experiences of those who have been marginalised in mainstream narratives of the community. His female characters are drawn from a range of linguistic, ethnic and religious backgrounds, including Kutchi/Ismaili, Punjabi/Hindu, Goan/Christian, Swahili/Muslim and European/Christian.

Vassanji's narratives trace multiple cartographical movements of his women protagonists, who cross boundaries both literally and metaphorically, leading to the "multi-sitedness of being" (Pascale 2006, p. 1). In *The Gunny Sack*, he traces Ji Bai's geo-cultural displacement as a 13-year-old child-bride from Bajupur village in western India to Tanzania, whereas in the *In-between World of Vikram Lall*, he recounts Mrs Sheila Lall's migration to Kenya upon her marriage to the Kenyan-born son of a Punjabi Hindu indentured labourer. Rita, in *The Book of Secrets*, elopes to England, whereas Vera migrates to Canada in *No New Land* (1991). A recurrent motif in Vassanji's work is that of the "half-breed" male. Characters such as Salim (*The Gunny Sack*), Pipa (*The Book of Secrets*) and Kamal Punja (*The Magic of Saida*) are "fathered" by the Ismaili community but "mothered" by black women who are often erased from the community's historical narratives. These include the gentle Swahili slave Bibi Terabit in *The Gunny Sack*, Mama Khanoum—Mukhi Jamali's African wife—in *The Book of Secrets*, and Kamal's Swahili mother in *The Magic of Saida*.

Sultan Somjee's *Bead Bai* (2012) focuses on the migrant experiences of the Satpanth-Ismailis (or Satpanth Khojas) who settled in Africa from the early 20th century onwards. He describes how members of this community traded in coloured beads with various ethnic tribes. In particular, he shares how the merchant's wife, mother and daughter, who would sort and handle the bead stocks, came to be known as "Bead Bais". His narrative offers invaluable insights into the entrepreneurial acumen of these women.

The novel's protagonist, Sakina, spends her afternoons with Maasai elder Ole Lekakeny, from whom she learns how to work with beads. Lekakeny tutors her on the intricate bead patterns of the *emankeeki* (a circular, beaded, neck-to-chest ornament resting on the shoulders, which married women wear). Sakina's creation becomes symbolic of a cultural synthesis, merging Asian and African artistic traditions and worldviews. By describing Sakina's involvement with Maasai's artistic practices, Somjee sheds light on an unknown facet of the lives of Indian women in East Africa in terms of artistic engagement, which adds to the complex layers of gendered Asian African identity.

In *Home Between Crossings* (2016), Somjee continues with the life of Sakina, now 28 years old and known as "Moti Bai", which suggests her identification with the beads as an integral part of her life. The novel takes us through the British colonial policy of creating a racial and class pyramid structure, with Europeans on top, Asians in the middle and Black Africans at the bottom. This is followed by the rise of Kenyan nationalism in the 1950s and the turbulent Mau Mau rebellion against colonial rule. The latter half of the book explores the growing anti-Asian hostilities in the post-independence phase. The narrative ends with Sakina's heart-wrenching dislocation from her home in Kenya and her emigration westwards to Canada.

Bead Bai also offers a rare, gendered perspective on the struggles of "othered" women who seek to escape the "*kothas*" (brothels) in Mumbai, only to fall into the flesh trade in their new land. Somjee reconstructs the fascinating journey of three women who leave a *kotha* in Mumbai and thus offers an insight into the hitherto unheard saga of women who set out for East Africa and who were widows and social outcasts.

Neera Kapur-Dromson's *From Jhelum to Tana* (2007) offers a valuable perspective on the Punjabi settler community in Kenya. Neera recounts the story of her grandfather, an indentured labourer who arrived in Kenya in 1898 to work on the railway line being constructed from Mombasa to Nairobi. There are important references in this book to the painful struggles of "othered" women—many of whom sought to escape the *kothas* of Mumbai, only to fall into the flesh trade in brothels set up along the railway line. There are studies available on indentured women who travelled to the Caribbean Islands (including beggars, widows and prostitutes) who viewed crossing the Kala Pani as a means of escaping severe social strictures such as the restrictions on widows. However, very little is known about socially and economically marginalised women who travelled to East Africa.

In *Shards of Memory: Woven Lives in Four Generations* (2002), Parita Mukta presents the history of three generations of women in her family in Kenya, through colonial and post-colonial times. The book traces the journey of her paternal grandmother in the 1920s, from Kathiawar/Saurashtra in western India to Kenya. In doing so, she charts the background of migration to East Africa by the Gujarati community. Mukta describes how her grandmother (Muktaben) arrived in Nairobi as a child bride and became a widow in her early 30s. Through the life story of her grandmother—referred to as "Ba"—Mukta illustrates the inclusion and exclusion practices enforced upon widowed women and how gender and class were used as mutually reinforcing systems of domination and subordination by the Gujarati community in Nairobi.

She thereby draws attention to power dynamics within an inherently patriarchal and non-assimilationist community. The book offers a sharp critique of intra-ethnic relations among upper-caste, Gujarati-speaking Kenyan-Asian Hindus. It sets the internal cultural and social divisions of the community against the broader socio-political processes of the colonial and post-colonial Kenyan nation-state.

In *The Settler's Cookbook: A Memoir of Love, Migration and Food* (2009), Yasmin Alibhai-Brown reconstructs her family's history through the interesting trope of food. She uses the structure of a recipe book to revisit her childhood in a lower-middle-class family in Uganda, and her family's subsequent relocation to the United Kingdom after the expulsion of about 90,000 Asians by military dictator Idi Amin in 1972. Yasmin throws light on the tension between her sense of belonging to Uganda, where she grew up, and her life in the United Kingdom, where she married and settled. She uses a particular aspect of the food trope to reconstruct the experience of migration and dislocation and draws on the format of the *Kenya Settler's Cookery Book and Household Guide* (1949), which was compiled for the wives of white settlers in Africa. A compelling aspect of Yasmin's book is how certain recipes have evolved from the original forms, deliberately modified to weave the long-silenced voice of the Indian diaspora into the narrative of the lands where they settled.

Dancing with Destiny (2014) is the autobiography of Urmila Jhaveri, who was born in 1931 in Pemba, Tanzania. Urmila was married to K.L Jhaveri, a high-profile lawyer and a close associate of Mwalimu Julius Nyerere, the first president of the new state of Tanzania. She was an active member of the Tanzanian national women's movement, *Umoja Wa Wanawakz Wa Tanzania* (UWT), and worked tirelessly to uplift the economic and social status of marginalised women, irrespective of class and race. Urmila traces her family's history 90 years back when her parents migrated from British-ruled India to the island of Pemba, and later to Dar es Salaam. While she had little memory of an actual India, the idea of a homeland was kept alive through several spatial connectors from her childhood such as her interactions with an elderly couple, Ada-Boghabapa (Grandpa) and Maa, who lived in a hut opposite her home. She recounts how her father taught the children to memorise the names of their ancestors up to eight generations. Yet, she reflects that as a child, it never occurred to her that her roots were in India or elsewhere. The latter part of the book provides an interesting account of Urmila's involvement in Tanzanian politics, and the women's movement in particular.

Russell King observes that creative reconstructions of the migration experience can provide additional insights that go beyond those offered by diaspora scholars in the fields of economics, politics and sociology. According to King, social-scientific research

> ... is often limited in its objectives, aiming to shed light on some single aspect of migration such as the decision to leave, residential location on arrival, or socio-linguistics. It fails to capture the essence of what it is like to be a migrant; and be, or not be, part of a community, a nation, a society—cut off from history and a sense of place. It fails to portray nostalgia, anomie, exile, rootlessness, restlessness (King et al. 1995, pp. ix–x).

Creative reconstructions, on the other hand, can offer insights that "are often infinitely more subtle and meaningful than studies of migrants which base themselves on cold statistics or the depersonalised, aggregate responses to questionnaire surveys" (King et al 1995, p. x).

The objective of this chapter has been to offer an alternative entry point to understanding how women had to negotiate a complex range of experiences in the process of crossing boundaries of ethnicity, race, language and culture. These experiences were often accompanied by both personal and familial clashes. Creative texts can, therefore, offer a deep insight into the finer nuances of the individual worlds of East African Asian women, and thereby link their historical past to that of the larger diasporic communities to which they belong.

References

Alibhai-Brown, Yasmin. *The Settler's Cookbook: A Memoir of Love, Migration and Food.* London: Granta, 2009.

Jhaveri, Urmila. *Dancing with Destiny: A Memoir*. New Delhi: Partridge India, 2014.

Kapur-Dromson, Neera. *From Jhelum to Tana*. New Delhi: Penguin Books, 2007.

King, Russell, John Connell and Paul White. *Writing across Worlds: Literature and Migration*. London; New York: Routledge, 1995.

Madhvani, M., and G. Foden. *Tide of Fortune: A Family Tale*. London: Manubhai Madhvani Bermuda Trust, 2008.

Mehta, Nanji Kalidas. *Dream Half-Expressed: An Autobiography*. Raj Ratna Nanjibhai Kalidas Mehta Centenary Celebration Committee. Bombay: Vakil & Sons, 1996.

Modi, Renu and Mala Pandurang. "Women as an Invisible Constituency: A Gendered Reading of the Life of Nanji Kalidas Mehta and Muljibhai Madhvani", *Journal of South Asian Diaspora* vol. 9, no. 2 (2017): pp. 179–92.

Mukta, Parita. *Shards of Memory: Woven Lives in Four Generations*. London: Weidenfeld and Nicholson, 2002.

Pascale, Herzig. *South Asians in Kenya: Gender, Generation and Changing Identity in Diaspora*. Munster: Lit Verlag, 2006.

Patel, Zarina. *Challenge to Colonialism. The Struggle of Alibhai Mulla Jeevanjee for Equal Rights in Kenya.* Kolkata: WorldView Publications, 1997.

Seidenberg, Dana April. *Mercantile Adventurers. The World of East African Asians. 1750–1985.* New Delhi: New Age International Publishers, 1996.

Somjee, Sultan. *Bead Bais.* Charleston: Create Space, 2012.

Vassanji, M.G. *The Gunny Sack.* New Delhi: Penguin Books, 1989.

———. *The Book of Secrets.* New Delhi: Penguin Books, 1994.

———. *The In-between World of Vikram Lall.* New Delhi: Penguin Books, 2003.

———. *The Magic of Saida.* New York: Vintage Contemporaries, 2012.

PART 4
African Art, Music and Cinema

Chapter 14

Lessons from African Arts: Experiences in Voicing Concerns for Marginalised Populations

Penina Muhando Mlama

Introduction

This chapter will highlight some of Africa's contributions to global cultural heritage. However, given that Africa is a huge continent with 54 sovereign states, each boasting a large variety of art and music, it is impossible to cover this large repertoire of artistic creativity in one chapter. Therefore, the terms "Africa" and "African art" will be used in a general sense.

The term "art" will also be used broadly to refer to fine and performing arts, painting, sculpture, posters, cartoons, dance, storytelling, recitation, poetry, drama, song and pop music.

Arts of the Ruling and the Dominated Classes

It is our contention that in any society structured by class, there are two types of arts: that of the ruling or dominant class, and that of the ruled and marginalised class. This division arises from the fact that, in such societies, power relations between the two classes are rooted in conflicting interests where the dominant or the ruling class seeks to economically and socially exploit and oppress the underclass, while the ruled and marginalised strive to free themselves from such bondage.

Both classes engage with the arts, though for different purposes. While the dominant classes promote and patronise mainstream arts that help cement their power, the exploited and marginalised use the arts as tools in their struggles against injustice and the violation of their human rights. Art becomes a form of resistance, a means of expressing dissent, and a platform to demand denied rights. It also serves as a way to organise and mobilise against oppression. In this context, the arts often play a key role in political mobilisation, awareness raising, inciting protests, and even supporting armed conflict.

The arts of the ruling class often become mainstream and are well-documented and preserved to record the history of the rulers and maintain their dominance.

For example, in Africa's feudal systems, the ownership of major means of production—particularly land—rests with the feudal rulers. The primary producers, however, do not own land but lease it from the king or chief, effectively placing them in a state of serfdom. The products of this land are considered the property of the rulers, who decide the percentage to be retained by the serfs.

The feudal rulers have produced unique works of art, including paintings, sculptures, murals, historical narratives and epics that are of the highest class. The Benin Bronzes, Egyptian paintings and the West African epics of the griots are noteworthy examples.

The serfs, too, have produced arts in protest against the exploitative feudal socio-economic structures. However, little information is available on the arts of this class. Similarly, we have scant remains of the arts through which Africa's oppressed populations have protested against slavery, colonialism, capitalism, imperialism and internal dictatorial regimes.

This chapter will focus on highlighting the protest and resistance arts through which the exploited and marginalised classes in Africa have sought to liberate themselves from various forms of bondage. This focus is driven by a deep concern that Africa has lost a huge portion of its artistic heritage, which is critical to the ongoing struggles for self-determination and identity. Furthermore, it is a call to researchers, academia and activists to pay more attention to this important yet often overlooked dimension of Africa's cultural legacy.

Africa's Contribution to World Arts

African artistic creativity has historically played a key role in advancing societal welfare. It has served as a medium for education, community mobilisation, the preservation of history and cultural heritage, the enforcement of values and attitudes, and entertainment. Many African artistic creations and styles have contributed tremendously to appreciation of art globally and to intellectual discourse on art history, theory and practice.

Renowned fine art styles from Africa include the ancient Egyptian paintings, the Nok art of Nigeria, the Benin Bronzes, the Tinga Tinga paintings of Tanzania and the Makonde carvings of southern Tanzania and northern Mozambique. Many African artists have gained international recognition for their work. These include Malangatana Ngwenya and Nástio Mosquito of Mozambique, Abdoulaye Konaté of Mali, Tracey Rose of South Africa, Sam Joseph Ntiro of Tanzania, El Anatsui of Ghana, Kudzanai Chiurai of Zimbabwe, Meschac Gaba of Benin, and Julie Mehretu of Ethiopia. African fine arts also influenced modern Western art, a well-known instance being the influence of African sculpture on Pablo Picasso's treatment of the human figure.

African popular music styles, such as Afrobeat (West Africa), Highlife (Ghana), Ndombolo (Democratic Republic of Congo), Bongo Flava (Tanzania), Makosa (Cameroon) and Kwaito (South Africa), have reverberated beyond the continent's borders. Afrobeat, in particular, is now present in mainstream pop music across the world. Celebrated African music legends with global acclaim include Youssou N'dour and Baaba Maal (Senegal), Fela Aníkúlápó Kuti (Nigeria), Miriam Makeba, Brenda Fassie, Lucky Dube and Ladysmith Black Mambazo (South Africa), Koffi Olomide (the Democratic Republic of the Congo), Salif Keita and Ali Farka Touré (Mali) and Angélique Kidjo (Benin), Manu Dibango of Cameroon, to mention a few. Notably, Ladysmith Black Mambazo and Angélique Kidjo have each won five Grammy Awards, while the Soweto Gospel Choir and Ali Farka Touré have earned three apiece, and Youssou N'Dour has won one. Among legendary music scholars is Ghanaian ethnomusicologist Joseph Hanson Kwabena Nketia.

Thousands of precious African art masterpieces are displayed in internationally famous museums, such as the Musée d'Ethnographie du Trocadéro, Musée Dapper in Paris (France), the Musée Barbier-Mueller in Geneva (Switzerland), the American Museum of Natural History and the Metropolitan Museum of Art in New York (USA), and the British Museum, London (the UK). Prominent private collections include those of Paul Guillaume, Charles Ratton and Louis Carré of Paris. The Musée du quai Branly in Paris alone features around 70,000 stolen sub-Saharan African artefacts.

The presence of these precious African masterpieces in European and American museums is ironic, given the colonial powers' systematic assault on Africa's cultural and artistic heritage—works they once dismissed as primitive and devoid of value to "civilisation". Yet it was these very colonial administrators, European missionaries and adventurers who pillaged some of the finest works of art the continent has produced. The Benin Bronzes, for example, were looted by the British in 1897 during the violent destruction of Benin City, carried out to punish the reigning monarch, Oba Ovonramwen Nogbaisi, for resisting colonial rule. Similarly, Asante gold artefacts, Yoruba sculptures, masquerade masks and thousands of other artworks were confiscated and shipped to museums across Europe and America, where many still remain to this day.

India also faced the plundering of her priceless art treasures under British rule. Notable among them is *The Trumpeters*, an 18th-century watercolour by court artist Nainsukh, now in the British Museum. Rakesh Krishnan Simha reports that the Victoria and Albert Museum in London holds the largest collection of Indian art treasures outside the subcontinent—over 40,000 pieces (Simha 2016).

As we explore the cultural linkages between India and Africa, it is important to acknowledge the significant loss of art treasures from both regions, now held in Europe and America. The call for the return of these stolen treasures to Africa, as emphasised in the 'Report on the Restitution of African Cultural Heritage' by Felwine Sarr and Bénédicte Savoy (2018), commissioned by French President Emmanuel Macron, marks a meaningful step in the right direction.

African Arts during Colonisation

To colonise the minds of their African subjects, colonial powers undermined Africa's rich artistic heritage and attempted to replace it with their own art forms, which they promoted as suitable for a "civilised person". European art was introduced through colonial education systems and Christianity, while the French policy of "assimilation" imposed French culture on West African populations, making them believe that by mastering the French language and culture, they could, in turn, become French.

As Mwalimu Julius Nyerere, the founding President of the United Republic of Tanzania, aptly stated in his Inaugural Presidential Address to Parliament in 1962:

> Of all the crimes of colonialism there is none worse than the attempt to make us believe that we had no indigenous culture of our own; or that what we did have was worthless—something of which we should be ashamed, instead of a source of pride... When we were at school we were taught to sing the songs of the Europeans... learnt to dance the 'rumba' or the 'chachacha', to 'rock'n'roll', to 'twist' and even to dance the 'waltz' and 'foxtrot'. But how many of us can dance, or have even heard of, the *Gombe Sugu*... play the African drums? (Nyerere 1966, p. 186)

The imposition of colonial art, however, did not prevent Africans from using their own artistic expressions to defy colonialism, as seen in the following Disumbi dance song from Tanzania, which opposed British domination:

> *Kingi Joji kingi Joji eeee*
> *Mlajoni chelu mlajoni*
> *Mundewa mlagiso*
> *Lekela Mandege*
> *Lekela Itumba*
> *Si nheifo uta ukole ee*
> *Fitung'ati ki delele*
> *Kingi Joji Kingi Joji eeee*
> *Mlajoni nyee mlajoni* (Mahuwi 2002)

Translation

King George, King George (reference to the then King of Britain)
He surely is uncircumcised
The king who rules from afar
Let go of Mandege area
Let go of Itumba area
Or else come yourself and hold the bow and arrow
And meet our mighty warriors
King George
He surely is uncircumcised.

When a British governor, before whom this song was once performed, asked its meaning, he was told it was in praise of King George. There were numerous instances of such protest art all over Africa, but owing to their oral nature, many have faded from memory.

The most vibrant arts of resistance, however, emerged during the liberation struggles in southern Africa. Brutal minority rule in Zimbabwe, Portuguese colonisation in Mozambique and Angola, and apartheid in Namibia and South Africa led to intense wars of liberation. The arts were extensively used to support these armed struggles. The Zimbabwe liberation movement, for example, used the Pungwe—an indigenous Shona ceremony involving dance and music—to mobilise mass support and recruit fighters. In South Africa, toyi-toyi dance songs of defiance were effectively employed during demonstrations to rally the masses against the apartheid regime.

Cultural ensembles were employed by the liberation movements of the African National Congress (ANC, South Africa), Frente de Libertação de Moçambique or Mozambique Liberation Front (FRELIMO, Mozambique), the South West Africa People's Organisation (SWAPO, Namibia) and the Popular Movement for the Liberation of Angola (MPLA, Angola) to rally support for the struggle all over the world. The ANC's Mayibuye and Amandla Cultural Ensembles toured extensively, using performance as a powerful tool to generate international solidarity. The ZoZoZu's Yinde Lendlela Esihambayo collection and EFF Azania's revolutionary songs available on YouTube, are examples of such music. Sadly though, the bulk of such liberation struggle artistic works remains unrecorded. It is critical that this artistic heritage of Africa's liberation be recaptured and preserved.

Resistance Arts in Post-independence Era

The exploitation and oppression of Africa's marginalised groups did not stop with the end of colonialism. In fact, the euphoria of independence was short-lived. Africa's majority poor soon realised that, despite achieving political independence, the systems that enabled their exploitation were still intact—only now administered by their own kith and kin. Kalikali, a Sukuma dancer from Tanzania, powerfully captured this reality in a 1964 song composed just three years after Tanzania's independence:

Ukitawala twitawalile A bana
Tanganyika Nghana twitawalile
BakulumbagawitawajiAbo bali na
milimo mitale Abo balipandika
magana Buli ng'weji
Al'abalimi ba baluba Nduhw'
iyakupandika Litingang' ili busese
Ililima lyingile Tubyulima buluba
Buguji bushike Guchel'
umpangoTuliginya sumba Ng'wana
Mbagule
Ming'wana gakwigutaga
Kulola ha sa kwesa
Na kumigija mu shitambala

Translation

We have really got independence
The people of Tanganyika

Truly we are independent
They are giving thanks to independence
The ones with big jobs
The ones who earn hundreds month after month
But the growers of cotton have nothing to gain
Prepare farms as the planting season come
Growing cotton, the prices fall
This is not a good plan
We are fattening other people, son of Mbagule
They are really eating
They are laughing and dancing
And blowing their noses with handkerchiefs
(Songoyi 1990, p. 57–8)

In recent years, Africa has been labelled "the rising continent" on account of the impressive annual economic growth—above 7per cent in many of her countries—compared to the global average of around 3 per cent. This is, however, negated by the stark reality that Africa is home to nearly half (413 million) of the world's poorest people, living on less than US$2 a day (World Bank 2019). Armed conflict, corruption, resource mismanagement, ethnic divisions and despotic rule continue to negatively impact the advancement of the majority poor. This situation has provided fertile ground for protest arts, particularly among marginalised communities, as illustrated by the examples cited below.

Pop Music

Pop music in many African countries has become a leading force in protesting oppressive conditions. Musicians known for their socially and politically charged pop music include Fela Aníkúlápó Kuti (Nigeria), Oumou Sangaré (Mali), Roma Mkatoliki (Tanzania), Gidi Gidi Maji Maji (Kenya) and Anselmo Ralph (Namibia), to mention just a few. Gidi Gidi Maji Maji's "Unbwogable" became a popular anthem of defiance that contributed to the defeat of President Daniel arap Moi in Kenya's 2002 general elections. Sangaré uses her music to confront gender injustice while Mkatoliki's "Amka Tanzania" (Wake up, Tanzania) is an exposé of corruption in Tanzania and its impact on ordinary citizens. Corruption also features in Eric Wainaina's Kenyan hit "Nchi ya Kitu Kidogo" (A Country of Something Small).

In Senegal, pop musicians put up a strong resistance against the erosion of democratic rule during the country's 2012 general elections, particularly in response to President Abdoulaye Wade's controversial decision to seek a third term—an act that defied the constitution. Didier Awadi's song "Ma Waxoon Waxeet" (I said it, now I take it back) ridiculed Wade for reneging on his earlier promise not to run for another term. Awadi summed up the role of musicians in what became a nationwide protest, stating, "Our role is to bring a consciousness to the people, so that they don't vote for people who pay them but for people who have a political platform. We have to be the watch-keepers of democracy" (Skelton 2012).

Rapper Keyti of Senegal, who also actively participated in the anti-Wade protests, said:

> I definitely believe in the crucial role of music and musicians in politics and in building a democratic society because they help bring a different perspective. Musicians are traditionally closer to the people and their opinions often less subjective than those of politicians. If that contribution is heard and taken to account, it can be a link between the politicians and the people (Skelton 2012).

Author and journalist Stanley Gazemba (2014) underscores the power of music as a tool for resistance, stating, "Certain songs grate on the ears of those in power because they criticise their excesses and cry out for the suffering masses. Often, they are silenced in the mainstream media but still find a way to reach listeners through underground channels" (Gazemba 2014).

In Congo-Brazzaville, composer and poet Franklin Boukaka emerged as a moral voice for the disaffected masses. His activism ultimately cost him his life—he was executed in 1972 after a failed coup attempt. Similarly, powerful soundtracks of music played a critical role in the Arab Spring that toppled oppressive regimes in Tunisia, Egypt and Libya.

Political Cartoons and Paintings

Political cartoons are another powerful art form employed against abuses and excesses of dictatorial regimes. As Lyombe Eko observes, cartoons are used as "counter narratives to undermine governments and political leaders. The caricatures are effective means of disrupting dominant power relations and open up spaces of resistance to the excesses of leaders" (Eko 2017).

Among Africa's most prominent political cartoonists is Zapiro (Jonathan Shapiro) of South Africa, renowned for his sharp critiques of human rights violations. His 2008 cartoon "The Rape of Lady Justice" was a jab at President Jacob Zuma for his blatant flouting of the justice system. In Cameroon, cartoonist Popoli (Paul Ntoogue) was forced to flee the country briefly in 1998 after publishing satirical cartoons critical of President Paul Biya. In Senegal, the 2010 cartoon of Omar Diakité, better known by his signature "Odia", took aim at the judiciary's ambivalent stance on the deterioration of freedom of expression. In Burkina Faso, Damien Glez's "Le Marabout Muet" (The Mute Marabou) criticised the media for their silence on the unresolved murders of four journalists.

In Kenya, Gado (Godfrey Mwampembwa) was dismissed by the Nation Media Group in 1992 for his critical depictions of government misconduct. One of his most striking works, a 1999 cartoon, portrayed President Robert Mugabe of Zimbabwe as a rampaging, club-wielding gorilla attacking the judiciary, civil society and the press. Kudzanai Chiurai also faced backlash for his political expression. In 2004, he went into self-imposed exile from Zimbabwe to South Africa after painting President Mugabe with horns and engulfed in flames. In South Africa, Chiurai continued to use his cartoons to challenge corruption, xenophobia and violence.

In Angola, Nástio Mosquito's provocative works are powerful as they disrupt political and social statements, while, in Mali, Abdoulaye Konaté's art conveys his critical thoughts on political tensions across the Sahel region.

Political Posters

Another powerful form of artistic expression used by marginalised populations across Africa is the poster. Posters are used in public demonstrations against human rights violations, often featuring images of perpetrators of injustice and slogans denouncing wrongdoing. In Tanzania, for example, rural communities display protest posters during mass rallies attended by the President, Prime Minister or other high-level government officials. These posters often highlight a wide range of grievances, including corruption, land grabbing, resource mismanagement, racism, police brutality, forced evictions, war and other human rights abuses.

In 2019, posters, wall paintings and graffiti played a key role in Sudan's months-long demonstrations that led to the eventual ousting of President Omar al-Bashir. Abdi Latif Dahir (2019) calls this phenomenon "revolution in art", describing how one "upshot of the uprising … has been the geyser of colourful and vibrant artwork that has dominated both the streets and the Sudanese social media". He notes how murals, paintings and graphic art have sprung up across the nation, agitating for peace, "extolling the place of demonstrators and martyrs, exhorting the world to stand up for the Sudanese people, and imagining a better future" (Dahir 2019). Indeed, many more examples could be cited to underscore the significant role that various forms of art and music continue to play in Africa as tools of protest and resistance against injustice.

A major concern is that much of these arts are still not properly recorded and preserved. As a result, the African continent has already lost—and stands to lose more—significant portions of its artistic treasures and musical heritage. Urgent action is required to reverse the situation. Efforts to recapture, record and preserve these treasures should be strongly encouraged, especially because the greatest losses are often among the arts of marginalised communities.

Similarities between India and Africa

In conclusion, we wish to raise the question of whether India has experienced a similar situation in which the art and music of marginalised populations have not received sufficient attention or proper documentation. If so, are there lessons that Africa can learn from India in addressing this challenge?

References

Bakari J.A. "Satires in Theatre for Development in Tanzania", in *Africa Theatre for Development: Art for Self Determination*, ed. K. Salhi, pp. 115–33. Exeter: Intellect Books, 1998.

Banham, Martin, et al. *The Cambridge Guide to African and Caribbean Theatre.* Cambridge: Cambridge University Press, 1994.

Boal, A. *Theatre of the Oppressed.* London: Pluto Press, 1979.

Cabral, Amilcar. "National Liberation and Culture", text of speech delivered at Syracuse University on 20 February 1960, translated from the French by Maureen Webster. Available online: https://www.historyisaweapon.com/defcon1/cabralnlac.html (accessed on 5 January 2025).

Chisiza, Zindaba. "Dialogical Theatre: Reconsidering the Role of Theatre for Development for Malaria Prevention in Malawi", in *Applied Theatre: Performing Health and Wellbeing*, eds. Veronica Baxter and Katherine E. Low. London and New York: Bloomsbury Methuen Drama, 2017.

Dahir, Abdi Latif. "Sudan's Street Protests have inspired another Revolution—in Art", *Quartz Africa*, 12 July 2019. Available online: https://qz.com/africa/1664733/sudans-protests-inspire-art-graffiti-revolution/ (accessed on 17 January 2022).

Daichendt, James G. "The History and Art of Protest Posters", 2017. Available online: https://www.kcet.org/the-history-and-art-of-protest-posters (accessed on 17 January 2022).

Divis, Craig. "The Power of Political Cartoons", 17 January 2015. Available online: https://mrdivis.wordpress.com/2015/01/17/the-power-of-political-cartoons/ (accessed on 25 January 2022).

Eko, Lyombe. "The Art of Criticism: How African Cartoons Discursively Constructed African Media Realities in the post-Cold War Era", *Critical African Studies* vol. 4, 26 July 2012.

Gazemba, Stanley. "Retracing Kenya's Songs of Protest", *Music Africa*, 21 November 2014. Available online: https://www.musicinafrica.net/magazine/retracing-kenyas-songs-protest (accessed on 25 January 2022).

Hammet, Daniel. "Political Cartoons, Post-Colonialism and Critical African Studies", *Critical African Studies* vol. 2, no. 4, 2010. Available online: https://www.tandfonline.com/doi/epdf/10.1080/20407211.2010.10530755 (accessed on 5 January 2025).

Kalipeni, Ezekiel, and Chris Kamlongera. "The Role of Theatre for Development in Mobilizing Rural Communities for Primary Health Care: The Case of Liwonde PHC Unit in Southern Malawi", *Journal of Social Development in Africa* vol. 11, no. 1 (1996): pp. 53–78.

Kerr, David, and Stephen Chifunyise. "The Growth of Theatre for Development: Case Studies of Botswana, Zambia, Nigeria and Kenya", in *A History of Theatre in Africa*, ed. Martin Banham. Cambridge: Cambridge University Press, 2004.

Lewela, Karest and Humprey Sipalla. "The Meaning of Protest Art in Society", 2014. Available online: https://www.pambazuko.org/arts/meaning-protest-art-society (accessed on 25 January 2022).

Livingston, Jo. "The British Museum's 'Looting' Problem", 2018. Available online: https://newrepublic.com/article/150642/british-museums-looting-problem_(accessed on 25 January 2022).

May, Chris. "Liberation Music: South Africa, Zimbabwe and Zambia", *Golden Afrique* vol. 3, 13 May 2007.

Mda, Z. *When People Play People*. London: Zed Books, 1993.

Mingren, Wu. "The Benin Bronzes: A Tragic Story of Slavery and Imperialism cast in Brass", 2017. Available online: https://www.ancient-origins.net/artifacts-other-artifacts/benin-bronzes-008565 (accessed on 25 January 2022).

Mlama, P.M. *Culture and Development: The Popular Theatre Approach in Africa*. Sweden: Motala Grafiska, Motala, 1988.

Musa, B.A. "Popular Theatre and Development Communication in West Africa: Paradigms, Processes and Prospects", in *African Theatre for Development: Art for Self Determination*, ed. K. Salhi, pp. 43–68. Exeter: Intellect Books, 1998.

Museum of Fine Art Boston. "Art of Africa and Oceania", 2020. Available online: https://www.mfa.org/collections/africa-and-oceania (accessed on 25 January 2022).

Nyerere, Julius. "President's Inaugural Address, 10 December 1962", in *Freedom and Unity—Uhuru na Umoja: A Selection from Writings and Speeches, 1952–65*. London, Nairobi, Dar es Salaam, Ibadan: Oxford University Press, 1966.

Peet, Sam. "Toyi Toyi: South Africa's spirited Dance of Protest, Culture Trip", 2020. Available online: https://theculturetrip.com/africa/south-africa/articles/toyi-toyi-south-africas-spirited-dance-of-protest/ (accessed on 25 January 2022).

Plastow, J. *African Theatre and Politics: The Evolution of Theatre in Ethiopia, Tanzania and Zimbabwe: A Comparative Study*. Amsterdam: Rodopi, 1996.

Preston, George Nelson. *African Art Masterpieces*. New York: Hugh Lauter Levin Associates, 1991.

Sarr, Felwine and Benedicte Savoy. "The Restitution of African Cultural Heritage: Towards a New Relational Ethics", 2018. Available online: http://restitutionreport2018.com/sarr_savoy_en.pdf (accessed on 25 January 2022).

Simha, Rakesh Krishnan. "Forget the Koh-i-Noor, the British looted far greater treasures from India", *Bharata Bharati*, 5 May 2016. Available online: https://bharatabharati.in/2016/05/05/forget-the-koh-i-noor-the-british-looted-far-greater-treasures-from-india-rakesh-krishnan-simha/ (accessed on 25 January 2022).

Skelton, Rose. "Musicians at the Forefront of Protests", *Freemuse* 13 March 2012. Available online: https://freemuse.org/news/senegal-musicians-at-the-forefront-of-protests/ (accessed on January 17, 2022).

Songoyi, Elias Manandi. "The Artist and the State in Tanzania: A Study of Two Singers, Kalikali and Mwinamila". Master's Dissertation, University of Dar es Salaam, 1998.

World Bank. "Poverty Overview", 2021. Available online: https://www.worldbank.org/en/topic/poverty/overview#1 (accessed on January 25, 2022).

Zapiro. "Rape of Lady Justice", 7 September 2008. Available online: https://www.zapiro.com/080907st (accessed on January 25, 2022).

Interview

Msagala Mahuwi. Interview with the author on dance as protest against colonial rule, 2002. Chibanhi, Kilosa, Tanzania.

Chapter 15

Bollywood Projections on the Screen of Angolan Culture and Imagination

José Luís Mendonça

> I am convinced that the whole sense and thrust of the future draws its force from an intensely felt consciousness of history, faithfully transmitted from generation to generation through education. In Africa, as elsewhere, this consciousness is one of the essential conditions of the independence, development and affirmation of peoples (M'Bow 1979, p. 5).

The rich scents of India have crossed the space of Africa since the 16th century. From the time of Vasco da Gama, maritime maps charting the sea route to India included Kongo—one of the kingdoms that would later give rise to the Angolan nation-state. During the colonial era, transatlantic navigations further connected Africa with India. Over time, many Indian customs, such as the use of curry and pepper, entered the daily lives of Africans. Indian immigrants have lived in Angola for centuries, contributing to mixed ancestry in the African territory. Similarly, Angolans also travelled to India for military service. By the 20th century, Bollywood had begun to inspire the synaesthetic fabric of the Angolan narrative.

Luís de Camões' epic poem *Os Lusíadas* (1572), translated as *The Lusiad: or, The Discovery of India: An Epic Poem* by William Julius Mickle in 1877, vividly describes Vasco da Gama's arrival in Calicut on the west coast of India:

And now, their ensigns blazing o'er the tide,
On India's shore the Lusian heroes ride.
High to the fleecy clouds resplendent far
Appear the regal towers of Malabar,
Imperial Calicut, the lordly seat
Of the first monarch of the Indian state.

(…)

Two infant rivers pour the crystal tide,
Indus the one, and one the Ganges nam'd.

(Camões 1877, p. 198–202)

This is how India's kingdoms were portrayed—in polished, decasyllabic verse celebrating Portuguese imperial conquests, which were taught in schools of pre-independence Angola. These texts usually depicted Angola as a land of defeated kingdoms and enslaved peoples. As a result, there grew among Angolans a huge thirst for knowledge about their own country's history as well as that of the entire African continent. This thirst was only partially mitigated in the post-colonial period, when novels and poetry began to create new narratives of the past and the present. The era of Angola's independence became a fertile ground for themes of great projection and literary inspiration.

Yet Angola's post-colonial history has been deeply marked by a continued subservience to the ideological matrices of the West. The country gained freedom from the Portuguese in 1975, so the formative years of the underdeveloped nation coincided with the height of the Cold War (1974–88). The newly independent Angola was torn apart by civil war and drained of its financial resources, especially those derived from oil, the country's main export. My first novel, *If Ministers Lived in the Slums* (2019), recreates this turbulent period. It reflects my identity as an African *homo culturalis,* broken into four constitutive structures of being-in-the-world introspection: the Bantu bloodline, the dust of political and social times, the forces of climate and nature, and the weight of both African and universal history on the thought and memory of the writer.

Transculturalism

Among the four structures that define the African *homo culturalis*, I wish to focus on the fourth: the weight of universal history. Through the interconnectedness of global cultures (the encounter of civilisations), the mental absorption of Indian films inspired the kinaesthetic fabric of *If Ministers Lived in the Slums*. Since the 1980s, theatres in Angola regularly screened Indian films. An important aspect of these films is their cultural substrate, conveyed through music, song and dance. The rhythms of Indian songs closely match Angolan and African rhythms. There is a shared musical soul in the Global South. In this sense, Angola and India mix their spiritual sounds.

Through the images that pass across the screen, one could discern similarities between the traditional costumes of the Besanganas[1] and the Indian sari, and the garments of Axiluanda fishermen and those of boatmen and ascetics on the Ganges.

I must mention one Indian film that deeply touched the hearts of Luanda citizens in the 1980s: *The Song of Happiness*, featuring actor Subir Kumar. The film had a huge projection and was screened in a cinema hall in front of an industrial school named after the Russian pedagogue Anton Makarenko. This was during the Cold War when Angola was aligned with the USSR. Three women from my neighbourhood watched the movie every single day for a month, which piqued my curiosity. My brothers and I still recall seeing them leave the cinema hall with tears in their eyes.

The film inspired a graffiti artist to paint a sublime phrase on the front wall of the Makarenko School that read: "*Subir Kumar, Descer Ku Rio*". This is a tricky expression to translate into English, as it plays subtly on the actor's name. In Portuguese, *subir* means "to go up", while "Kumar" sounds like *cu mar*—a homophone for "my sea". The graffiti artist then humorously added, *descer cu rio* (to go down with the river).

1 A term of respect for wives of Axiluanda fishermen on Luanda Island, it means "Your blessing, my Lady" in Kimbundu.

The critical appreciation of Indian movies inspired me to include various illustrative elements of Angolan culture in my novel—especially its rich musical background and traditional dance. It has a vivid description of a parade during the Luanda Carnival, the grandest celebration of the Angolan people. Carnival, or Shrovetide, was originally introduced by the colonial rulers of Angola. But over the centuries, elements of the Bantu culture have become more dominant in the celebrations.

> Carnival is a celebration... It is, above all, the celebration of historical tenacity and resistance over five centuries, in which fishermen absorbed cultures, religions and rituals from all over the world, making them an integral part of Carnival, very characteristic of Luanda (Birmingham 1991, p. xx).

The Scatological Drama of the Black Man

The theme that runs through *If Ministers Lived in the Slums* is the construction of the post-colonial Angolan state. Put simply, after being the grout of the New World—having helped build America and Europe with his blood and sweat—the African man is still denied the basic benefits of Western civilisation: things as simple as piped drinking water, electricity and basic sanitation.

According to German philosopher Friedrich Hegel, the highest conceivable value in the phenomenon of slavery lies in its role in the progress of humanity. Hegel described the institution, in its transience, solely in terms of the need for the historical progress of humankind—a transitional moment leading towards a higher phase of development (Hegel 2001, p. 117). However, when we extend this conceptual framework to our present time, we find that the "progress of humanity" is a restricted and not universal concept for two reasons. First, the economic, technical, scientific, social and philosophical advancements were largely made possible by the liberation of the coloniser from manual labour, which was achievable only at the cost of centuries-long exploitation of African slaves. The fruits of this coerced labour contributed to human progress that was geographically limited to Europe, Eurasia, North America and parts of Asia, where the so-called G8 countries are located.

A disproportionate share of global wealth is confined to a group of millionaires in these regions. Second, Africa—the birthplace of the enslaved people who kneaded the raw materials for Europe and Americas—remains trapped in conditions of extreme poverty and underdevelopment even today.

Sociologist Boaventura de Sousa Santos places this ongoing inequality on the axis of neocolonialism. He writes: "We were all so socialized in the idea that the anti-colonial liberation struggles of the 20th century ended colonialism, that it is almost heresy to think that after all colonialism is not over, it has just changed its shape or clothing, and that our difficulty is above all to properly name this complex process of continuity and change" (Santos 2018, p. xx).

The other axis lies in the political choices we have made—and continue to make—in countries such as Rwanda, Eritrea, Uganda, Congos, Zimbabwe, Somalia and Angola. These choices often stem from decisions that fail to take into account the cluster of former African nations that are confined within artificial borders. From the independence that the installed powers project, we see the denial of the Other as a full citizen, one with equal rights to live and participate in politics, even at the highest levels of government.

A date that decisively shaped the reality the Angolan people are experiencing today was 27 May 1977. It was around this event that I wove the narrative of my novel. The current scatological drama of the black man stems largely from the world order dominated by superpowers, as well as from the privatisation of the Angolan state by the ruling elite. History too often concentrates on the leaders of humanity, but it is literature that gives voice to the anonymous heroes of everyday life.

The Cultural Isolation Syndrome

African countries are currently facing a crisis of cultural communication. In the southern region of the continent, European languages present themselves as barriers to the construction of an idealised cultural fraternity among Angola and its neighbours—the two Congos, Zambia, Namibia, Zimbabwe and Gabon, and even Mozambique, a fellow Lusophone country—as well as other

SADC (Southern African Development Community) and African countries. This cultural dialogue has been challenging for SADC governments, partly due to the Euro-linguistic insularities inherited from colonisation. There are two sides to the coin: one permeable to dialogue with the distant West, and the other impermeable to cross-cultural regional dialogue.

Article 30 of the Charter for African Cultural Renaissance recognises the importance of establishing inter-African cultural cooperation. This cooperation is key to promoting mutual understanding and the enrichment of African cultures—both within the continent, with the African Diaspora, and with the rest of the world.

More than ever, African leaders need to listen, not only to their private advisers but also to non-party intellectuals who articulate the aspirations of African civil society. The Ebola epidemic has proved that Africa has reached a critical point where it must re-evaluate cultural practices and heritage that no longer are in line with the demographic explosion and urban expansion in cities like Luanda.

This historic moment demands a fundamental change in the sociocultural paradigm, anchored in two poles: first, a model of endogenous development (unveiling the "immense smallness" of problems made invisible by the cloak of macroeconomics); and second, a decisive break from extemporaneous traditions, paving the way for a real renaissance.

I agree with Stuart Hall when he says that the notion of "a fully unified, complete, secure and coherent identity is a fantasy". He underscores the emergence of new identities that fragment the modern individual and describes modern nations as genuine "cultural hybrids" (Hall 1992, p. 297).

Here, I raise another question—one related to the much-celebrated expression, "cultural diversity". The most developed nations always preserve a residual cultural background, largely shaped by language, even when they are made up of a mix of different peoples and nations. In southern Africa, however, the Bantu substrate is slowly being diluted. With each passing decade, it is becoming obsolete, and one of its key elements—the local languages—is gradually falling into disuse.

Nowadays, the panorama of national cinematography in Angola no longer revolves around Indian films as it once did. Hollywood has now taken over Angolan cinema halls. Films from other parts of the African continent are rarely shown, despite Nigeria's film industry being the second largest in the world by volume (Bright 2015). In this sense, Africa is too far from Angola, or perhaps Angola is too far from Africa.

The same can be said of African literature, which is conspicuous by its absence from Angolan bookstores and libraries. This is partly due to the challenge of translation, which has to do with Angola's linguistic isolation within the continent. Secondly, there is the problem of cultural exchange being almost non-existent among African nations, many of which have adopted different forms of Western expression as a result of multiple colonisers, leaving us with a fragmented linguistic heritage that disrupts the Pan-Africanist spirit.

References

African Union. *Charter for African Cultural Renaissance*. Khartoum, 24 January 2006. Available online: https://au.int/sites/default/files/treaties/37305-treaty-Charter_for_African_Renissance_ENGLISH_digital_0.pdf (accessed on 30 December 2024).

Birmingham, David. "O Carnaval em Luanda", *Análise Social* vol. 26, no. 111 (1991): pp. 417–29.

Bright, Jake. "Meet 'Nollywood': The Second Largest Movie Industry in the World", *Fortune*, 24 June 2015. Available online: https://fortune.com/2015/06/24/nollywood-movie-industry/ (accessed on 30 December 2024).

Campos, Diego de Souza Araújo. "Um Estudo sobre a Escravidão em suas Relações coma Hierarquia Social Heranças e Particularidades da Instituição Escravocrata" (A Study on Slavery in its Relations with the Social Hierarchy: Inheritances and Particularities of the Slavery Institution). Unpublished dissertation, Pontifícia Universidade Católica do Rio de Janeiro, 2007. Available online: https://www.maxwell.vrac.puc-rio.br/11408/11408_1.PDF (accessed on 30 December 2024).

Davis, John B. *The Theory of the Individual in Economics: Identity and Value.* London and New York: Routledge, 2003.

De Camões, Luís. *The Lusiad: Or, the Discovery of India: An Epic Poem.* Translated by William Julius Mickle. London: George Bell and Sons, 1877.

Hall, Stuart. "The Question of Cultural Identity", in *Modernity and its Futures*, ed. Stuart Hall, David Held and Anthony G. McGrew. Cambridge: Polity Press, 1992.

Hegel, G.W.F. 2001. *The Philosophy of History*. Translated by J. Sibree. Ontario: Batoche Books, 2001.

M'Bow, Amadou Mahtar. *The General History of Africa*, vol. 1, Paris: UNESCO, 1979. Available online: https://unesdoc.unesco.org/ark:/48223/pf0000045083 (accessed on 30 December 2024).

Santos, Boaventura de Sousa. "O Colonialismo e o século XXI" (Colonialism and the 21st Century). *Centro de Estudos Estratégicos da Fiocruz Antonio Ivo de Carvalho*, 6 April 2018. Available online: https://cee.fiocruz.br/?q=boaventura-o-colonialismo-e-o-seculo-xxi (accessed on 30 December 2024).

Chapter 16
African Culture in the World: An Epistemological Reassessment

Martial Ze Belinga

Introduction: Can Africa's Influence on Culture be Described in Words?

Understanding Africa—its continuities and changes as well as its vital cultural contributions to the world from the dawn of humanity to the present day—is not necessarily a self-evident proposition. To comprehend an Africa on the move implies that this continent—the discourse around which has largely been scripted by outsiders—can be analysed through logic and that the procedures of cause and effect, along with rationalities customarily reserved for the so-called "civilised" world, can be equally applied here.

These initial presuppositions, however, are not much in tune with the old Africanist vocabulary, which, through a kind of nonlinear continuity, persists in overdetermining perspectives and discourses on Africa and the world. Africa is still discussed and referred to using specialised terminology that highlights dialects, patois and idioms rather than languages, and "wild tribes" rather than organised human groups and entities. It is said to have no religions, only superstitions; little beauty, but an abundance of exoticism.

Such perspectives persist even in the highest levels of global institutions. Dominique Strauss-Kahn, former Managing Director of the International Monetary Fund (IMF), remarked in a 2018 report on the CFA franc—the old currency of the French colonies which is still used by 14 African countries—that "… Africa can be differentiated from the rest of the world by its difficult 'passage to Statehood', a political concept that is alien to pre-colonial Africa and in contradiction with its enduring tribal traditions, but that the Westphalian world order ineluctably calls for" (Strauss-Kahn 2018, p. 34). Such a statement, as assured as it is sententious, made by an important person, whose mission for years was to provide economic guidance to indebted countries, shows that the perception of an inferior Africa—at least in terms of the historical adoption of the notion of State—remains deeply rooted at the very heart of development institutions.

It comes from a type of thinking and an arrangement that dominate global knowledge, one in which Africa and Africans do not build knowledge but merely cobble together retrograde beliefs. Vast geographical separations, therefore, seem to position the continent as a world "without" history, states, scripts, or moral systems—subjected instead to civilising efforts from a privileged world, that is Promethean and European. The vocabulary used to describe these two worlds is radically different and, in fact, quite opposed, with the terminology for one serving as the negative of that used for the other.

Such a pejorative nature of discourse and knowledge could only succeed in portraying Africa's influence as, at best, irrelevant and, at worst, harmful. Any answer to the question of Africa's cultural contribution to the world would be shaped, and constrained, by the lexical categories imposed upon it. These categories are based on the experiences and perceptions of the so-called Black, sub-Saharan peoples, often described in reductive and stereotypical terms: tribal, ethnic, sentimental, lazy, instinctive, violent, barbaric and unhistoric, as argued by philosopher Hegel, and prelogical, according to anthropologist Lévy-Bruhl.

This "colonial library"—to borrow the seminal expression of Congolese philosopher V.Y. Mudimbe—though enduring and even highly polished with its salient expressions, does not fully succeed in masking the paradoxes that dot the interstices of narratives about Africa, both of yesterday and today. How were peoples, labelled as having "no history" and no genius, able to produce artefacts so prized by the developed and European world, and to unleash a predatory accumulation and speculative international economy based on their cultural heritage as early as the 15th century? How were the aesthetics of peoples deemed to have no civilisation able to alter the canons of art and creativity for the 20th-century European avant-garde, influencing the likes of Pablo Picasso, Henri Matisse, Georges Braque and many others? (Ze Belinga 2003).

In 2007, at a forum organised by UNESCO in Benin, it was estimated that between 90 per cent and 95 per cent of African art objects were locked away in private, public and denominational collections in the West (UNESCO 2011, p. 63). In response, African states have increasingly called for the restitution of these cultural objects, most of which were looted during colonisation. Is this not a case of facts contradicting the categorically declared inferiority of Africans and their cultural contribution to the world?

Putting an end to this paradox—of an Africa that is absent from the world and omitted from authorised discourse, yet simultaneously marked by an unimaginable accumulation of looted African artefacts—would require an epistemological investment that enables the characterisation and removal of coloniality from the discursive structures that continue to disparage Africa. It is only when the continent can be described, objectified and understood through reason and experience that its culture can be explained in terms of its relationship with the modern world. We suggest the decolonisation of the dominant presuppositions and paradigms of the social sciences as a crucial precondition for understanding Africa, with its continuities and changes, in terms of its cultural contributions to the world.

Following our disruptive epistemology, we will present, through diachronic cross-sections, illustrations of African cultural influences in both ancient and contemporary contexts. Much as the continental experience will be mobilised for the early and ancient histories, the African diasporas will be considered as representative vectors of complex contemporary African continuities.

Despite their visibility, we will set aside cultural industries—such as music, arts, crafts, cinema, publishing, fashion, and gastronomy—that have made African culture a perceptible part of everyday life around the world. As the issue at hand is epistemological and decolonial, our focus will be more on making the silences speak and revealing the absences that shape the discourse on Africa and its cultural influence.

We will adopt a broad and multidimensional approach to culture, situated at the intersection of anthropology and biology, drawing from the work of David Bidney and Julian Huxley (Huxley 1956). According to Huxley, culture is a complex system of mechanisms of maintenance, reproduction and transmission, which includes artefacts, sociofacts and mentifacts shared in a society. Artefacts refer to the material basis of culture; mentifacts denote systems of knowledge and representation; and sociofacts include kinship structures, matrimony rules and social status.

When it comes to altering the way the world thinks of and perceives Africa, the challenge lies in the effort required to restore the world's capacity for a fair and pluriversal comprehension of humanity and to foster an inclusive dialogue among all peoples regarding the common path forward.

Decolonisation of Humanities, a Prerequisite for the Objectification of Africa

It is likely to be very difficult to demonstrate Africa's cultural influence on the world due to the conceptual barriers imposed by the dominant discursive regimes on colonised peoples. These remnants of distorted discursive and thematic structures, which we refer to using the established term/paradigm "coloniality" (Quijano 1991), take us back to a hegemonic state of legitimised knowledge. This knowledge is still influenced by "colonial sciences" and the historical administrative practices of subjugating Africans. The cognitive frameworks produced by this process of subjugation proved to be particularly tenacious, the more so as they were internalised by former colonies, including within academic circles, and "naturalised" through education and the so-called modern schools. Identifying the characteristics of this art of making statements in a colonial manner—epistemological coloniality—makes it possible to derive an alternative understanding and an insider's perspective on the African historical and cultural experience.

"The Conventions" of Colonial Writing in the World

Although the colonised peoples initially pitted their own cosmovisions and interpretations of history against the hegemonic ones found in the utterances of the slave traders (both Arab and European) and colonial rulers, it was the writings of the 'victors' that prevailed and spread throughout the world.[1] Many contemporary researchers have tried to identify what Mohamed Sahli (1965) terms "the conventions" of this colonial writing, which are still more or less explicit within the discourse on Africa. The work on UNESCO's General History of Africa (1964–1988) and that of Sahli, who speaks of the "ideological conventions" of the colonial regime, or Congolese historian Elikia M'Bokolo, among others, examine the characteristics of this historiography, which can be summed up in a few points:

- Essentialism: This approach presents Africans and their cultures as ontologically inferior. The need to colonise was instrumental in this essentialising of the subjugated.
- Mesological determinism: Linked to geography, sociology, ethnicity and race, this view reduces colonised peoples, considered incapable of thwarting the prognosis of their environment, to mere products of their unyielding climate, geography and racial identity.
- Diffusionism: A consequence of inferiority, it implies that the facts of science and civilisation are meant to move inevitably in a single direction—from superior emission centres, such as Europe (the ultimate), towards "others" (passive receivers).

1 For example, Kimpa Vita, the 17th-century prophetess of the Kongo Kingdom, advocated a Christian theology that reintegrated Kongo traditions into the pantheon of the saints of the Church, making her a pioneer of the African theology of liberation for some, but equally of the decolonisation of the humanities.

- Teleology: A product of essentialism and determinism, but also of Eurocentrism, this implies that the colonised and inferior will necessarily follow the path already traced by "civilised" and "developed" societies.
- Eurocentrism: The paradigm organising colonialism, which, as a matter of principle, explains and/or evaluates in relation to an idealising presumption of European achievement. These two forms of Eurocentrism—positive or explanatory, and normative—define the horizons of the discourse on colonised peoples and Africa.

These characteristic features de-historicise dominated societies and erase culture itself—this complex whole that has evolved over time from the collective experience of peoples. To shield oneself from the influence of the cognitive modes that produce such problematic content on the African experience, it would be useful to outline an epistemological formalisation of it. In fact, the persistence of essentialist visions goes far beyond a vocabulary that needs to be cleaned up; its roots run deep in a grammar of speech and presentation, from which emerge, almost automatically, defects, a provincial reality, and an annihilated Africa.

The PSC Model, a Formalisation of Epistemological Coloniality

The coloniality of knowledge can be understood and ultimately overcome by dissecting narratives and highlighting *perspectives*, thought *structures* and *concepts* mobilised by the authors. Indeed, our PSC model (Perspective-Structures-Concepts, UNESCO n.d.) tries to capture a grammar of epistemological bias.

Perspective generally determines the rest. A natural drift of speech, speech at rest, and perspective often adopt the position and designs of the speaker vis-à-vis the subject under consideration. For the perspective of a master speaking about subordinates and culturally deprived peoples to prevail, specific structures and appropriated categories are needed to organise, arrange and sort content. The inferior and "underdeveloped" will be "discovered" by "explorers", and one will not speak of people reduced to slavery, but of slaves, as though it were a natural fact of life. The temporal categories will compress history around the colonial experience, leading to notions of an indefinite precolonial period, the colonial as a founding moment in history, followed by a postcolonial period, suggesting that the history of the colonised peoples began with the white man.

The spatial categories help to describe the territorial adventure of the masters and reduce the culture of the colonised to outlandish residues of an unimportant past. “Continental”, “black”, “white”, “Moorish”, “interlacustrine”, “English-speaking”, “Portuguese-speaking”, “Spanish-speaking”, “sub-Saharan Africa”—all refer to the external gaze and the names of European possessions. The mobilisation of meta-categories (transverse categories) such as languages, ethnonyms and toponyms, writings, sources and cartography is not neutral in the restitution of the cultural influence of peoples. “Language-cultures”, as Beninese linguist Olabiyi Babalola J. Yäi calls them, are encyclopaedias, memories of ancient knowledge. On their own, they offer subjects of narration that do not spontaneously appear in other languages.

We can also re-examine the assumptions of disciplines aimed at offering a scientific understanding of non-Western peoples. Anthropology, as the study of distant and primitive peoples, separates those who are observed and studied (anthropos), from those who observe and study (humanitas). Economics defines underdevelopment and its unique teleological horizon—“development”—through the transfer of knowledge and funding from the West.[2]

As for philosophy, many assert that it began with “the Greek Miracle”, notwithstanding the long period of learning on African soil, particularly in Egypt, by ancient Greek scholars such as Thales, Pythagoras, Socrates, etc. (James 1954). The constituent disciplines of the modern humanities, along with their Eurocentrism, leave little room to portray Africa as anything other than servile and mediocre, with no cultural impact on the world, an infertile repository for external inflows.

---

2 Most notably, it was US President Truman who promoted the concept of “underdevelopment”.

This episteme of a prejudged and disparaged Africa is perpetuated as much by its invasive "white noises" (constantly repeated pejoration) as by its own silences, which by default affirm the significant hegemonic paradigms. Thus, the Haitian Revolution of the 19th century—the only one to be carried out and won by enslaved populations—is almost completely ignored in mainstream world history (Trouillot 1995). Africa's demography prior to the slave trade remains surprisingly shrouded in mystery and is often presumed to have been small, although the meticulous work of demographer Louise Marie Diop-Maes estimated the population at around 600 million people in the 16th century and only 200 million in the middle of the 19th century (Diop-Maes 1996).

Silencing can lead to the manipulation of evidence: it is the falsification of history according to historian and Egyptologist Cheikh Anta Diop (1954). Re-examining this global cognitive and epistemological order, which is both a product of and a resource for the domination of people, is indispensable for the restitution of the humanity of formerly colonised peoples, and for reassessing their cultural contributions to the world.

African Cultural Influence in the World

Through the prism of a decolonial and disruptive approach to history and humanities dedicated to Africans around the world, Africa's cultural influence appears massive and long-standing—yet often rendered invisible through its very banality or through "silencing processes" (Depelchin 2005). A few illustrations can support this epistemological correction of the object "Africa", tracing a continuous, vital and global presence from the first steps of humankind to the present day.

From Homo Sapiens to Ancient Egypt, Africa—the Source of Human Knowledge

The first major sequence in human history established Africa as the cradle of humanity—the incubator of the first people who resembled contemporary humans and are believed to have appeared around 300,000 years ago. Logically, human culture too should have first manifested in Africa. However, it was only after the excavations at the archaeological site of Blombos Cave in South Africa in the 1990s that Africa was also recognised as the starting point of human culture. Many artefacts found in the Blombos Cave—some of which date back to 70,000 BCE—bear testimony to early human "artistic" activities: latticework, engravings of geometric signs, shell ornaments, etc.

This discovery was crucial, as scientists had previously leaned towards placing the emergence of human creativity in Europe, where the Chauvet Cave paintings in France (30,000 BCE) were considered defining evidence (Morin 2018). The discovery of the Blombos Cave pushed back the timeline for the first manifestations of creativity and abstraction, dating them to a period prior to the dispersal of early humans, who, as they moved around the planet, took with them the "cave art" practised by their ancestors. This would thus be one of the oldest bequests of African cultural heritage to early humans and civilisations. This creative ability seems so intrinsic to humankind that it is seen as inherent to all cultures, thereby rendering Africa's influence invisible.

Ancient Egypt, that is Pharaonic Africa, represents one of the oldest cultural and scientific archives in what we call the modern world, such has been its intellectual influence on surrounding peoples, many of whom later became dominators. It is also one of the most manipulated and instrumentalised objects of knowledge, which, since the colonial period, has witnessed an amplification of the huge paradox surrounding its origin and identity. While Cheikh Anta Diop notes that Greek contemporaries of the Egyptians always described them as Africans with "black complexions" and "frizzy hair"—as recorded by scholars like Herodotus, Diodorus of Sicily or Strabo—European scholars since the colonial period have never ceased to paint this civilisation as white (Diop 1954). This theory—based on an accident of geography—made it possible to stay silent about African influence on the Eurasian world, especially on Greece, whose earliest philosophers were educated by the Egyptians themselves, the keepers of ancient knowledge recorded in writing in temples or transmitted orally. The different modes through which African knowledge from the Pharaonic period was transmitted to Greek scholars are explained in the illuminating work of George G.M.

James, *The Stolen Legacy* (1954). The paradigms of an ahistorical and oral Africa, supposedly devoid of written traditions, were inapplicable to Pharaonic Egypt, which meant that it had to be given as un-African an identity as possible. This also served to legitimise, through its obvious superiority, the rationale for rendering Africa as savage—an essential part of the long process of enslavement and colonial domination.

African influence, especially from Egypt, is truly inestimable and cannot be described here in detail. However, a few examples will give us a broad sense of its impact. Cheikh Anta Diop's *Civilisation ou Barbarie* presents a compelling discussion of Africa's contributions to modern philosophy and science, from which the following examples are drawn (Diop 1980).

Indeed, it was Egyptian cosmogonies that introduced several major archetypes that later developed into the Abrahamic religions and philosophy. For example, in the history of religious thought, concepts such as an autogenous god (Ra), a primordial fertile divine couple (Osiris and Isis), creation through the spoken word, resurrection (Osiris), life after death, and the Trinity (Osiris, Isis, Horus) were all expressed in Egyptian cosmogonies before being adopted by Mediterranean or Eastern civilisations. The idea that water, air, earth and fire are the four constituent elements of the universe—attributed to philosophers from the pre-Socratics to Plato—also originates from the cosmogonies of Pharaonic Africa. These broad archetypes are believed to form the theological foundations of the Abrahamic religions and flourished for thousands of years on African soil before nurturing the so-called "revealed religions". Locally re-appropriated African cultural influence is thus essential even today in the spiritual life of a major section of humanity.

According to Diop, the Egyptian cultural environment also influenced the philosophical idealism and materialism developed by the Greeks, particularly through concepts such as "creation by the spoken word" on the one hand, and "original matter" (*nun*) on the other. Pharaonic Africa also passed on to the world, among other legacies, one of the earliest known figures to be venerated as a scholar: Imhotep, a man of immense knowledge, who lived around

3,000 BCE. Deified by tradition, he was not only a thinker and doctor but also an architect-cum-builder of pyramids and a high-ranking member of the Egyptian state during the reign of King Djoser.

In the light of Egypt's contribution to the world in fields of spirituality, philosophy, and, by extension, the sciences and humanities (medicine, mathematics, architecture, aesthetics, etc.), it is necessary to reassess the epistemological order under which Africa's contributions are so often undervalued.

The "New World" and the Transfer of African Knowledge

The transmission of continental knowledge, skills and attitudes to the Americas, the Arab–Muslim world and the Indian Ocean region constitutes an important instance of Africa's cultural influence globally. The vast movements of African populations over time were the primary means by which there occurred this migration of knowledge and its social worlds towards the "New Worlds" to which Africans were deported. The slave trade and voluntary migrations dispersed Africans and their unique resources, creating diasporas that became islets—African cultural territories or territories cross-bred with Africanness—in the Americas and former slave societies of the Arab–Muslim world, physically distant from the African continent. Their lifestyles, gastronomy, languages and leisure activities, although locally adapted, still often bear indelible traces of their original African roots.

Since Roger Bastide's seminal work *The African Religions of Brazil* was published in 1960, the impact of African spiritualities on American societies has become better known. The religion called "Vodou" in Haiti, "Candomblé" in Brazil, and "Santeria" in Cuba—along with variants like "Voodoo" in Louisiana or "Hoodoo" in South Carolina among the Gullah (a subgroup of the African American ethnic group)—has largely contributed to the establishment of social life, imaginary worlds, systems for interpreting the world, and the development of musical, pictorial and sculptural aesthetics in the Americas. This religion originating in West Africa within the cultural area of the Aja–Tado peoples (present-day Benin, Togo, Ghana and Nigeria) spread, adapted, and syncretised in the Americas, finally forming an effective form of cultural resistance that supported insurrections like the Haitian Revolution of the 19th century. Beyond its role in manifesting resistance, the strength of this religion—its adaptations, traditions and view of the world—contributed to transforming and building the Americas, partially liberating them from the exclusive mould of Christian and slave imagery.

Historian Paul Lovejoy (UNESCO 2013), a specialist in African diasporas in the Atlantic world, has studied the transfers of African knowledge in the "New World". Two examples, amongst others, illustrate the immense contribution of Africa: agriculture and textiles.

Judith A. Carney (2001) recalls that the cultivation of rice was introduced to the Americas by West Africans, who brought with them both the techniques for processing this crop and a gendered organisation of labour. Regions such as North Carolina and northeastern Brazil still bear traces of this African agricultural legacy, although it has largely been forgotten. "Uncle Ben's", the world-famous American rice brand, is high-quality rice grown by an African American farmer named Ben, which was later industrially processed and commercialised.

Another notable example is the introduction of stimulants such as the kola nut, native to West Africa, which became the base ingredient for many cola drinks in the Americas from the late 19th century, including the world-famous "Coca-Cola". Coffee, whose cultivation and consumption originated in Ethiopia, was later disseminated through the Arab-Muslim world and eventually globalised. Today, a significant portion of the world consumes coffee without realising that it is an African product that has become an integral part of modern lifestyles.

Cotton and indigo cultivation also illustrate how West African knowledge was transferred to the host countries through the diaspora. These products, along with their techniques and societal uses, travelled and were adapted to new contexts and redeployed in a predominantly capitalist and industrial environment.

Africa's cultural contribution is omnipresent across the world and commensurate with the wide dispersal of populations who carried their cultures with them. Today, African influences are still visible in the music industry, through rhythms that have become "universal", such as American Blues, the Cuban salsa, Brazilian samba and capoeira dance. Gwoka (the art of percussion) from the French West Indies—inscribed on UNESCO's Representative List of Intangible Cultural Heritage of Humanity—is one such social, artistic and cultural expression of African populations who were reduced to slavery and resisted their commodification by ensuring the survival of their imaginary worlds, often through the syncretic route of reinvention.

We also find indirect African influences, for instance, in the work of Jean-Michel Basquiat, the iconic New York painter and street artist. Born to a Haitian father, Basquiat's life and artistic expression were deeply marked by Voodoo spirituality which he inherited from his family (Mirande 2015).

The adaptability and resilience of the Africans—their values of resistance and their belief in liberation from slavery and segregation based on their African origin—have inspired many Afro-descendants to excel in fields like science and technology in the US. As a result, today there is an impressive number of "Black inventors" who have filed for patents for innovations including electric lamps, motor lubricants, combine harvesters, convertible sofa beds, fire extinguishers, gas masks, traffic lights, lifts, and laser surgery for cataracts (Antoine 2012).

Conclusion

The image of an Africa that continues to suffer in more ways than one and has not quite recovered from its recent history, which could well have wiped it out both literally and figuratively, is hard to reconcile with the "discovery", despite a thousand prejudices and preconceived notions, of a geo-human space whose cultural influence on humanity is real, ancient and profound.

It is at the cost of a consummate asceticism—weaning away from inherited modes of thought, and from the silences and certainties of a Eurocentric episteme—that Africa emerges from the caves of Blombos, the Ishango bone (Congo, 20,000 BCE), and Egypt, the earliest teacher of modern knowledge. The long history of African migrations and diasporisation has been a conduit for an enormous transfer of knowledge, particularly to pro-slavery societies and other regions where Africans and their descendants settled.

African culture—through artefacts, mentifacts and sociofacts—helped build the societies to which Africans were forcibly deported or to which they voluntarily moved. When reassessed through an epistemological break, the profound influences of African culture—expressed in languages, syncretic social and religious practices, and eating habits—not only reflect Africa's enduring legacy but also bear witness to the strong international appeal of the continent's creative industries.

A global Africa—shaped through contact with pre-existing American worlds or forged by the labour and knowledge of its daughters and sons—remains actively engaged in adapting its customs and placing its sacred spheres in global contexts, thereby embodying new, decentred, and partly unprecedented forms of modernity.

References

Antoine, Yves. *Savants et inventeurs noirs.* Paris: L'Harmattan, 2012.

Carney, Judith Ann. *Black Rice: The African Origins of Rice Cultivation in the Americas.* Cambridge: Harvard University Press, 2001.

Depelchin, Jacques. *Silences in African History: Between the Syndromes of Discovery and Abolition.* Dar es Salaam: Mkuki na Nyota Publishers, 2005.

Diop, Cheikh Anta. *Nations nègres et culture.* Paris: Présence africaine, 1954.

———. *Civilisation ou Barbarie.* Paris: Présence africaine, 1980.

Diop-Maes, Louis-Marie. *Afrique noire, démographie, sol et histoire.* Paris: Présence africaine/Khepera, 1996.

Huxley, Julian. "Evolution, Cultural and Biological", in *Current Anthropology: A Supplement to Anthropology Today,* ed. William L. Thomas, Jr. Chicago: The University of Chicago Press, 1956.

James, George G.M. *The Stolen Legacy.* New York: Philosophical Library, 1954.

Lovejoy, Paul. "African Contributions to Science, Technology and Development", Collective Volume. *The Slave Route Project.* Paris: UNESCO, 2012.

Mirande, Marion. "L'héritage haïtien de Jean-Michel Basquiat" in Grandpalais.fr, 28 January 2015. Available online: https://www.grandpalais.fr/fr/article/lheritage-haitien-de-jean-michel-basquiat (accessed on 13 April 2020).

Morin, Hervé. "Dans une grotte d'Afrique du sud, un dessin vieux de 73,000 ans", in *Le Monde,* 12 September 2018. Available online: https://www.lemonde.fr/archeologie/article/2018/09/12/un-dessin-vieux-de-73-000-ans-trouve-dans-une-grotte-sud-africaine_5354166_1650751.html (accessed on 5 January 2025).

Quijano, Anibal. "Colonialidad, modernidad/racialidad". *Peru Indigerna* vol. 13, no. 29 (1991): pp. 11–29.

Sahli, Mohamed C. *Décoloniser l'histoire. Introduction à l'histoire du Maghreb.* Paris: Cahiers Libres Issue 77, Maspéro édit, 1965.

Trouillot, Michel-Rolph. *Silencing the Past.* Boston, Beacon Press, 1995.

UNESCO. n.d. "General History of Africa, vol. 9". In press (TBC 2022–2029).

Ze Belinga, Martial. "Économie des arts et artisanats africains: Attractivité internationale versus prédation globale", *Présence Africaine* vols. 167–8, nos. 1–2 (2003): pp. 36–54.

Chapter 17

Musical Traditions of Africa and Similarities with India

Manjari Sinha

The musical traditions of Africa are abundantly diverse. As a huge continent with 54 countries—each with multiple ethnic groups that have their own varieties of music—Africa has a vibrant cultural heritage with refreshingly sumptuous diversity. Music and songs have long been integral to rituals and religious ceremonies, much like in India, where music flourished under the patronage of temples and was performed as an offering to the presiding deity. In both India and Africa, music has been an oral tradition, passed down from generation to generation like the continuous, unbroken flow of a river.

These oral traditions played a vital role in preserving the dynamism of performance through people's remembrance. Myths, legends, epics, oral histories and life stories were just some of the genres that embodied social and cultural memories of African societies. Motion and action are central to the aesthetic principles of many performing groups.

African performance is an interesting amalgam of arts that are difficult to separate, much like the intermingling of arts in India. The very thought of music and Africa brings to mind the definition of "nātya" in the *Nātyaśāstra*—the ancient treatise on Indian performing arts attributed to Bharata Muni:

न तज्ज्ञानं न तच्छिल्पं न सा विद्या न सा कला |
न स योगो न तत्कर्म नाट्येऽस्मिन् यन्न दृश्यते ||

na tajjñānaṃ, na tacchilpam, na sā vidyā, na sā kalā
na sa yogo na tatkarma, nāṭye'asmin yanna dṛśyate

There is no knowledge, no craft, no learning, no art, no yoga, not any activity which is not seen in *nātya* [the theatrical art]' (Chapter 1, Verse 116, Kumar, p. 41)

The musical tradition of Africa is very similar to the Indian notion of *nātya*, which is not solely music, dance, drama or theatrical art, but an amalgamation of all these disciplines. The Indian understanding of the interrelationship between artistic forms can be illustrated through a story from the *Vishnudharmottara Purana*, where King Braja, fascinated by a piece of sculpture, goes to a master to learn the art. The master asks him, "Have you ever learnt drawing and painting? You must first learn how to draw and paint what you want to sculpt." When King Braja goes to learn drawing and painting, the master asks him, "Have you learnt to dance? How can you understand your lines without learning dance?" and sends him to a dance teacher. The dance teacher, in turn, sends him to learn music to which the dance would be performed. Finally, the music teacher sends him to study literature, so that he knows the poetry to be sung in the dance. The story thus underlines the interconnectedness of various forms of Indian art.

The same holds true for African arts, where the musical, dramatic and visual forms act together and are conceived as intertwined. The natural versatility of performers brings together singing, playing musical instruments and dancing. Along with masquerade and drama, these form a single conceptual package. All of these art forms are closely linked to social life; they are not enjoyed as isolated performances but are part of the ebb and flow of life.

Music, in essence, is an integral part of life in Africa, and its impact is visible all over. In Ghana, for instance, Highlife songs are famous for their use in political campaigns. In rural areas, day-to-day work is often coordinated and energised by music—for example, bush clearers work to the accompaniment of instrumental ensembles. There are no demarcations through prejudicial terms like "folk", "popular", and "art" music in African contexts, where aural traditions are highly developed, and these methods of transmission are not regarded as any less competent or effective in artistic creation. It is no surprise, then, that performing is considered as normal as speaking in many African societies.

Music remains an integral part of African religious ceremonies and rituals, social gatherings where stories are passed down through generations, and special occasions like celebrations. Traditional music is frequently performed in natural surroundings and often involves active participation from the audience. Just as India has songs that accompany harvesting and household chores like grinding grain, and *sanskar geet* that accompany occasions like childbirth (*sohar* songs) and weddings (*vivah geet*), Africa has songs for work, childbirth, marriage, hunting and political activities. Music is also used to ward off evil spirits and pay respects to benevolent ones, the dead, and the ancestors. None of these musical expressions are performed outside their intended social context, and most are accompanied by a specific dance form.

Historically, Africa's music has been shaped by several interacting factors: language, environment, cultural diversity, politics, and population movements. Ethnic groups that evolved in different parts of the continent ate different foods, lived in different climatic conditions, and came in contact with different groups. Each moved at different rates and to different places, and was influenced by different historical and cultural circumstances. Systems of governance also varied, which too influenced musical traditions.

Popular African music—expressed through styles such as Afrobeat from West Africa, Highlife from Ghana, Ndombolo from the Democratic Republic of Congo, Bongo Flava from Tanzania, Makosa from Central Africa, and Kwaito from South Africa—has reverberated beyond African borders. Afrobeat is present in pop music around the world, much like the way Africa's visual arts have influenced the evolution of modern art worldwide. This universal popularity of African music has survived the Western yardsticks applied to dismiss or eliminate its indigenous quality and character.

African musical instruments fall into five primary categories: membranophones, chordophones, aerophones, idiophones and percussion. In membranophones, the sound is produced by striking or rubbing against a membrane stretched over a frame; these include drums, kettles, clay pots and barrels. Chordophones are string instruments like the harp, lute, lyre, zither and fiddle. Aerophones are wind instruments like the flute and trumpet. Idiophones are percussion instruments, such as cymbals, xylophones, rattles and shakers made of naturally sonorous materials. The percussion category also includes foot tapping and hand clapping.

The wide range of African percussion features traditional instruments like the talking drum and djembe in West Africa, water drums in Central Africa and various types of ngoma or algoma drums found in Central and Southern Africa. There are also slit gongs and double bells. Some of these instruments have achieved international recognition. The above-mentioned are among the most popular, but people make and use a vast array of instruments besides these. Often, a close, almost human-like bond develops between musicians and their instruments.

The Sub-Saharan musical tradition relies predominantly on percussion instruments—xylophones, djembes and drums—complemented by tone-producing instruments like the mbira or thumb piano. There are complex rhythmic structures where multiple rhythms interact to form polyrhythms. The most common polyrhythm plays three beats against two as a triplet played against straight notes. These highly rhythmic elements express life in all its manifestations through the medium of sound.

Polyrhythm is one of the most ubiquitous characteristics of Sub-Saharan music and may be contrasted with polyphony in Western music. Unique instruments have evolved to facilitate the simultaneous playing of contrasting rhythms—for example, the mbira, kalimba, kora and ngoni. They often organise notes not in a single linear sequence from bass to treble, but across two separate rows or arrays, which make it easier to play cross-rhythms.

With some exceptions, African music does not follow a written tradition, which means there is little or no written music available for study or analysis. It is almost impossible to accurately notate the melodies and harmonies of African music using Western staff notation. There are subtle variations in pitch and intonation that do not easily translate into the Western system.

Apart from the predominance of rhythm, African music also differs from Western music in that the various parts of the music do not necessarily blend in a harmonious fashion. Instead, each instrument or part may represent a particular aspect of life or a distinct character, and the participation of each instrument matters more than the way they fit together as a whole.

Since it does not rely on a written score and is highly improvisational, African music shares several features with Indian music. Much like the *sawāl-jawāb* (question-answer) in Indian music, a distinguishing feature of African music is "call-and-response", where one voice or instrument plays a short melodic phrase that is echoed or answered by another.

This interactive style extends to rhythmic patterns as well: a master drummer plays a central rhythm, which is then repeated or responded to by other drummers. Typically, a core rhythmic pattern is maintained, with drummers then improvising new patterns over the static original patterns. This is like the different combinations of beats that characterise the *jāti* patterns of Indian *tālas*: *tisra* (three), *chatuśra* (four), *khaṇda* (five), *miśra* (seven) and *sankīrṇa* (nine). African musicians revel especially in syncopation because of their perfect sense of rhythm.

African music closely adheres to Western tetratomic (four-note), pentatonic (five-note), hexatonic (six-note), and heptatonic (seven-note) scales. Indian *raga* music, which requires at least five notes (*swaras*) to form a *raga*, does not include tetratomic *ragas*. However, comparisons can be made with *audav jāti* (pentatonic) *ragas*, *ṣadav jāti* (hexatonic) and *sampūrna jāti* (heptatonic) *ragas*. Similarly, in African music, the harmonisation of melody is accomplished by singing in parallel thirds, fourths, or fifths, which is comparable to the *swar samvād* in Indian classical music, such as the *śadja–gāndhār samvād*, *śadja–madhyam samvād* and *śadja–pancham samvād*.

African music has a close connection with the tonal languages of the region. Some communities use vocal sounds and movements in their music. In singing, the tonal patterns or the text puts some constraints on the melodic patterns. In instrumental music, a native speaker of the language can often discern textual elements from the music itself. This effect is seen in drum languages, such as the talking drum. This could easily be compared to the language of Indian *talas*.

The vibrant music and dance traditions of the African diaspora have given rise to several genres, including soca, calypso and zouk in the Caribbean, and samba, conga, son, rumba, salsa, bomba and cumbia in Latin America. These genres, based on the music of enslaved Africans, have greatly influenced contemporary African popular music. Although African American music is widely known and loved, it is not as popular as North American music which in fact emerged from it. Similarly, South American music also has strong African roots.

Moreover, the musical traditions of Irish and Scottish settlers in America merged with African American musical elements to create genres like old-time and bluegrass. African music was a major factor in shaping what we know today as Dixieland, blues and jazz. These have all borrowed from African rhythms and sounds, brought over the Atlantic Ocean by slaves.

While the music of Sub-Saharan Africa is generally characterised by its upbeat, polyrhythmic and joyful nature, the blues should be viewed as an aesthetic response to the conditions of slavery in the New World. Twentieth-century American instruments like the gravikord were influenced by the kora, which, along with the ngoni, facilitated polyrhythmic structures and voice techniques such as complex hard melisma and yodelling that produce vocalisation in song.

Non-commercial African American radio stations played a crucial role in promoting African music as part of their cultural and political missions during the 1960s and 1970s. African music also found receptive audiences at Historically Black Colleges and Universities (HBCUs) and appealed particularly to activists in the civil rights and Black Power movements. Certain Sub-Saharan African musical traditions also had a significant influence on such works as Disney's

The Lion King and *The Lion King II: Simba's Pride*, which blend traditional with Western music. Songs such as "Circle of Life" and "He Lives in You" combine Zulu and English lyrics, as well as traditional African styles of music with more modern Western styles. The film also incorporates words from the Bantu Swahili language, such as "*hakuna matata*", which means "no worries".

Most contemporary genres of African popular music are created through cross-pollination with Western popular music. In particular, they have adopted Western musical instruments and recording studio techniques. However, just as India makes conscious efforts to guard its musical and cultural heritage, Africa is equally aware of its rich musical inheritance. In Zimbabwe, 75 per cent of airtime has to be given to local music. Although Sony Music launched in Africa in 2016 by opening an office in Nigeria, traditional services of major international Western studios are still unavailable in Africa. These protective actions have led to the rise of new genres, like Urban Grooves in Zimbabwe, which, while modern, remain deeply rooted in African musical tradition. Indian music looks forward to creative collaborations with the African music.

Reference

Kumar, Pushpendra, ed. *Nāṭyaśāstra of Bharatamuni*, vol. 1. Delhi: New Bharatiya Book Corporation, revised edition, 2010.

PART 5
Textile Traditions of Africa and India

Chapter 18

Textile Linkages between India and Africa: The Case of Tanzania

George Danford Nahimiani

Introduction

India has a rich history of textile traditions with spinning, weaving, dyeing and printing being popular cottage industries for centuries before the formal colonisation by Britain in the 1770s. In fact, it is known that there was stiff competition between India and the British East India Company in textile marketing, to the extent that India was eventually ordered to reduce textile production in favour of British competitors.

Through travel and trade, textiles from India found their way to Tanzania. The arrival of Indians in Tanzania as traders, skilled craftsmen and professionals took place just over 200 years ago, and their influence on the cultural life of Tanzanians is immense. Any discussion on Swahili culture and art in Tanzania, therefore, is incomplete without mentioning the Indian influence on various aspects of culture, such as food, language, textiles and fashion design.

The geo-cultural position of Tanzania has attracted visitors as early as the 1st century CE (Meier 2000, p. 26), but most resident Tanzanian Indians are the descendants of either early traders who settled along the coastal areas or workers recruited by Britain in the early 19th century to work at various government departments in the then Tanganyika Territory. In Zanzibar, during the reign of Sultan

Sayyid Barghash bin Said (1870–88)—who had spent two years in exile in Bombay after his rebellion was put down in 1860 (Sheriff 2008, p. 79)—Indian architects and builders were invited to build his palaces, such as the House of Wonders (*Beit el-Ajaib*), which featured 13 intricately carved doors (Fig. 1). Some of these doors have their origins in Gujarat and are now considered part of Tanzania's heritage of visual art.

Fig. 1: A Zanzibar door.

Source: Kimbokota K. 2018.

Modern textile linkages between India and Tanzania were strengthened when Mwalimu Julius Nyerere, the first President of Tanzania, made a state visit to India in January 1970, during which he emphasised trade ties between the two nations. He remarked, "Many of the things which Tanzania is accustomed to buying in Europe may be obtained from those developing countries—like India—which are some steps ahead of us in economic development … ."

In April 1970, while opening the Preparatory Conference of Non-Aligned Nations in Dar es Salaam, he reiterated his call for economic cooperation: "…in economic matters we non-aligned states, as a group, can help ourselves … to bolster our freedom from economic domination by working together, by co-operating for our mutual benefit". These statements from a head of state clearly set the stage for trade relations between developing nations like India and Tanzania.

It is no accident, therefore, that India invested heavily in Tanzania's textile industries, including manufacturing of *khanga* fabric. Further, India-based textile factories continue to export *khanga* to Tanzania, competing with China, Japan and Oman, among others.

It is against this background that this chapter will focus on the textile linkages between India and Tanzania. The leading cultural object is the *khanga*, which illustrates that cultural life does not take place in a vacuum. Its presence reveals the dynamic interplay of cultural practices within the broader context of African and Indian Ocean trade.

The *Khanga* Textile Material

Fig. 2 and Fig. 3: Khanga textile designs.
Source: Author (2020).

India has been a great manufacturer of *khanga* cloth during the colonial as well as postcolonial periods in Tanzania. According to historian Kax Wilson (1979), the *khanga* originated in the port city of Zanzibar in the early 1850s, where it was initially hand-printed by an Indian merchant using black-coloured woodblock prints on white cotton cloth.

Fashion designer Faroque Abdela (2008, p. 101) notes that a simple black-on-white design (*mera*) was block-printed onto white cotton rectangles using vegetables such as sweet potatoes or onions. Later, Abdulla Essak, who established his business in Mombasa in 1887, became the first person to handprint *khanga* cloth that featured proverbs written in Arabic script.

The earliest *khanga* designers were inspired by the guinea fowl (known in Swahili as *kanga*), whose body is characterised by white spots on a black background.

Before the *khanga* became popular, the textile favoured by peasants and traditional healers was the *kaniki*, often referred to as black calico. Among the coastal Zaramo ethnic group, for example, Finnish anthropologist Marja-Liisa Swantz (1986, p. 300) observed, "In spirit rites when a person goes into trance, great care is taken that the *kaniki* cloth which a woman wears does not slip out of place". *Kaniki* is a black-printed cotton fabric imported from India. The rectangular piece of cloth was commonly worn during ritual dances and farming activities. It could be worn for weeks without washing, as its dark colour concealed dirt easily.

Later, Muslim traders from Kutch in India introduced a version of the *khanga* that was symmetrical in design, featuring a central motif and a border with script, something that is still seen today. However, contemporary *khanga* is no longer symmetrical but rectangular, measuring 254 cm by 91.5 cm (10 feet by 3 feet). Made of very thin cotton, it is worn as a casual dress at home or draped over clothing as a form of veiling—an alternative to the head-to-foot black *baibui* or the Arabian *hijab* worn in public. In this form of draping, the *khanga* serves both Islamic and local identities.

The floral designs often seen on *khanga* are in line with Islamic doctrine, which traditionally discourages the depiction of human and animal images in art. However, this principle is not observed when *khanga* is used to advertise churches, companies or political parties. For example, following the death of President Nyerere in 1999, *khangas* bearing his portraits were produced and purchased by Muslims and non-Muslims alike as memorabilia.

The introduction of Computer-Aided Design (CAD) has made digital printing of *khanga* fabrics easier and faster. The cloth has since become part and parcel of the cultural pattern of Tanzanians and serves in a variety of social roles. The existence of over 14 Indian-owned textile factories in Tanzania—most of which produce *khanga*—is a clear indication of the demand for this fabric. This demand has led to cultural co-production in Africa (Ressler 2012, p. 1), and this is true of Tanzania in particular.

Ritual Roles of *Khanga*

The invention of the *khanga*, often manufactured using locally grown cotton, has been a blessing in disguise for many families. Expectant mothers, for example, are instructed by hospital midwives to bring with them ten pairs of *khanga* and three pieces of *kitenge* cloth at the time of delivery. It is common practice for mothers to wear a *khanga* during childbirth, after which the newborn baby is also wrapped in one (see Fig. 4).

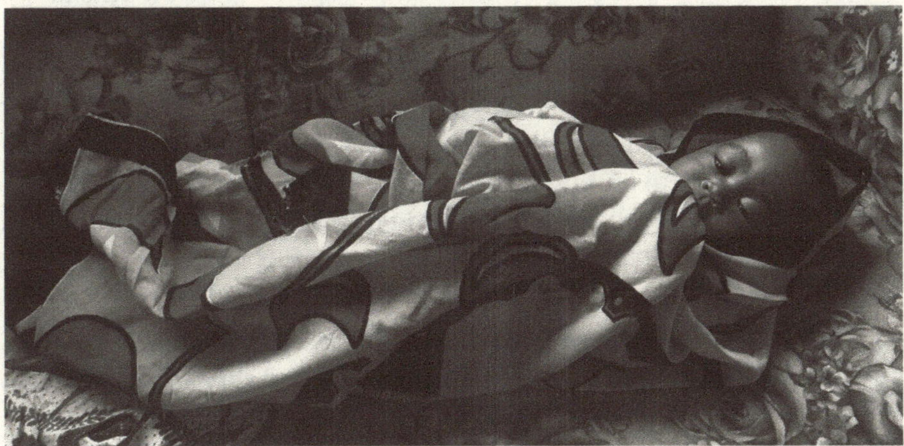

Fig. 4: A baby wrapped in *khanga*.

Source: Author (2020).

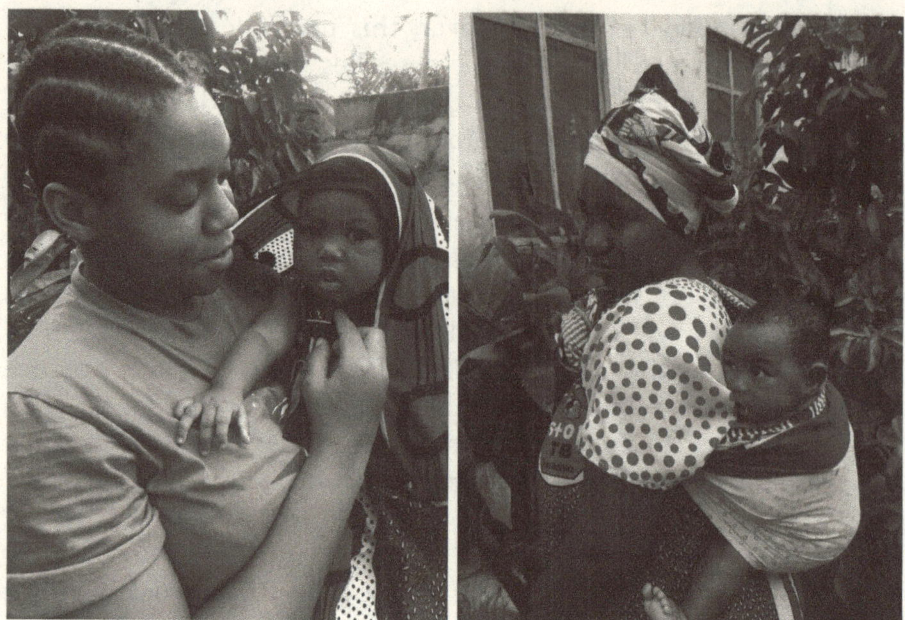

Fig. 5 and Fig. 6: The babies covered and carried using the *khanga.*
Source: Author (2020).

This light material allows air circulation to take place naturally as excessive body heat escapes while cool air passes through, keeping the body at its normal temperature. At the age of three months or so, the baby is carried on the mother's back using the *khanga*, a practice known in Kiswahili as *mbeleko* (see Fig. 5 and Fig. 6).

At the age of puberty, most daughters are given a new pair of *khanga* by their mothers and are instructed on how and when to wear it. Some girls are even taught to care for the *khanga* by perfuming it and drying it in the shade after washing. In some communities, boys are also offered *khangas* by their mothers after their circumcision ceremony, marking their transition into manhood.

The *khanga* may also be used as a shroud, especially in villages. Among Muslims, it is common to tie one around the *jeneza* (wooden coffin carrier) used to carry the body of a woman. Most women attending burial ceremonies wear *khangas* over their regular dress—such as jeans and a blouse, or a black dress made from *kaniki* material—to symbolise grief. Some women cover their heads

Fig. 7: Women attending a burial ceremony.

Source: Author (2020).

completely with *khangas* as a sign of modesty (see Fig. 7). *Kaniki* cloth is widely used in funerals as mourning attire. Men, women and children wear black dresses, often made from *kaniki* of different textures, during the mourning period, which lasts about one month.

Khanga and Marital Life

The *khanga* always comes in pairs, and it is common to see married couples wearing matching *khangas* at night: as a loincloth for the husband and as a wrapper for the wife. In some Muslim communities, when a couple decides to divorce, each keeps one half of the pair as a symbol of the hope or intention to restore the relationship (Abdela 2008, p. 102). There is, however, a special bridal *khanga* known as *kisutu* (Fig. 8 and Fig. 9).

It has a different design from ordinary *khangas* and is worn mainly by some Swahili wives on special occasions to communicate various unspoken messages to their husbands. The typical *kisutu* is printed in symbolic colours of red, white and black. In Lamu, Kenya, brides wear such *khangas*: red indicates their virginity, black represents the pain of deflowering while white symbolises the colour of the male seed she will receive for the first time (Ressler 2012, p. 5). So, whenever we come across a *kisutu* with a black background and red-and-white patterns, it can be regarded as the original *kisutu* fabric.

Fig. 8 and Fig. 9: *Kisutu* designs.

Source: https://www.bing.com; https://www.pinterest.com/pin/389068855281935957/

Weddings and send-off parties in many local communities are important occasions where *khangas* are gifted to the mothers of the bride and groom. A mother may receive over 30 pairs of *khangas* at one sitting. She usually donates some to her close female relatives as a gesture of family solidarity. She may even use them at the time of her daughter's delivery.

Khangas as Media of Communication

The popularity of *khanga* has made it a common medium for communicating important messages in society. Political parties, football clubs, manufacturing companies, churches and others design *khangas* to celebrate special occasions, such as anniversaries, by inserting proverbs, quotations, mottoes and statements. Messages in Kiswahili, such as "*Sina swali nina jibu*" (I only have the answer, no question), and "*Asemae hajapata, aliyepata hasemi*" (The one who has does not speak, the ones who haven't, speak) are often used as polite warnings to those who brag about what they have, even if their claims are untrue. Most *khanga* designers target specific customers, especially women, by printing *khangas* with special messages known in Kiswahili as *mipasho*, to warn against issues like anti-social behaviour in marital life. At funerals, many women in Tanzania prefer wearing *khangas* with printed messages expressing condolences.

It has been observed that the majority of women are more attracted to the printed messages on *khanga* than to their motifs or colour schemes, most of which depict exotic flowers and symbols that are rarely recognisable to the local people. The growing literacy rate among women has made it possible to select *khangas* that are relevant to their diverse needs. For instance, during the visit of the then US President Barack Obama to Tanzania in the mid-2000s, some female political enthusiasts bought *khangas* bearing his portrait, mounted them on stretchers, framed them like works of art and hung them on their walls. This shows how versatile and affordable *khangas* can be.

Khanga and *Kaniki* in Music and Dance

The use of the *khanga* has no ethnic boundaries in Tanzania. As such, almost any ethnic group can use it as a costume in dance and music. However, there are local dances in which all women dancers have to be clothed completely in either *khanga* or *kaniki*, which have symbolic significance in terms of the origin and meaning of the dance. In matrimony-related dances held in seclusion, for example, all middle-aged Swahili women wear *khangas* of a uniform colour scheme. *Kaniki* assumes special significance in dances where it is the costume for both genders. In the Wagogo dances of peasants in central Tanzania, for instance, all dancers wear *kaniki*. When *khanga* is used by both genders in dance, it is usually designed in a single colour scheme to create the uniformity desired by the choreographer. However, the dance leaders wear different colours.

Conclusion

India and Tanzania have made unique contributions to the *khanga*, a flexible fabric that for over 150 years has documented trends, ideas, influences and historical events through its images and text. Many motifs have their roots in both India and Tanzania, such as local fruits and flowers. The use of the human image gives this fabric the power of posters and billboards in social and cultural communication. For some people, printed text is what makes a *khanga* authentic and worth collecting for the different groups using it. Its authenticity as traditional Swahili art is beyond reproach, as it is closely associated with the social and spiritual concerns of the Swahili people living along the Indian Ocean. It is traditional art not in the sense that it conveys objects, ideas and contexts of use that are past, static and unchanging. The *khanga* has been subjected to a variety of contemporary uses, but its intrinsic roles remain deeply ethnic, especially among the Swahili people along the Indian Ocean. In this way, the *khanga* is both a cultural and social text, a fact used by manufacturers to market the cloth. This has proven to be an effective commercial strategy which has given *khanga* wide popularity among the literate population of consumers in East Africa. It continues to shape the cultural identity of the Swahili people of the East Coast, as it has a big role in day-to-day affairs.

Fig. 10 and Fig. 11: Della dress.
Source: Author (2020).

It should not, however, be forgotten that India and Tanzania share climatic characteristics that are conducive to cotton growth. This has been one of the strongest linkages insofar as *khanga* manufacturing is concerned. An extension of *khanga* production has been the introduction of the *della* dress, made from light cotton yarn similar to that of *khanga*. The dress, which is becoming extremely popular among local women, is imported from India or China. However, *khanga* fabric is most often used for the production of the *della* because of its lightness of texture.

The contributions of India and Tanzania in *khanga* manufacturing are likely to inspire many innovations in the use of *khanga* fabric that would help in the evolution of textiles.

References

Abdela, Farouque. "Mimi Kama Kanga, Nafa na Uzuri Wangu" (I am like a Kanga Cloth. I Die in all my Beauty), in *Art in Eastern Africa*, ed. Marion Arnold. Dar es Salaam: Mkuki na Nyota, 2008, pp. 95–101.

Kimbokota, S.K. "A Study of Swahili Carved Doors", Unpublished MA Dissertation, Department of Creative Arts, University of Dar es Salaam, 2019.

Lichtenstein, Amanda Leigh. "Kanga's Woven Voices", 2017. Available online: https://www.aramcoworld.com/Articles/November-2017/Kanga-s-Woven-Voices (accessed on 7 February 2022).

Machado, Pedro. "Cloths of a New Fashion: Indian Ocean Networks of Exchange and Cloth Zones of Contact in Africa and India in the Eighteenth and Nineteenth Centuries", 2009. Available online: DOI: 10.1163/9789047429975_004 (accessed on 9 January 2025).

Meier, S.A. "Swahili Art as a Cultural and Political Text". Unpublished MA Dissertation, Graduate College, University of Iowa, 2000.

Nyerere, J.K. "The Indian Ocean as a Link", in *Freedom and Development/ Uhuru Na Maendeleo: A Selection from Writings and Speeches, 1968–1973*. Dar es Salaam: Oxford University Press, 1974, pp. 257–61.

———. "Developing Tasks of Non-Alignment" in *Freedom and Development/ Uhuru Na Maendeleo: A Selection from Writings and Speeches, 1968–1973*. Dar es Salaam: Oxford University Press, 1974, pp. 159–72.

Ressler, Phyllis. "The Kanga, A Cloth that Reveals: Co-production of Culture in Africa and the Indian Ocean Region". Textile Society of America Symposium Proceedings, Paper 736 (2012). Available online: http://digitalcommons.unl.edu/tsaconf/736 (accessed on 13 January 2022).

Sheriff, Abdul. "Swahili Culture and Art between Africa and the Indian Ocean", in *Art in Eastern Africa*, ed. Marion Arnold. Dar es Salaam: Mkuki na Nyota, 2008, pp. 65–84.

Swantz, Marja-Liisa. *Ritual and Symbol in Transitional Zaramu Society*. Uppsala: Scandinavian Institute of African Studies, 1986.

Wilson, Kax. *A History of Textiles*. Boulder, Colorado: Westview Press, 1979.

Chapter 19

Reading the Palimpsest: Mapping *Kanga* in the Indian Ocean Maritime Zone

Salome Mshai Mwangola

Introduction

No single textile is as intimately associated with the Eastern African region—particularly the nations of Kenya and Tanzania—as the rectangular pieces of cloth known as *kanga* or *leso*. Popular discourse and much academic research focus primarily on the textile's emergence in the latter part of the 19th century in the Swahili Coast seaports of Mombasa (historically known as Mvita) and Unguja (the main island of Zanzibar).[1] In the century since, *kanga* has become

1 The term "Swahili Coast" refers to the region encompassing a loosely connected network of city-states along the western rim of the Indian Ocean, stretching from present-day Somalia to present-day Mozambique. Linked by a shared culture—including language and religion—these city-states were autonomous, each with its own distinct system of governance. Historically, they functioned as liminal spaces where cultural and economic exchanges took place between the African hinterland and other civilisations, peoples and regions via the maritime bridge of the Indian Ocean. For a comprehensive overview of the history of the Swahili Coast, see Kusimba (1999). In this article, I will refer to these ports using both their historical and contemporary names. Mombasa (in present-day Kenya), for example, was once known as Mvita, a name still in use today, primarily in reference to a parliamentary constituency within what is now both a city

ubiquitous in these two countries and is also found in many others in the Eastern African region.

The *leso* is celebrated as "the cloth that speaks", mainly for two reasons. First, the majority are inscribed with a pithy legend that forms a prominent feature of the design. This not only distinguishes them but, more importantly, allows them to be strategically deployed as a means of communication. Second, *leso* have historically played a cultural role in several East African communities, especially among the Swahili. The mere presence of the cloth—whether worn on one's body, used in daily tasks, or displayed prominently—can be interpreted, within a context, as a form of performance (Rayya and Swaleh 2016; Zawawi 2005).

Here, I explore a third sense in which *kanga* "speaks". I reflect on the *kanga* as a palimpsest that offers a glimpse into the rich history of the pre-20th century Indian Ocean worlds. I consider how the very fabric itself—and the elements associated with it—point to the vibrancy of the cultural, social, political and economic interactions that have shaped the Eastern African seaboard over the centuries.

A note on nomenclature: In this paper, *kanga* and *leso* will be used interchangeably for reasons that will become clear in the discussion that follows.[2]

The Cloth That Speaks

The *leso* is a rectangular piece of cloth characterised by its distinctive material as well as its visual and verbal elements, which may vary from one design to another but retain an overall coherence. Traditionally made of cotton, *leso* is now also produced using other fabrics, including polyester blends. Their weight can range from light or heavy, depending on the thread count, making them suitable for different uses and contexts and determining their durability and

---

and a county. In this paper, "Mombasa" refers specifically to the historical city-state. Unguja is the principal island of the Zanzibar Archipelago (in present-day Tanzania), though the name "Zanzibar" is sometimes used to refer to Unguja itself.

2 Words in Kiswahili and other languages that have enriched standard English spoken in East Africa are indicated in italics.

Source: S. Mshai Mwangola.

Fig. 1: *Kanga.*

Jina: *Mwenyezi Mungu ndie atake nisaidia* (Almighty God is the one who will help me).

Copyright: Mali ya Chavda Zanzibar Jayshri ID 144*.

Design: *Mji*: Squares composed of circles enclosed by flower outlines in brown, placed above intricate green and brown four-pointed motifs reminiscent of *henna* patterns, set against a white background dotted with green.

Pindo: A row of brown heart shapes formed by leaf wreaths surrounding circles, on a black background.

---

* Jayshri (Fig. 1) and Atlas (Fig. 2) are textile companies in India that manufacture *kanga* for export to East Africa.

quality. They vary in size, ranging from 150 to 165 cm in length, and 105 cm to 115 cm in breadth.

Today, *leso* are manufactured commercially and sent to traders in rolls, with each roll having a width equivalent to that of a single piece. Each piece is marked off by a thick line running along the weft, where the trader cuts or tears off the fabric, usually in pairs known as *gora* (or *dhoti*). These pairs are then further separated into two identical pieces, which are traditionally finished by hemming along all four edges.

In the 21st century, *leso* material is often cut and sewn into a variety of items—clothing, furniture accessories, bags, and more—though traditionally the cloth was left intact as a versatile piece of fabric that could be purposed in different ways.

In addition to its characteristic size, the design unique to *kanga* consists of two distinct elements—visual and verbal—arranged in three zones. The largest of these is the *mji* (town), which occupies the central area of the fabric and is framed by a clearly defined border known as the *pindo*. The *pindo* is often set off from the *mji* by a series of boundary lines. At the four corners of the cloth, nestling between the intersecting lines of the *pindo*, are the *kilindo* (guards). This layout forms the foundation of the visual design.

Within this map, patterns are created by a variety of motifs. In the *mji*, one may find either a single giant motif surrounded by smaller contrasting ones—or even by empty space—or an intricate pattern of small, repetitive motifs, usually arranged in neat lines. This pattern may, in turn, consist of a single motif or a mix of motifs repeated to form a field. The motifs may be geometric shapes or representations of objects, both man-made and natural.

A contrasting arrangement of the same or different motifs is found in the *pindo*, which usually runs parallel to the edge of the cloth. The *kilindo*, sometimes inserted in each corner, consists of a single motif that is distinctly set apart from the others in the *pindo*. The visual pattern can give a particular design its *jina* (name) and suggest its use. For example, the iconic *kisutu* design, traditionally worn as bridal attire among the Swahili in Kenya and Tanzania, has since been adopted as a symbol of Giriama identity, and it remains one of the most popular designs in contemporary fashion.

The final visual element is colour. Designs are produced in a palette of five colours, with each design using two to four colours. Colour is in some cases a critical factor in determining meaning and use, but in most contexts, its choice is a matter of personal preference.

Source: S. Mshai Mwangola.

Fig. 2: *Leso* edge featuring *kilindo.*

Jina: *Hamtugombanishi mapenzi yetu hayaishi* (You will not provoke us to quarrel, our love will not end).

Copyright: Atlas Design Number 9134.

An orange peel-off sticker bears the legend: *Kiboko yao* Special *khangas* Atlas. 100 per cent cotton.

Design: *Mji* featuring a floral outline reminiscent of *henna* designs, detailed in dark brown with lighter brown shading, set against a yellow background with leaf motifs.

Note: Decorative brown borders separate the *mji* from the *pindo*, and the *pindo* from the dark brown selvedge, evoking the aesthetic of *bandhani* art.

Note: *Kilindo* motif contrasts with a line of *korosho* (cashew nut) motifs, all rendered in shades of brown and yellow.

These three zones are also important when it comes to the verbal elements of the *kanga*. The most prominent of these is the text box which contains the *msemo* (saying), which often gives the cloth its *jina* (name). This box is found along the lower border of the *mji*, just above the lower *pindo*. The *jina* may be derived from any number of sources—a proverb, riddle, popular song lyrics, literary quotation or simply a witty aphorism. It might respond to a specific issue or event, or be centred on a particular individual or collective. It could be a slogan of a political party or candidate, the motto of a civic education campaign, the name of a corporate body, or a brand catchphrase. While most of these sayings today are in Kiswahili, English and other languages, such as Arabic, occasionally appear as well.

A second verbal element, commonly found on *kangas*, is usually tucked away along the outer edges of the *pindo*. It consists of details of intellectual property such as the name of the design's owner, along with production information like fabric material, place of origin or place of manufacture.

More rarely, written text is incorporated into the visual design within the *mji*. This is almost always seen in *leso* commissioned by institutions or individuals, often intended to commemorate events or celebrate particular people.

It is the combination of these elements that gives *kanga* its distinctive identity and makes it such a versatile and valued medium for expressing cultural meaning, particularly among the Swahili people from whom it originated. Much has been written about the cultural role of specific designs such as *kisutu* in performing identity or establishing social roles as well as the ways in which women have used *kanga* to assert agency and "speak out" on issues of personal or communal significance, especially in socially sensitive contexts (Beck 2001; Yahya-Othman 1997).

While firmly rooted in Swahili culture, *kanga* has become a widely recognised and utilised garment across East Africa, cutting across boundaries of class, religion, nationality, ethnicity, and race. It has found its place in the religious and secular rites of passage conducted by East Africa's different communities, from naming and baby-welcoming to initiation, and from weddings to funerals.

Although traditionally associated with the Swahili people, who are predominantly Muslim, *kanga* today is embraced by people of diverse faiths and cultural ancestries. It is not uncommon, for example, to see Catholic nuns wearing *kangas* over their habits, or to find *kangas* bearing overtly Christian messages such as "Merry Christmas".

It has proved versatile as a cultural signifier, continually adapting to different contexts. A substantial body of historical documentation also traces the evolution of *kanga* designs over time as well as the ways in which individual designs have recorded significant events or amplified celebrations of momentous achievements, whether at individual, communal, organisational, national, or even regional and global levels (Ressler 2012; Ryan 2013).

How did the simple *leso* come to carry such powerful meaning? What drove its transformation into a vessel for diverse personal and collective narratives, rich with social, cultural, economic, and political significance? And how has it managed to retain its association with the Swahili as a distinct community, while simultaneously reflecting the stories and influences of so many others?

To answer these questions, I step back in time to peel away the layers of the palimpsest, hidden in plain sight within the material, visual and verbal elements of this unique textile.

The Fabric of Life

As noted above, the history of the *kanga* is deeply entwined with that of cotton. Only in the early 21st century did manufacturers begin experimenting with alternative fabrics—a shift some connoisseurs see as contradictory, given *kanga*'s strong association with cotton. Its origins are closely linked to the story of cotton within what I call the Indian Ocean Maritime Zone (IOMZ): a world system that is both geographical—in encompassing the physical lands and civilisations connected by the Indian Ocean—and socio-cultural, in the importance of exchange and complementarity.[3]

3 See also Fatima Harrak, "Conceptualising Globalisation in Africa", CODESRIA 15th General Assembly Plenary Session 2. Available online: https://www.youtube.com/watch?v=vSVLDjRbjRg (accessed on 6 January 2025).

Source: S. Mshai Mwangola.

Fig. 3: Contemporary *leso*, commissioned by a corporate company.

Jina: *Tulipe ushuru, tujitegemee*! (Let's pay tax, we become self-sufficient!).

Copyright: Design No: 6053 Made in Kenya.

Design: *Mji* featuring the name and logo of the commissioning organisation, Kenya Revenue Authority.** A lion head in profile, enclosed in a circle, is prominently displayed midway down the *mji*, with the organisation's motto as the *jina* in the text box below. The design uses the brand colours—white, black and red.

Pindo: Intricate black and white borders framed by two decorative bands: one with black and white motifs, the other with a line of red dots enclosed by circles. The pattern includes leaves and flowers reminiscent of *henna* designs.

** The Kenya Revenue Authority is the national agency responsible for tax collection in Kenya. The decorative border, featuring the *korosho* motif, styled as a flowering plant, symbolises prosperity. Similarly, the red line of dots inscribed inside circles might recall the coins with holes in the middle that once circulated in the region.

Scholars of the Indian Ocean have documented the rich and complex exchanges among civilisations in the region, from antiquity up to the 16th century, when a new global order began to take shape.

Describing the Indian Ocean as "the cradle of globalization", Shanti Moorthy, senior lecturer in Anatomy at Monash University, and Ashraf Jamal, senior lecturer in Art History and Visual Culture at Rhodes University, argue that "any study of the Indian Ocean will reveal the collision of the global and the local, not as a site for vulgar power and conquest, but [of] genuine and, by and large, peaceable exchange, prior to the development of European expansionism" (Moorthy and Jamal 2010, p. 3).

Since at least the 10th century, cotton has dominated the trade between Eastern Africa and Southern Asia, a relationship sustained by reliable monsoon winds that powered vessels across the waters.[4] But beyond its economic significance, the IOMZ was also a lively zone of cultural exchange—a space where diverse peoples met and where ideas, practices, and goods moved fluidly across shores.

Thus, the story of cotton in the IOMZ is not just about mapping trade routes or quantifying the flow of goods between ports but it is also about how those engaged with cotton, both as producers and consumers, shaped and were influenced by the wider social, cultural, political and economic contexts in which this trade unfolded.

The people of Eastern Africa have traditionally used a variety of plant and animal materials to produce clothing and textiles. Among these, cotton has held a particularly important place for centuries. Its use has steadily grown over time—both in terms of volume and the range of areas where it gained popularity—surpassing alternatives such as leather (from hide) or barkcloth. Although cotton was cultivated and processed into cloth in Eastern Africa as early as the 10th century—for example, in and around Mogadishu on the northern Swahili Coast—the region has also imported cotton for many centuries (Presthold 1998, pp. 27–29).[5]

4 On the historic evidence of trade between these two points dating back to the first century CE, and the importance of cotton among other goods traded over time, see Meera Venkatachalam, Renu Modi and Johann Salazar, *Common Threads: Fabrics made in India for Africa*, Leiden: African Studies Centre, vol. 76, p. 34.

5 Other fabrics, notably silk, were also produced but were generally too expensive for all but the most affluent; consequently, the use of cotton gradually increased over time until it came to be regarded as the material of the people in this region.

Two key factors contributed to this. First, cotton's versatility and adaptability made it so popular that, over time, demand began to outstrip local supply. Second, the fine quality and distinctive designs of imported cotton added prestige and affluence, increasing its desirability. So much so, by the 16th century, cotton was valued not only for everyday use but also as a form of economic, political, and diplomatic currency across the region.[6]

Historically, most of the imported handwoven cotton came from the Indian peninsula and was exchanged for animal products such as ivory and hides as well as agricultural produce like grain. While the slave trade did exist during this period, it was relatively small in scale compared to later times.

By the 15th century, cotton from Asia—particularly from Kutch and Gujarat in the Indian subcontinent—had become one of Eastern Africa's most significant imports. Seaports like Mombasa became the entry points for this trade, with goods destined not only for the coastal areas but also deep into the hinterlands, reaching as far as Ujiji (on the shores of Lake Tanganyika) and beyond.

By the time the first European vessels came to the Indian Ocean in the 15th century, trade was already a commercial mainstay along the Swahili Coast. With the coming of the Portuguese—the first Europeans to gain a foothold in the region in the 16th century—the culture of the IOMZ began to change substantially. Although these new entrants initially appeared interested only in establishing new trade partnerships and seemed destined to play a peripheral role in existing networks of exchange, they soon introduced two disruptive forces: advanced weaponry and a philosophy of violent domination that would irrevocably alter the prevailing order of the IOMZ and pave the way for European imperialism.

It was more by serendipity than strategy that Portugal found itself ahead of other European powers that would soon flood into the IOMZ, attracted by its wealth. Portugal established a foothold in Goa on the

6 Venkatachalam et al (2020), pp. 40, 45, 48.

Indian peninsula and, for about two centuries, struggled to control the lucrative trade routes that provided access to it. Ultimately, they did not sustain their dominance in the region, although they did hold sway for a time over several key ports critical to the Eastern African trade zone, stretching from present-day Mozambique to the northern city-states of what is now Somalia.

Portugal's economic grip on the Swahili Coast was finally broken in the late 17th century by the arrival of a multi-state force led by the Sultan Seyyid Said of Oman. Responding to appeals from leaders of city-states such as Mombasa, the Omanis came as liberators but they did not retreat once the Portuguese had been expelled. Instead, they settled down, establishing themselves as the new rulers of the very city-states they had helped to free. Sultan Said eventually moved the capital of his sultanate from Muscat to Zanzibar.

By the mid-18th century, Zanzibar had become a sultanate in its own right, ruled by Majid bin Said, one of Sultan Seyyid Said's sons. Though nominally independent, Majid's sultanate continued to pay tribute to Oman. The Omanis had firmly established themselves as the new power brokers along the Swahili Coast, controlling the ports that served as gateways to the lucrative trade with the hinterland.

Not only did they increase the volume of goods passing through the island but Seyyid Said also established large clove plantations to take advantage of the expanding global spice market. These plantations would eventually make Zanzibar the world's leading producer of cloves. The Omanis became the principal intermediaries in regional and long-distance trade, making Zanzibar the political and economic centre of the Swahili Coast.

With the Portuguese retreating south into Mozambique and north to Goa, other Western powers began to enter the region, engaging in trade and competing both with one another and with the long-established partners of the IOMZ. The Industrial Revolution in Europe further transformed the cotton economy in Eastern Africa, flooding the market with cheap, machine-woven textiles from countries such as Britain and the Netherlands.

Over time, however, European dominance in the textile trade was matched, and then eclipsed, by a rising Western power: the United

States of America—which entered the market with a superior brand of cotton that would soon become the standard bearer in the region.

All newcomers importing cotton into Eastern Africa in this period quickly learnt that the market was a highly discerning one. Those who assumed they could trade inferior cloth in the hinterland soon found that this approach would not do. The region's consumers were highly sophisticated, with fashion trends changing rapidly and consumers becoming increasingly selective. Spoiled for choice, they were exacting about the quality of cloth they were willing to purchase and use, forcing traders to adapt to the local market as opposed to the other way around.

This consumer-driven environment created an optimum environment for the proliferation of a dazzling variety of fabrics in the East African market, where, by the 19th century, cotton cloth had come to dominate. There was increasing demand for the products of the region, as companies from Boston to Manchester, and from Bombay to Amsterdam, competed for a foothold in this lucrative and influential market.

With Eastern Africa gaining a global reputation for exporting high-value luxury goods such as spices, ivory, gum copal and animal hides, there was no shortage of international buyers eager to trade. As a result, the region became a dominant player in the global economy. Manufacturers around the world scrambled to meet the demands of East African consumers, making the region a powerful catalyst for technological innovation, particularly in the growth of the textile industry, in economies as far apart as the US and India.

As Professor Jeremy Prestholdt observes, "In choosing to buy immense amounts of Indian cloth, East African consumers... stimulated Bombay's industrialisation". For, in order to serve this market, "Salemites built the first steam-powered textile mill in the United States while Bombay embarked on a program that would make it the industrial centre of the Indian Ocean region by the end of the 19th century" (Prestholdt 2004, p. 779).

American dominance over the cotton trade was established by the early 19th century. The distinctive cotton grown in the southern

United States and exported from New England ports acquired a reputation for durability and longevity earning it the local moniker *merikani*. The main competitors were the British, although Indian merchants also sought creative ways to sustain their centuries-old trade relationships with the region. The latter had one big advantage: unlike their Western counterparts, who relied heavily on middlemen, Indian traders had long-standing ties with established partners in the region (some of whom traced their ancestry back to India), and could therefore navigate the market with greater ease and trust.

To reduce costs and remain competitive, the British began exporting cotton manufactured in factories they had set up in India. For a while, this became the source of so-called "British" cotton in the region. Although more affordable than the superior American product, it could not displace *merikani* from its position of prestige, especially amongst the elite. It was only when the American Civil War disrupted supply chains and reduced the availability of *merikani* that the American share of the market began to fall, and finally dwindle into relative inconsequence.

If the British expected to reap the spoils of the American retreat, they were to be disappointed. Their factories in India soon came under pressure from new, locally-owned competitors, as Indian entrepreneurs adopted Western production techniques and set up their own textile mills. By 1880, it was these Indian-owned factories in Bombay that were leading the exports to Eastern Africa, leveraging the priceless human connections provided by their intermediaries on the ground. These middlemen made it possible for their Indian partners to anticipate shifting fashion trends and produce cloth in patterns, designs, colours and sizes that appealed to the region's diverse consumer taste.

This responsiveness became particularly important, as it grew increasingly cost-effective for manufacturers to move away from the plain, unbleached cotton that had dominated for centuries, and towards mass production of a range of coloured and patterned fabrics. This shift laid the foundation for the emergence of the distinctive cloth we now know as *leso* or *kanga*.

What's in a Name?

While there is no certain date for the emergence of this textile and competing myths of origin exist, some facts are generally agreed upon. First, it emerged as a distinct cloth with a unique design in the second half of the 19th century. Second, it was women who were primarily responsible for its development, even though male merchants played an important role in midwifing it into being. And finally, the port cities of Unguja (Zanzibar) and Mombasa are central to its evolution, and thus this cloth bears witness to the multiple cultures and rich histories of the geographical and socio-cultural context that shaped it.

The two names, by which the textile is known, *kanga* and *leso*, reflect the most popular accounts of its origin. The most widely used term is *kanga*, which historically is associated with the southern part of the Swahili Coast, and most specifically with Unguja in Zanzibar. It is this dialect of Kiswahili—ki-Unguja—that forms the basis for what is today known as Kiswahili Sanifu (Standard Swahili), which has been formalised as the "official" version of Kiswahili.[7] Perhaps this is why *kanga* is the name by which the cloth is best known. *Leso,* on the other hand, is the term more commonly used in the northern Swahili-speaking regions, particularly in the ki-Mvita and ki-Amu dialects spoken in Mvita (Mombasa) and Lamu, respectively. That both words exist is a reminder of the historical autonomy of the city-states, which began to wane under Omani rule, even though people's sense of identification with their cities did not entirely disappear.

---

7 Each of the Swahili city-states had a unique identity and culture, most notably marked by dialect. The traditional dialect of Unguja (ki-Unguja) became the basis for the earliest bilingual dictionaries developed by the English after Zanzibar became a British protectorate in 1890. Later, Britain ventured inland, eventually establishing the East African Protectorate, then the Kenya Colony (1920). In 1947, mainland Tanganyika became a United Nations Trust Territory under British administration. Kiswahili emerged as the region's lingua franca, and to facilitate its use as an administrative language across all the areas under its control, the British regularised the use of this standard dialect. After independence, Tanzania (formed after the legal union of Tanganyika and Zanzibar) and Kenya adopted Kiswahili as their national official language. It is also recognised as the official language of the East African Community.

Kanga is the name of a bird, the guinea fowl. One of the oldest *kanga* pattern motifs is said to recall the guinea fowl's distinctive black and white plumage. According to popular lore, some thought that a group of women clad in the fabric resembled—and even sounded like—a flock of guinea fowls. But there may also be a more poignant history behind the name.

Source: S. Mshai Mwangola.

Fig. 4: *Kanga* (Guinea fowl) mural on the wall of Moi International Airport Mombasa, Domestic Departures Lounge.

Artist credit: Theo of Spyrocraft, Nairobi.

As previously mentioned, the advent of Omani rule brought a rapid expansion of trade to and through Zanzibar, including the trafficking of enslaved people. Many remained on the island, working in households and on the spice plantations that became an important economic mainstay during this period. The clothing provided to these people was generally a length of unbleached cotton, which women would wear in the standard two-piece style popular across the region. The cloth was roughly sized to wrap securely around the female body.

For enslaved and impoverished women who could not afford *merikani*, the alternative was cheaper, lower-grade cotton imported from or via India such as *kaniki,* which was dyed dark to conceal stains. In contrast, the status of free-born or emancipated women was often indicated by the quality of the cloth they wore. Those who could not afford *merikani,* decorative prints or finely dyed or hand-stamped cloth are believed to have created their own decorated prints, using indigenous and endogenous techniques of block printing to soften the severity of the cloth.

The easiest design to replicate was simply the addition of myriad white spots on dark cloth or the reverse—a motif that enterprising merchants quickly commissioned from factories in India and imported in bulk, making it even more affordable and available. The rest, as they say, is history.

There is a footnote to this discussion: some prefer the spelling "*khanga*" over "*kanga*". Author Sharifa M. Zawawi points to the onomatopoeia of the Arabic words *karquah* (piece of cloth) and *kharq,* referring to the action of tearing across the weft to produce individual pieces. She wonders whether these terms may have influenced the naming of the cloth (Zawawi 2005, p. 129). If so, this connection may reinforce the Omani-era origins, reminding us that the prototype for the *khanga* was likely a length of cotton cloth, torn to an appropriate size for use as a wrapper.

The word *leso,* on the other hand, is derived from the Portuguese word *lenço,* meaning handkerchief or bandana. These cotton bandanas were square pieces of cloth with a standard design that consisted of a pattern of motifs in the centre with a decorative border. The *lenço* were imported in rolls, which merchants would cut into individual pieces for sale. According to oral histories, women began sewing together two rows of three *lenço* to create a single, inexpensive, yet beautifully decorated printed cloth large enough to cover the body. This garment became known as *leso ya kushona* (sewn-together *lenço*).

Once again, merchants took note of its popularity and began commissioning factories to produce cloth in a new size, using the dimensions of the *leso ya kushona.* The new, full-length printed cloth, dubbed *leso* as a nod to its origins, quickly became a staple item in local markets. In this way, the word *leso* continues to evoke the historical presence of the Portuguese on the Swahili Coast.

Is one story more accurate or earlier than the other? Does it matter? It is highly likely that the cloth's emergence was influenced by both ancestries. Taken together, the origins of the three names—*kanga, khanga* and *leso*—reflect a history of cultural interaction among peoples across continents. They stand as a testament to the cosmopolitan nature of the socio-cultural spaces from which this fabric arose.

Layers of Meaning

The history sketched above sets the stage for understanding the material elements of *kanga.* It helps explain why cotton emerged as the fabric of choice at the time that it did, and how its wide availability made quality cotton accessible in sufficient quantities to become affordable to many across the region. In addition, it contextualises the rationale behind other elements that have since become distinctive features of what we now know as *kanga.* I will briefly consider some of these below.

As mentioned earlier, *leso* is gendered in that it is generally associated with women, even though several communities have, over time, adopted and adapted *kanga* for male use. Among the Swahili, however, *leso* was and still is primarily a marker and performer of female identity. It is, therefore, not surprising that *leso*'s unique size is linked to its mythic origins as a piece of cloth designed first and foremost to be wrapped around a woman's body.

While there have always been some variations in style, these can be traced back to traditions of women's dress from this era within the larger region that produced the prototype known as *nguo mbili*—two identical pieces of cloth used for clothing. The size of each piece was determined by an approximation of the length needed to wrap around the average female body, with enough width to extend from just under the arms to somewhere about mid-calf.

This size of cloth was by no means standardised when *leso* first emerged at the end of the 19th century, and not all manufacturers were enthusiastic about adjusting their production to suit the dimensions women preferred. Since women would also use a second piece of cloth either as a headdress or as an additional body wrap running from the hips to the feet, *leso* were generally packaged and, as mentioned, sold in pairs.

The inclusion of verbal elements in *kanga* design is also part of the historical layers that give the cloth its cultural meaning. Most iconic of all is the *misemo* that have become the focus of much scholarly and popular interest. And this, too, has a fascinating history.

Kaderdina (Abdulkader) Hajee Essak, popularly known as Abdulla, was a cloth trader in Mombasa credited with pioneering the use of sayings in *kanga* designs. In 1843, his father, Essak Bharadia, arrived in Zanzibar from Mandvi (in Kutch, India) at the age of 13, in search of a better life. After working for a trader in Zanzibar for several months, he moved to Mombasa, from where he embarked on several expeditions into the hinterland, in trade caravans where calico cotton was part of the merchandise. Eventually, he saved enough to start his own business in Mombasa. He later returned to Kutch to marry before settling back in Mombasa with his family.

His son Kaderdina took over and established his own business in 1887. He is credited with standardising the inclusion of *misemo* as a design element. This was not an entirely original idea, as it was already common at the time to find text added to cloth in Arabic script, often with religious (Islamic) content. An innovative move made by Kaderdina was to notice how women, who patronised or worked in his shop, named the different designs to distinguish them. He found a way to make these names part of the printed design itself.

Sometimes the names referred directly to a motif on the cloth. At other times, women associated the patterns with lines from literature, music or witty sayings. Kaderdina began collaborating with these women to select *misemo* that captured the spirit of particular occasions or seasons when the *kanga* might be bought or worn. They chose easily recognisable lines of literary or musical texts, gathered "quotable quotes" from everyday speech, or coined trenchant messages that conveyed meaning in a range of contexts.

Initially, the text was inscribed in Arabic script, which was in use at the time among the Swahili. However, in the 20th century, after the Sultan handed over administration of what came to be known as

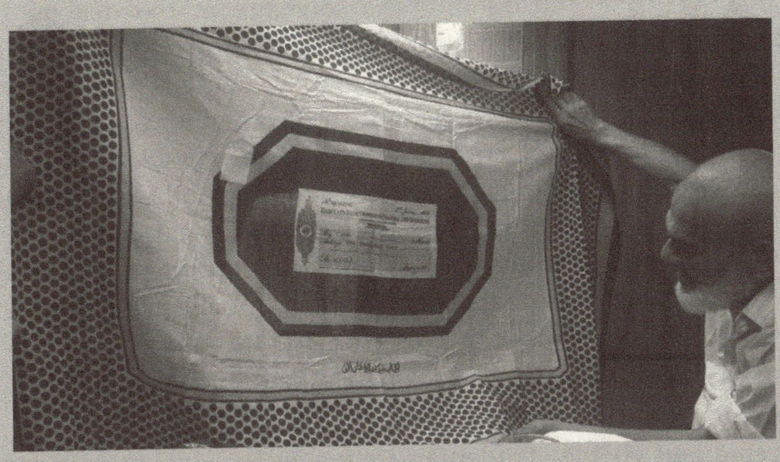

Source: S. Mshai Mwangola.

Fig. 5: Historic (Commissioned) corporate *leso*.

Abdulhamid Kaderdina of Kaderdina Hajee Essak Limited displays a 1938 *leso* from the archive.

Design: *Mji* features a Barclays Bank (Dominion, Colonial and Overseas) cheque for 10,000 shillings, set on a brown hexagonal shape outlined in yellow and bordered in brown.

Note: Includes a legend in Arabic script, reportedly indicating the cheque amount of 10,000 shillings.

the Coastal Strip to the British, the colonial authorities imposed the Latin alphabet in which the majority of the texts would be printed.

The descendants of Essak continued to run the family business, popularly known as Duka la Abdulla, serving as an enduring reminder of the generations of merchants from the Indian subcontinent who settled in Eastern Africa and became part of this history.[8]

8 This business is today best known as the home of the famous "Mali ya Abdull" *leso* brand (widely regarded as one of the most prestigious Kenyan *leso* copyright brands). The shop also offers a variety of other *leso* brands and other cloth products. It has been located at its current premises on Biashara Street, Mombasa, for over a century.

As noted earlier, tucked into the selvedge of the design, just beneath the *pindo*, is information relating to copyright and/or the origin of the cotton used to make a particular *leso*. This practice dates back to the competitive era when manufacturers stamped unbleached cotton with assurances of authenticity, such as *merikani* from New England. Well-known manufacturers often included their trademarks on the cloth as well. Wearing this quality cloth became a matter of pride, with people prominently displaying the trademark, much like today, when some consumers buy or wear brands associated with superior quality as a symbol of prestige.

While this information was printed in the selvedge so it could be hidden in the hem of the *kanga*, some found ways to ensure the brand remained visible. Trademarks such as "Lowell" were signs of prestige proudly displayed by those wearing authentic *merikani* in the 19th century. This tradition of quality verification continued into the 20th century, with printed copyright details automatically added to certain brands, designers and copyright holders.

Many connoisseurs today only purchase or wear *kanga* from particular factories, manufacturers or designers.[9] Choices are also influenced by the origin of the cotton. In different historical eras, cotton from particular regions in Africa, Asia, Europe or North America was in high demand within specific market sectors, making it commercially advantageous to highlight that information on the cloth. This could be due to patriotic pride or consumer beliefs that cotton from certain places is of superior quality.

Related to this are the differing attitudes people hold towards *leso* that is not made of 100 per cent cotton. Some consumers are wary of *kanga* that does not declare its cotton content, either because they feel *kanga* must be made entirely of cotton or because they regard cotton as the most versatile fabric.

---

9 This is comparatively rare, as copyright is usually held by the commissioning business. However, some designers have become iconic in their own right, such as Tanzanian designer Kassamali Gulamhussein Peera, popularly known as Miwani Mdogo ("small spectacles") and Hashim A. Nakanoga, as documented by Ryan (2016, pp. 426–7).

Fig. 6: Three *kanga pindo.*

From top:

(A) K.H.E. Regd. Maliya Abdulla Mombasa – Kenya (http://www.maliyaabdulla.com).

Design: Motifs of *korosho* or *embe* (mango) in brown and yellow, resembling calabashes, on a white background. Black border along the selvedge.

(B) "Design no. 6053 Made in Kenya" (see Fig. 3).

Design: Geometric elements (dots, circles, ovals and lines) in black and red. Features a stylised plant with *korosho*-like leaves and flower motifs reminiscent of *henna,* set on white with a black selvedge border.

(C) *Nida Nzito kanga* (heavy *kanga*) *Pamba ya* Tanzania (Tanzanian cotton) Giga: 7424.

Design: Contemporary heart shapes combined with traditional dots, lines and circles in dark brown, on an orange background. Dark brown border along the selvedge.

Finally, it is worth noting how the visual elements of *kanga* design reflect the region's history and multi-stranded traditions. The origins of the basic design have been discussed in relation to the three zones traditionally found—the *mji*, *pindo* and *kilindo*. One of the most fascinating aspects of *kanga* design is the selection of the motifs that adorn the fabric. Some of these are geometric shapes, often considered to represent a distinctly African aesthetic. Notably, one of the most popular motifs is the simple dot that is credited with giving the cloth its name. To this day, it remains so popular that some do not consider a *kanga* authentic unless dots are present in its design.

Yet others look for another beloved motif, the *korosho* (cashew nut) or *embe* (mango) whose curved shape is instantly recognisable to those familiar with the classical Indian *ambi* motif. It is surely no coincidence that this shape is seen as a symbol of fertility in both the Indian subcontinent and along the Swahili Coast. In this, and in artistic traditions such as *bandhani* and *henna*, which clearly reflect the influence of other civilisations of the IOMZ, we are constantly reminded of the generosity and reciprocity of the cultural exchanges that have defined and sustained this region for centuries.

Conclusion

In this reflection on the unique East African textile known as the *leso* or *kanga*, I have demonstrated how it functions as a reminder of the rich cultural, socio-political and economic history of the Indian Ocean Maritime Zone. I have examined the material, visual and verbal elements that distinguish it from other textiles and explored how they encode layers of meaning documenting human interactions along the Swahili Coast and deep into the eastern hinterland of the Africa over a period of 10 centuries. I show how cultures from four continents—Africa, Asia, Europe and North America—contributed to the emergence of this cloth, thus challenging notions of globalisation and cosmopolitanism that are tied to the present moment. In doing so, I celebrate this unique palimpsest, a "common treasure" whose riches await discovery by the keen excavator.

Acknowledgements

I am grateful to the proprietors and staff of Kaderdina Hajee Essak Limited, particularly the family patriarch and immediate past Managing Director, *Mzee* Abdulhamid Kaderdina, as well as his son, the current Managing Director, Muneeb Kaderdina, for sharing with me the history of this longstanding family business. The interview was conducted on 18 September 2019 at the Kaderdina Hajee Essak Limited business premises (Duka la Abdulla), Biashara Street, Mombasa.

I also thank Abubakar Zein Abubakar for introducing me to the ways in which maritime civilisations, such as the Swahili, anchored since time immemorial along the shores of the Indian Ocean, understood the ocean not as a wall that divided them but as a bridge that facilitated connections among the peoples of the region.

References

Beck, Rose Marie. “Ambiguous Signs: The Role of the Kanga as a Medium of Communication”, AAP 68 Swahili Forum, vol. 8 (2001): pp. 157–69.

Harrak, Fatima. “Conceptualising Globalisation in Africa”, CODESRIA 15th General Assembly Plenary Session 2. Available online: https://www.youtube.com/watch?v=vSVLDjRbjRg (viewed on 6 January 2025).

Kusimba, Chapurukha Makokha. *The Rise and Fall of Swahili States*. Altamira Press, Walnut Creek, 1999.

Moorthy, Shanti, and Ashraf Jamal. “Introduction”, in *Indian Ocean Studies: Cultural, Social and Political Perspectives*. New York: Routledge (2001), pp. 1–30.

Prestholdt, Jeremy. “‘As Artistry Permits and Custom May Ordain’: The Social Fabric of Material Consumption in the Swahili World, circa 1450–1600”, PAS Working Papers 3 (1998).

———. “On the Global Repercussions of East African Consumerism”. *American Historical Review* vol. 109, no. 3 (2004): pp. 755–81.

Ressler, Phyllis. “The Kanga, A Cloth that Reveals: Co-production of Culture in Africa and the Indian Ocean Region”. Textile Society of America

Symposium Proceedings, Paper 736 (2012). Available online: http://digitalcommons.unl.edu/tsaconf/736 (accessed on 6 June 2020).

Ryan, MacKenzie Moon. "The Global Reach of a Fashionable Commodity: A Manufacturing and Design History of *Kanga* Textiles", Doctoral dissertation, University of Florida, 2013.

———. "Kanga Textile Design, Education, and Production in Contemporary Dar es Salaam, Tanzania", Textile Society of America Symposium Proceedings 1002 (2016): pp. 424–33. Available online: http://digitalcommons.unl.edu/tsaconf/1002 (accessed on 6 June 2020).

Timmamy, Rayya, Amiri Swaleh. "Ulimwengu wa Kanga". *The University of Nairobi Journal of Language and Linguistics* vol. 5 (2016): pp. 195–203.

Venkatachalam, Meera, Renu Modi and Johann Salazar. *Common Threads: Fabrics made in India for Africa.* Leiden: African Studies Centre, 2020.

Yahya-Othman, Saida. "If the Cap Fits: Kanga Names and Women's Voice in Swahili Society". *Afrikanistische Arbeitspapiere* (AAP) no. 51 (1997): pp. 135–49.

Zawawi, Sharifa M. *Kanga: The Cloth that Speaks.* The Bronx, New York: Azaniya Hills Press, 2005.

PART 6
India–Africa Partnership

Chapter 20
The Indians in Madagascar

Michèle Rakotoson

The History of the Indian Population in Madagascar

Indians have been present in Madagascar for at least four centuries, as per historical records (Blanchy 2008, p. 3). Madagascar is part of the Indian Ocean region, which includes the west coast of India, the southern part of the Arabian Peninsula, East and Southern Africa, Comoros, Madagascar and the Mascarene Islands (including the Republic of Mauritius).

In Madagascar, the community is primarily made up of Gujaratis. Before the 18th century, Gujaratis traded with East Africa, exporting silk fabrics, cotton and medicinal plants in exchange for slaves, gold and ivory. Above all, they wove a web of economic relations between India, Persia, the Gulf countries and Africa. This led to the development of a distinct culture, the Shirazi (Somali) culture, which is still very visible in western and northern Madagascar and in the Comoros Archipelago. The national museum displays numerous artefacts found in Madagascar—earthenware, silver jewellery (particularly bracelets), wood carvings, raw silk weaves, men's clothing from Malabar, and carved doors—that are often attributed to the Arabs though, in fact, they are of Indian origin.

The Indian influence in Madagascar is considerable as they are scattered throughout the country. Even in small villages, one can find hardware dealers and jewellers. The jeweller to the last queen was an Indian whose descendants still live in Madagascar. During royal festivals at the palace, there were men and women who dressed in Indian costume. The prime ministerial palace has a dome, likely the work of an Indian architect whose name was not recorded, simply because he was not European.

It is in Western Madagascar that the Indian influence is strongest. Trade is dominated by Indians, and their descendants are now entering the political arena, serving as members of parliament representing the Malagasy regions they come from. Yet, this contribution is rarely acknowledged in ethnological and historical works on Madagascar. While much is said about the negative aspects, such as various kinds of trafficking, this represents a veritable case of concealment of a very important aspect of Malagasy history.

The second wave of Indians arrived in Madagascar at the end of the 19th and the beginning of the 20th centuries. These migrants were mostly indentured labourers from the poorest sections of society. From 1848 onwards, with the introduction of the indentured labour system, the largest contingent of Indians arrived from Gujarat, which was facing an economic crisis at the time. The Bohra, Khoja and Baniya communities settled along the west coast of Madagascar. The migration peaked between 1910 and 1915.

Novelist Raphaël Confiant tells the story of the exodus to Martinique and how Indians integrated with the local population in *La panse du chacal* (translated as *The Cane Cutter's Song* by Vidya Vencatesan). In Madagascar, apart from a few Indians who arrived much earlier but did not settle, the majority of Indians came as indentured labourers during the colonial period, when the foundations of the Malagasy kingdom were undermined. Integration was more difficult during this time, as local communities had closed in on themselves in an effort to resist the colonial bulldozer.

This generation of migrants came from a background that had assimilated more elements of Western culture. For them, the backup plan was to try and acquire French nationality, while still remaining distinctly "Indian" and nurturing their own traditions. They brought with them a culture that was better equipped to resist colonisation.

However, the problem today is that many of their descendants are stateless.

Moreover, it should be noted that greater integration in the western part of Madagascar was due to the stronger religious impact of Islam, resulting from the Shirazian culture. Malagasy people of Persian origin—the Antalaotras—worked more closely with the Indians than Indian Muslims did with Malagasy Christians, who were harder to influence. The expansion of Christianity during this time was so dynamic that other communities kept themselves inconspicuous. In this context, however, we must mention the increasingly important role played by Hindus on the humanitarian front and their significant contributions to social and cultural foundations.

The Impact of the Indian Community in Madagascar

Madagascar has less than 15,000 people of Indian origin, though the number would be higher if we include those of mixed racial origin and the stateless. In terms of population, they represent less than 0.10 per cent of the total. However, this minority is prominent due to its economic heft. The majority of its members run businesses or industrial enterprises, ranging from humble to highly developed, and play an important role in the country's economy, contributing a third of the Malagasy GDP.

This economic role has a long lineage. The 1894 Directory shows that Indians exclusively controlled trade on the western side of Madagascar. There was considerable trading activity, especially with the east coast of Africa, which was almost entirely carried out using dhows. Most Indians never went back home and instead reinvested their profits locally. This commercial activity was largely managed by family-owned businesses dispersed across Madagascar, particularly along the west coast. There are also some important companies in Antananarivo, the capital.

Realities of the Indian Community in Madagascar

In Madagascar, the Indian community is known as Karana. Formerly written as *Karany*, the term derives from the Koran (as the majority of Indians in Madagascar are Muslims), but it also has Gujarati roots.

In the last century, Gujaratis used the term *karianjee* or *karany* to refer to one of the three people in charge of Indian merchant vessels: the *malam* (captain responsible for navigation), the *tandel* (head of crew and supplies), and the *karany*, who was in charge of the cargo and its entry and exit registers. This indicates an ancient trading tradition, which enabled them to prosper in Madagascar.

Unfortunately, the Indian community currently faces several barriers to full integration. The law regulating foreigners restricts their professional activities, barring them from certain professions and prohibiting the acquisition of real estate without prior authorisation. As a result, Indians must repeatedly apply to renew their residence permits, as any stay beyond three months means a life-long stay, from birth to death. However, some who have settled in Madagascar for generations have been granted permanent residence permits.

Socially, the Indian and Malagasy communities are both endogamous, which makes mixing between them almost impossible, thereby rendering the situation delicate.

This problem is less serious on the western and northern coasts, where integration is more vibrant and where many "mixed-race *karana*" play an important socio-economic role. Currently, a lot of work is being done by young Indians, in particular by those who establish and direct foundations, like the Hiridjee, Akbaraly and Aga Khan Foundations. These organisations are mainly active in the social domain: setting up schools, promoting women's education and increasingly contributing to the field of culture, as seen with the Akbaraly Prize.

The findings may appear discouraging, but if we consider the realities on the ground and acknowledge the potential for dual nationalities, these young Malagasys of Indian origin (third and fourth generation) could be the go-betweens, alongside the Malagasy youth. It is important to remember that poverty remains widespread in the country—80 per cent of the population may never board a flight and risk being excluded from many forms of development. This reality is reflected in everyday life: mechanics repairing old cars often turn to Indian suppliers, pharmacies sell affordable generic drugs made in India and much of the solar equipment in use also comes from India.

References

Blanchy, Sophie. "The Impact of Political, Economical and Juridical Context on Identifications in the Indian Gujarati 'Diaspora'", HAL, 24 February 2008. Available online: https://hal.science/hal-00988227v1/document (accessed on 1 January 2025).

Confiant, Raphaël. *La panse du chacal* (translated as *The Cane Cutter's Song* by Vidya Vencatesan). Paris: Mercure de France, 2004.

Chapter 21

India and Africa: For a Dynamic Cultural Partnership

A. Racine Senghor

My subject is inspired by my experience as Head of the Monument of the African Renaissance and by the close institutional ties between this body, under the Ministry of Culture of Senegal, and India, facilitated through the diplomatic representation of this longstanding partner and friend of Senegal.

I would like to re-look at the history of India and Africa with a view to the future, to recall the cooperation initiated by President Léopold Sédar Senghor, to highlight Mahatma Gandhi's influence on the course of the world, and, in conclusion, to offer some perspectives on the partnership between India and Africa.

Africa and India share historic ties that are both ancient and deep. Both regions were colonised, endured its consequences and were profoundly shaped by it, making colonisation a significant part of their collective history. This history is important insofar as it represents a form of encounter between peoples, perhaps not the most desirable kind, but an encounter nonetheless. At the very least, it offers lessons from which we can learn. These lessons help in building the future—a future often marked by struggle, resistance, bullying and the blending of races.

When two peoples meet, conflict often arises, but cultural mixing always occurs. Colonisation inherently involves a desire for 'culturicide': to negate or alienate the culture of the colonised. The strongest resistance to this alienation is to remain true to oneself.

India and Africa have, for the most part, succeeded in this struggle against alienation, safeguarding their native cultures. It is on this invaluable and particularly "fruitful" ground that their partnership should be built.

The Monument of the African Renaissance, situated on one of the two hills known as "Les Mamelles", is a sculpture symbolising an African family. It faces the Atlantic, the Americas and the wider world. The family emerges with an irrepressible force, pushing beyond the shackles of the past towards the radiant light of a future founded on dignity, built by Africans themselves, without xenophobia.

This monument has become a site with which Africa and its children scattered across a vast diaspora around the world strongly identify. It is, above all, a recreational space and a preferred venue for intellectual, cultural and artistic exchanges. It has also established solid relations with the Embassy of India, hosting many activities with the Indian community in Senegal. It houses a square developed by India, named India Tiranga Park. The name is significant: the word *Tiranga* exists in both Indian languages and Wolof. In India, it refers to the "three colours" of the national flag, while in Senegal, it conveys the spirit of hospitality.

Shared Values Inspired by Mahatma Gandhi

If one were to ask who is the subtle inspirer of this beautiful "fusion", the answer would be Mahatma Gandhi, whose life and work were the focus of a year-long exhibition, and whose bust, gifted by the Embassy of India, figures prominently in the great hall for the monument. In my opinion, Gandhi should serve as a guiding figure in efforts to boost our partnership. His legacy and the reflections it continues to inspire are excellent benchmarks for meaningful action.

Gandhi's assassination on 30 January 1948 reverberated across the globe like an earthquake. The trauma of the Second World War still haunted minds; eyes remained haggard with grief, mourning the millions of soldiers and civilians from five continents who had perished in an unprecedented wave of human barbarism (a barbarism which, alas, still persists today in less spectacular but equally tragic, inhuman and unacceptable forms).

Peace was still uncertain. The international community had only just begun to set up institutions like UNESCO in the hope of securing a lasting peace. And it was in this setting of a fragile, breaking dawn that the greatest defender of peace the world had known fell to blind bullets. Announcing this devastating loss to the people of India and the world, Jawaharlal Nehru's words were deep and chilling: "The light has gone out from our lives and there is darkness everywhere. And I do not know what to tell you and how to say it. Our beloved leader, Bapu as we called him, the Father of the Nation, is no more" (Nehru 1984, p. 35).

For me, as for millions of others, Gandhi, the charismatic apostle of non-violence, will always remain an indelible representation of moral idealism. His image reminds me of Master Thierno, a symbolic character from the novel *The Ambiguous Adventure* by Senegalese author Cheikh Hamidou Kane (1961). This "photographic", and perhaps even spiritual, connection has existed in my mind since my high school days. Through my readings, I came to know these two figures—so distant in terms of their countries and so different in culture, societal roles and professional paths, yet bound by a shared moral authority.

Master Thierno is depicted as a deeply religious man, uncompromising in his reverence for the Word of God and the purity of Islam. This devotion leads him to exert physical discipline on his frail disciples—actions not meant as cruelty, but as expressions of love, intended to steer them along the path he has traced towards God and salvation.

Gandhi, by contrast, is the apostle of non-violence, yet equally a man of faith devoted to the cause of humanity, which he understood as the custodian of universal values and mutual respect. The similarity I sensed both as a child and later as an adult was their shared concern to shape a new kind of human being: one who embodies a pure ideal and helps chart a path forward that all people, regardless of background, belief or race can walk together.

Cheikh Hamidou Kane bases his stories on real people and situations. For me, Gandhi embodies Thierno, giving him a visible and tangible presence through his daily engagement with the "children of the earth". Thierno, the master, is described as follows: "The man is old, thin and emaciated, shriveled up due to his macerated skin". There is, therefore, a strong physical resemblance between the two as well as a similarity in their ideals.

Naturally, when I think of Thierno, I see Gandhi. In a similar way, through what one might call a translational effect, I also see other Senegalese religious figures: men wholly devoted to prayer and meditation, who sought to elevate people to their true human dignity through the channels of peace. These figures from my country and culture reflect an ideal image of a man whose life is dedicated to the collective destiny of his people. Their humility lies in their commitment to safeguarding that destiny; their gaze is cast not on themselves but on those whose burdens and sorrows they carry. Among them are the Sufi Cheikh Ahmadou Bamba Mbacké (1853–1927) who led a peaceful campaign against colonialism; the religious leader El-Hadji Malick Sy (1853–1922); the warrior-king Samory Touré (1830–1900); and many others—men whose faces were wasted from fasting, yet whose foreheads shone with the determination to succeed in their struggle.

I chose to begin my remarks on India and Africa with a literary work because literature opens up perspectives by transforming people into characters through its symbolism. Continuing in this vein, I interviewed Léopold Sédar Senghor (1906–2001), the poet-president of Senegal and champion of Negritude. I noted his great admiration for India and its civilisation, its centuries-old art and its architectural wonders. He writes, "I have contemplated the Taj Mahal; I found it splendid".

The splendours of India are found not only in its works of art; they are, first and foremost, embodied in its people, the creators of these masterpieces underpinned by high and beautiful thought, clarity of vision and relevance. Speaking of how he developed the notion of Negritude, Senghor wrote, "In our political struggle for African emancipation ... we were inspired by both the methods and ideas of

Mahatma Gandhi and Pandit Nehru". This method and philosophy are based on dialogue, a spirit of sharing, and a quest for symbiosis, which enables us to reach understanding and agreement by resolving contradictions. Inspired by Senghor, and before him by the wisdom as old as the great civilisations of Africa, the cradle of humanity, Senegal has always been identified as a "land of *teranga*".

What makes Gandhi so compelling is his vast culture, which enabled him to grasp the major issues that convulsed the world far beyond the borders of his own country. Moreover, we cannot overlook the role Africa played in shaping his conceptual legacy.

Beyond the static image of Gandhi immortalised in statues, it is his ideas—peace, non-violence, and *Satyagraha*—that endure. This unique form of struggle empowers the oppressed to disarm the oppressor and compel him—often despite himself—to question his own cause and to humanise himself so as not to lose face, for the human face of the world is reflected in our mutual recognition and respect for each other.

Disarming the oppressor through civil disobedience involves exposing the absurdity of his positions, which are detrimental to human dignity. This is all the more remarkable because it represents the will of the majority rising against an insignificant, albeit arrogant, minority. *Satyagraha* is the manifestation of Truth and Justice, ideals to which all people aspire, for we are all sentenced to share the world and must therefore learn to "live together". In my country, wise men have conceptualised this as "a shared desire for living together".

For the philosophy of non-violence to serve as a practical modus operandi, it must be rooted in long practice—an exercise in self-control, in testing one's senses and spirit—so as not to succumb to the easy impulses of unchecked vivacity, subjectivism or the faculty which induces regret after a misdeed.

Gandhi is also a model. Not like a tailor's model or a sewing pattern that ensures exact reproductions and is therefore soulless but an inspiring reference point that adapts itself to different contexts and their specificities. Originating in South Africa in defence of the rights of Indian workers in a country where racism was rampant, his approach evolved, adapting to local conditions and to the culture of India.

It is no coincidence that enlightened minds across the world have adopted Gandhi's model to lead their struggles for human rights to success. Among those who contributed to building a humanity free of negative slag was the black pastor Martin Luther King Jr., a descendant of slaves—victims of the "greatest crime against humanity". He delivered this far-reaching message:

> Let us not seek to satisfy our thirst for freedom by drinking from the cup of bitterness and hatred. We must forever conduct our struggle on the high plane of dignity and discipline. We must not allow our creative protest to degenerate into physical violence. Again and again, we must rise to the majestic heights of meeting physical force with soul force (King 2013, p. 187).

This was the bedrock of his dream, which showed him what would happen 40 years later: a black man, Barack Obama, became President of the United States of America!

The United Nations, particularly UNESCO, has striven, through education, science and culture, "to raise in the minds of men, the defenses of peace". Then there is the Dalai Lama and Dr Albert Schweitzer, who at the age of 21 had a profound dream: "In 1896 ... the idea suddenly seized me that I should not accept my happiness as something quite natural and that I had to give something in return." Thus was born his hospital in Lambaréné, deep in the Gabonese forest!

Finally, there is Nelson Mandela! Here is a man who suffered torture in the jails of the apartheid regime for almost 27 years; who carried on "his perishable shoulders" the hunger for peace and justice of his whole community. Yet, when he was finally released and entrusted with the heavy burden of power, he advocated non-violence to build a united South Africa—a rainbow nation where all communities could live together in peace. Mandela was deeply inspired by Gandhi, whose fight he continued decades later. Gandhi championed an unvarnished humanism, using the plight of the weakest, often the majority, as a pretext, offering his intelligence and unfathomable internal forces to convince others.

Greater Sharing of Values in a Dynamic Partnership

When we observe India, a vast subcontinent of more than a billion inhabitants with a unique and diverse culture, embodying the dynamism of those who have faith in themselves and the future, we begin to understand the magnitude of Gandhi's positive legacy. India is firmly rooted in its traditions while being resolutely committed to modernity. Its interests offer us the possibility of exemplary cooperation.

It is by observing India that I have come to fully appreciate the significance of Gandhi for Senegal and Africa. Aimé Césaire, poet and former President of the Regional Council of Martinique, once said that Africans should demand more than any other people, based on the deep scars of history and the immense challenge of bridging the gap between Africa and the rest of the world in meeting essential needs. The African renaissance, like what Gandhi helped India achieve, must be founded on great self-sacrifice and both individual and collective dedication to the common cause. This requires, first, awareness and then commitment through work to develop national skills and wealth. To love others, yes, but to have boundless love for yourself, which leads to national preference, is what guarantees a solid economy. I speak here of respecting our products, our cultural assets and our values.

Bearing in mind Gandhi's legacy, this renaissance should place great importance on training human resources in all fields, particularly in science and technology. India offers us a powerful example.

Gandhi is even more relevant today than in the past. As science and technology turn everything upside down and "aggravate" the pressures of globalisation, he urges us to distinguish between the essential and incidental, and to keep alive the cordial and human aspects within each of us. Digitisation and easy mobility create an interpenetration of peoples, which, without deep altruism, could lead to the ruin of our species.

Gandhi embodies this message because he remained Indian and drew on the inexhaustible resources of his people and culture to bring forth innovative, dynamic and effective thinking. Beyond

India, his charisma permeates the blood of all humanity, of all those who cherish the values we fight for to uphold human rights, at any place and at all time. May Gandhi continue to enlighten the world's march towards peace!

I have sought to outline the objective foundations of a partnership. Its implementation calls for a focus on the following points:

- Africa undoubtedly has an even greater need for openness in today's interconnected world. But this requires a genuine desire to live and fulfil that need for interconnection, to diversify relationships and break free from classic patterns without denying one's history or allies. Africa has strong arguments to make and valuable contributions to enrich life in this global "give-and-take" space. In this perspective, we will focus on:
    - New technologies and their growing impact on the creation of a new civilisation
    - Helping youth searching for their bearings to gain self-esteem and to adopt models such as those offered by India
    - Our common ways of life, along with artistic and cultural bonds
    - Opportunities that we discover beyond culture—economically and socially
- There will be artistic and literary exchanges, such as the Teranga Festival. These must be expanded by encouraging creativity on both the Indian and African sides. The two-way flow of cultural actors should be strengthened, vibrant cultural industries developed, and a diversified market created for a sector that continuously reinvents itself. An Afro-Indian or Indo-African Festival would provide an excellent platform to strengthen cultural ties. Developing and equipping spaces for cultural creation and dissemination throughout our countries would allow the exchanges we hope for, alongside training cultural actors in relevant skills and nurturing a culture of inventive boldness.
- If there is a focal point in this partnership, it is research, especially in the humanities, to continue what Léopold Sédar

> Senghor initiated. This research will provide a scientific foundation for our closeness and reinforce our duty to ensure cultural cooperation. Professor Cheikh Anta Diop laid the groundwork for this; we must capitalise on and deepen it.

India and Africa are the future of humanity. They need to look at each other more closely, and their common future will first take the route of culture, which is "at the beginning and at the end of everything".

References

Césaire, Aimé. *La Tragédie du Roi Christophe*. Paris: Présence Africaine, 1963.

Kane, Cheikh Hamidou. *L'aventure Ambigue*. Paris: Julliard, 1961.

King, Martin Luther. Speech of 28 August 1963, reprinted in *A Time to Break Silence: The Essential Works of Martin Luther King, Jr., for Students*. Boston: Beacon Press, 2013.

Nehru, Jawaharlal. *Selected Works of Jawaharlal Nehru*, ed. Madhavan Palat, Second Series, vol. 5. New Delhi: Jawaharlal Nehru Memorial Fund, 1984.

Senghor, Léopold Sédar. 1976 *La civilization indienne*: J Nehru. Dakar: R. Ethiopiques.

———. 1979. *Elégies majeures*. Paris: Le Seuil.

Chapter 22
Africa–India Media Connectivity

Suhas Borker

I was watching a BBC television programme (BBC HARDtalk, 2020), in which Stephen Sackur interviewed John Kani—the renowned South African actor and playwright, celebrated both for his work in Hollywood blockbusters and his acclaimed play in the West End.

"Were you disappointed by the 25 years of ANC[1] rule?" was the question put to John Kani. And there it was: a Western narrative, symptomatic of a lingering colonial hangover, reducing the rich and complex saga of South Africa's post-apartheid journey to an oversimplified binary thought process of an on–off or yes–no. In that moment, I told myself how critical it is for local narratives to take the lead. Now, in the 2020s, it is essential that we tell our own stories—stories of the struggles and triumphs of our women and men in both Africa and India—and share them with one another to foster a deeper, more authentic understanding of each other.

1 The ANC, or African National Congress, has been the ruling political party of post-apartheid South Africa since the election of Nelson Mandela in 1994. Cyril Ramaphosa, the incumbent President of South Africa, had led the ANC since 18 December 2017. The author was invited to speak at the plenary session of the ANC's Third International Solidarity Conference, held in Pretoria from 25 to 28 October 2012.

There is an urgent need to strengthen Africa–India media connectivity and to build a bridge of local narratives that can bring the people of both regions closer together. As Africa and India strive towards a shared vision of democratic, pluralistic, inclusive, participatory and equitable development, the role of media in fostering mutual understanding becomes crucial. Yet, media connectivity remains a largely missing piece in the relationship between the two. At present, both Africa and India receive only marginal visibility in each other's media landscapes: Africa is scarcely represented in Indian media, and India is similarly underrepresented in African media.

I asked my African friends if they had ever seen any news about Africa in Indian newspapers or on Indian television. Their response was telling: Africa only makes the headlines in India when there is a major disaster, a terrorist attack or a coup.

Currently, there are no Indian journalists based in Africa, and no African journalists stationed in India.

Given that Africa and India together account for approximately 2.6 billion people—roughly one-third of the world's population—this gap is not just striking, it is troubling. The lack of mutual media presence has led to a significant disconnect in awareness and understanding between our peoples.

But it was not always like this. There was a time when Indian and African media enjoyed a vibrant and meaningful relationship. Let us look back at the various ways in which this connection once thrived—grounded in shared struggles, solidarity, and a commitment to telling each other's stories.

Gandhi: First Indian Journalist in South Africa

In May 1893, Gandhi arrived in South Africa to defend the case of an Indian company in Durban, Dada Abdullah and Company. As veteran journalist Sailen Chatterjee notes in his article titled "The Journalist in Gandhi", "The political situation in South Africa not only made him a Satyagrahi, but a thorough journalist." Gandhi worked as the South African Correspondent for *India*, a journal founded by

Dadabhai Naoroji, through which he sent dispatches about the situation in South Africa, with particular reference to the grievances of Indians living there.[2]

Gandhi believed that the sole aim of journalism should be service (Chatterjee 1965, pp. 31–32, 83, 118). During the Boer War, Gandhi, with his band of Indian volunteers, tended to the sick and wounded while also working as a war correspondent.

Ten years after his arrival in South Africa, on 4 June 1903, Gandhi, with the help of fellow Indians, launched his first newspaper *Indian Opinion* in Natal. The publication aimed to give voice to the feelings of Indians living under apartheid in South Africa. He wrote the first editorial, titled "Ourselves", in which he stated: "We need offer no apology for making an appearance. The Indian community in South Africa is a recognized factor in the body politic, and a newspaper voicing its feelings and especially devoted to its cause would hardly be considered out of place. Indeed, we think it would supply a long-felt want" (Narasimhan 1997, p. ii).

With just 1,000 subscribers, *Indian Opinion* made a significant contribution to sensitising South African Indians to the unequal treatment meted out to them by white rulers and instilled in them the courage to resist injustice. Initially, the paper was published in four languages: English, Gujarati, Tamil and Hindi. However, the Hindi and Tamil editions were later discontinued due to a shortage of writers (Narasimhan, 1997).

Gandhi not only wrote for the journal but also covered its expenses (Chatterjee 1965, p. 23). The paper accepted no advertisements,

2 Dadabhai Naoroji was one of the founder members of the Indian National Congress (INC) in 1885 and served as its president in 1886, 1893 and 1896. He famously stated, "It is in Parliament (London) that our chief battle has to be fought" (Chavan 2017). In 1892, he made history by becoming the first Black and first Asian member elected to the British House of Commons, representing the Central Finsbury constituency of London on a Liberal Party ticket (Pillai 2017). Naoroji was a strong supporter of women's suffrage and Indian self-rule. He also formulated the drain-of-wealth theory, which became India's cornerstone argument against British rule and the first major economic critique of colonial rule in India.

and the press took no external job work. Henry Polak, a British-born lawyer, journalist and activist in South Africa, recounted the difficulties faced by *Indian Opinion* in those days: "The printing press, where the type setting was done by hand, was run by a decrepit oil engine which frequently broke down. When this happened, the settlers had to resort to hand power to turn out the paper in time for the usual dispatch of mails." There were no servants or peons; the press workers themselves had to print the paper, fold it, paste the addresses, make bundles and take them to the railway station (Chatterjee 1965, p. 15).

When Gandhi left South Africa, he entrusted *Indian Opinion* to Polak. In 1916, he sent his 23-year-old son, Manilal Gandhi, to oversee the Gujarati edition and take charge of the English edition. From time to time, he wrote to Manilal, offering guidance on managing the paper. "The editor has to be patient and seek for the truth only ... You should write what is the truth in the *Indian Opinion;* but do not be impolite and do not give way to anger. Be moderate in your language. If you err, do not hesitate to confess it" (Chatterjee 1965, p. 42).

Later, in his autobiography, *The Story of My Experiments with Truth*, Gandhiji wrote:

> In the very first month of *Indian Opinion*, I realized that the sole aim of journalism should be service. The newspaper Press is a great power, but just as an unchained torrent of water submerges the whole countryside and devastates crops, even so an uncontrolled pen serves but to destroy. If the control is from without, it proves more poisonous than want of control. It can be profitable only when exercised from within (Gandhi, 1948, p. 349).

Media Connectivity in the Past

Swahili was the first "Africa service" of All India Radio (AIR), launched in May 1953 (All India Radio n.d., p. 10). Apa Sahib Pant, independent India's first envoy to what was then British East Africa, initiated this move to support the freedom movements in Africa, specifically the Mau Mau insurgency against colonial rule in Kenya (Pereira n.d.). Since there were few Swahili speakers in India at the time, resource persons were brought from East Africa to New Delhi to run the service.[3] This one-hour daily service in Swahili continues to this day.

A few months before the Swahili service began, AIR had launched a French service on 2 October 1952, targeting West and Northwest Africa (All India Radio n.d.). These initiatives were part of All India Radio's External Services Division, which today broadcasts for about 72 hours daily in 15 foreign languages and 12 Indian languages.

Many Indian journalists devoted their lives to covering Africa, with Hari Sharan Chhabra standing out as the best example. In 1961, he launched *Africa Diary*, a weekly digest of news from the continent. Published from New Delhi, it became an important resource for researchers and scholars around the world. Chhabra was among the first students of the Department of African Studies, established at the University of Delhi in 1955. Africa became the "focus" of his life (Chhabra 2012). There was hardly a visit to Africa by an Indian President or Prime Minister where he was not a part of the delegation. He wrote many books on Africa, the last being *South African Foreign Policy: Principles, Options, Dilemmas*, which was released by Prime Minister Inder Kumar Gujral aboard Air India One during a flight from Kampala to Johannesburg in October 1997.[4]

In the 1960s, Ajit Gopal was a special correspondent for *Hindustan Times* in Nairobi for more than five years, covering Africa south of the Sahara. A barrister-at-law by training, he was regarded as an authority on African affairs (Grover 1992, p. 237). Around the same time, Batuk Gathani regularly filed reports from Nairobi for *The Hindu*, one of India's leading national newspapers.[5]

---

3 Sourced from an article by Veena Sharma, Head of All India Radio's Swahili Service, which has been broadcasting every day in Swahili for 22 years.

4 The author was on this flight on 5 October 1997 as part of the media team accompanying the Indian Prime Minister on an official visit to Uganda, South Africa and Egypt.

5 The Hindu, "The Hindu returns to Africa", 22 August 2012. Available online: http://www.thehindu.com/news/national/the-hindu-returns-to-africa/article3804615.ece (accessed on 11 January 2024).

In December 1965, when a young Indian Foreign Service officer, Ranjit Gupta, received his first posting in Egypt, he found four Indian journalists based in Cairo—"the largest number in any capital in the world at that time". This was "despite huge financial constraints and severe restrictions on the use of foreign exchange operating in India".[6] India, of course, had a special relationship with Egypt, which went beyond their shared leadership of the Non-Aligned Movement (NAM) and Nehru's close bond with President Gamal Abdel Nasser. India strongly identified with the struggles of African nations emerging from colonialism. The eighth NAM Summit took place in Harare in 1986. After that, N.V.R. Swami was posted as the Representative of the Press Trust of India (PTI) in Harare and covered the Indian President's visit to Zimbabwe in June 1989.

M.S. Prabhakara was the Africa correspondent for *The Hindu*, reporting from post-Apartheid South Africa throughout the 1990s until 2002.[7] In 1997, Ashok Sengupta, a senior officer of the Indian Information Service, was posted as a roving correspondent for AIR, based in Johannesburg.[8]

During South Africa's transition to democracy in 1993–94, Indian journalist Sidharth Bhatia reported extensively for Indian newspapers. Vijay Naik, the then Chief of Bureau in New Delhi of *Sakal*, a leading Marathi newspaper of Western India, wrote a series of 19 articles after his visit to South Africa in 1996.

A few freelancers have reported from New Delhi for the South African Broadcasting Corporation's (SABC) Lotus FM, a national radio station based in Durban that originally catered to the South African Indian community. Launched in 1983 as Radio Lotus, the station has since broadened its listenership across South Africa.

---

6 "Interview with Indian Ambassador (ret.) Ranjit Gupta: Cairo, Egypt—The First Posting (1965–1968)", 26 February. Washington: Middle East Institute. Available online: https://www.mei.edu/publications/interview-indian-ambassador-ret-ranjit-gupta-cairo-egypt-first-posting-1965-1968 (accessed on 12 January 2024).

7 Ibid.

8 The author met Ashok Sengupta in Johannesburg in October 1997.

Until recently, S. Venkat Narayan, a senior Indian journalist based in New Delhi and President of the Foreign Correspondents' Club of South Asia, was associated with Lotus FM as well as Radio 702 (Johannesburg) and Cape Talk (Cape Town). In addition, the SABC has had a stringer in New Delhi, Neha Poonia, who reported on follow-up stories related to the controversial Gupta Brothers in 2018.[9]

As a point of comparison, *Prensa Latina*—the Cuban News Agency with headquarters in Havana—has maintained a full-time correspondent in New Delhi for many years.

On the media training front, India continues to provide fully funded opportunities to African media professionals. Between 2009 and 2012, 45 African journalists received training in Indian media institutes, and during the same period, 90 African journalists were hosted on short familiarisation trips to India.[10]

Case Study: Aman Sethi, The *Hindu*'s Correspondent in Africa

On 22 August 2012, *The Hindu*, one of India's leading national newspapers, announced its return to Africa with the headline: "*The Hindu* returns to Africa". The announcement said that the newspaper had posted a correspondent to Addis Ababa, Ethiopia "in keeping with Africa's growing importance for India and its rising weight in the global economy and international politics".

The Hindu was returning to Africa, the continent that had "changed", after a decade. Its last correspondent, M.S. Prabhakara, had reported from post-Apartheid South Africa until 2002. The newspaper's commitment to "reporting Africa through Indian eyes"

9 "The Gupta brothers' hometown, Saharanpur", SABC News, 1 March 2018. Available online: https://www.youtube.com/watch?v=2WV2o4M87tk (accessed on 5 January 2025).

10 Avtar Singh Bhasin, "India's Foreign Relations – 2012 Documents". New Delhi: Geetika Publishers, in cooperation with Public Diplomacy Division, Ministry of External Affairs, Government of India, 2013, p. xx. Available online: http://mea.gov.in/Images/pdf/India-foreign-relation-2012.pdf (accessed on 9 January 2024).

meant "'seeing not just the wars and tragedies which is all that the West sees but the hundreds of little triumphs that no one talks about'" (The Hindu, 2012).[11]

The young journalist chosen for the job by *The Hindu* was Aman Sethi. Not quite 30 at the time of his posting, Aman, an alumnus of the Asian College of Journalism, Chennai, and Columbia University's Graduate School of Journalism, New York, had already made a name for himself as *The Hindu*'s Chhattisgarh correspondent. His extensive two-year reportage on the Maoist insurgency in the state earned him the International Red Cross Committee award in 2011 for articles on humanitarian issues.

Aman extensively covered the African continent, and here I would like to pick on two stories he reported from Zimbabwe. The first was during his time in Harare covering the 2013 Zimbabwe elections, where he found himself "fascinated by the controversial fast-track land reform process". His article, "Dispatches from an unfinished African revolution" datelined MHONDORO-NGEZI and dated 7 September 2013, reported on the land redistribution process.[12]

The report highlighted how "a growing body of academic work contradicts the narrative that the land invasions were masterminded in Harare by a small coterie including Mr Mugabe." Critics viewed Zimbabwe's fast-track land reform as "violent, state-sponsored property theft that destroyed the national economy and cemented the Western characterisation of President Robert Mugabe as a ruthless despot". Many argued that the government seized land for President Mugabe's cronies in the Zimbabwe African National Union–Patriotic Front (ZANU-PF), the party ruling Zimbabwe since 1980. However, Aman pointed out that "the sheer scale of land redistribution

---

11 The Hindu, "The Hindu returns to Africa", 22 August 2012. Available online: http://www.thehindu.com/news/national/the-hindu-returns-to-africa/article3804615.ece (accessed on 11 January 2024).

12 Aman Sethi, "Dispatches from an Unfinished African Revolution", *The Hindu*, 7 September 2013. Available online: http://www.thehindu.com/opinion/op-ed/dispatches-from-an-unfinished-african-revolution/article5101534.ece (accessed on 5 January 2025).

suggests the process has been more broad-based, and productive, than previously assumed". He also noted that "those involved in the struggle say their actions were autonomous, and intended as a protest against the government, which the invaders felt had compromised on the rallying cry of the liberation" (Sethi 2016).

This report was on Indian social media the same day, where Aman posed a thought-provoking question: In the context of the ongoing debate surrounding India's Land Bill, does Zimbabwe's experience suggest that questions of land are best resolved outside the ambit of the state?[13]

The second report, "A steel deal not yet sealed", was published on 6 October 2013.[14] It was about the Indian conglomerate Essar Group's US$750 million acquisition of the debt-ridden Zimbabwe Iron and Steel Company (ZISCO), a state-owned steel company, in 2011. The acquisition was envisioned as the keystone of a US$3.5 billion transnational project that included refurbishing the steel mill, settling ZISCO's US$340 million debt, constructing a 1,000 MW power plant and developing a rail corridor to transport surplus ore and steel products to Beira in Mozambique. There, Essar planned to build a terminal capable of exporting 20 million tonnes of material each year to India, China and markets across Africa. The deal was projected to account for 70 per cent of all foreign direct investments (FDIs) in Zimbabwe over a three-year period.

Aman wrote in 2013,

> Two years on, this grand vision stands suspended as Essar and the Government of Zimbabwe negotiate over ZISCO's vast iron ore reserves. The stakes could not be higher. For Zimbabwe, ZISCO's privatization signals that this southern

13 Aman Sethi, "Is Bypassing the State the Best Way to Push for Land Reform?", Kafila, 7 September 2013. Available online: https://kafila.online/2013/09/07/is-bypassing-the-state-the-best-way-to-push-for-land-reform/ (accessed on 5 January 2025).

14 Aman Sethi, "A Steel Deal not yet Sealed", *The Hindu*, 6 October 2013. Available online: https://www.thehindu.com/business/Industry/a-steel-deal-not-yet-sealed/article5204743.ece (accessed on 5 January 2025).

> African economy has reopened for business after a decade of turmoil, sanctions and capital flight. Essar has invested in processing plants such as 10 million tonnes per annum steel facility in Hazira, Gujarat but remains the only Indian steel major without a domestic captive resource. Mine allocations in Chhattisgarh have been stymied by legal claims and Maoist guerillas have repeatedly disrupted an ore-slurry pipeline that supplies pellets from NMDC's operations in Bailiadila. The company has sunk (US) $80 million into its Zimbabwe project already, but the deal is worthless without the mines.

A few months before publishing these two Zimbabwe stories, Aman participated in a Q&A session on Facebook on 19 May 2013 titled "Are Indian companies 'land grabbing' in Africa?"[15] This session was organised after he had reported about Indian corporate involvement in Ethiopia and Mali. Two key questions from the session stand out:

The first question was: Are Indian companies adding to the capacity building of locals there? Do they hire locally or bring in workers from India? Aman responded: "On labour—the Ethiopian government is very clear that they want companies to train local workers. Last year, I wrote about how liquor baron Ponty Chadha had come up with a plan to bring farmers from Punjab to Ethiopia—but the plan was shot down by the government. Most governments allow companies to bring in highly skilled technicians and managers, but try to get companies to train people to become machine operators etc."

The second question was: Do you think the government needs to put in place some minimum standards for corporates operating abroad so that locals are not abused in the process of these investments, or should it be a self-restricting corporate code of conduct? To this, Aman replied, "I think most governments have legal frameworks to safeguard the rights of project-affected communities—however, many

15 Saldanha, Ayesha. "Are Indian companies 'land grabbing' in Africa?", farmlandgrab.org, 19 May 2013. Available online: http://farmlandgrab.org/post/view/22099-are-indian-companies-land-grabbing-in-africa (accessed on 5 January 2025).

(much like in India) cannot effectively monitor these companies. In Karuturi's case for instance, no laws have been broken—but there seems to be a structural problem with the way the project was conceived—so I think we probably need to think beyond a legal regime and perhaps begin by trying to understand these processes as best we can. It's easy to say 'neocolonial land grab' and end the discussion—but that doesn't help our understanding of the world—rather it restricts engagement because the discussion is effectively over".

Aman not only brought Indian readers closer to the ground realities of Africa but his reportage also brought to the fore the local narratives often overlooked by the Western media paradigm. "As Africa struggles to take its rightful place in the world"—to quote again from the announcement of "*The Hindu* returns to Africa" of August 2012, Aman was there to "report the story" faithfully to *The Hindu* readers for about a year and a half till the end of January 2014. His last story titled "A broken army lies at the heart of conflict in South Sudan"[16] was filed from Juba on 24 January 2014.

Needless to say, this case study reinforces the urgent need to have Indian correspondents posted in Africa and African correspondents in India to foster deeper people-to-people connectivity.

Indians reporting on India/Africans reporting on Africa

Indians reporting on India and Africans reporting on Africa—and having their reports shared through print, television, radio and social media across both regions—would go a long way in positively reshaping and correcting the imbalances in the global flow of information.

"Can Africa tell its own stories?" asks Simon Alison, Africa correspondent for the *Daily Maverick,* based in Johannesburg. He has previously reported from Egypt, Palestine and Somalia for *Asia Times* and *Agence France Presse,* and holds a master's degree from the

16 Sethi, Aman. "A broken army lies at the heart of conflict in South Sudan", *The Hindu,* 24 January 2014. Available online: https://www.thehindu.com/opinion/op-ed/a-broken-army-lies-at-the-heart-of-conflict-in-south-sudan/article5610264.ece (accessed on 5 January 2025).

School of Oriental and African Studies, London.

Here, I would like for Simon Alison to tell his own story.

> There is not a lot of money in African journalism. As an African journalist, I know this all too well. An illustrative example: I was in South Sudan in November 2012, on a trip I was financing myself. Weeks of staying in flea-ridden hostels culminated in a four-day visit to a refugee camp near the border with Sudan.
>
> I was the only reporter there and pleased with myself for getting a story that no one else had. Not so fast.
>
> On my last day there, a small plane descended unannounced on the tiny airstrip and disgorged four foreign correspondents in their khakis and combat boots.
>
> They represented two of the biggest and best-known international media outlets. They spent a total of two hours in the camp. One of them had filed his story even before he left.
>
> As they hijacked my interviews, I chatted to their fixer who whispered to me that they had spent $8,000 to hire the plane for the morning.
>
> To me, this was an unimaginable sum: their morning cost more than four times my entire two weeks in South Sudan. And, of course, they missed the story.
>
> In four days, I barely scratched the surface of what was going on in the camp, but in their two hours, they could not even get beyond official statements.
>
> For aid workers and the camp's refugee leadership, this was a common complaint: journalists, invariably foreign, screeched in for a few hours and got the story wrong (Simon Alison, *The Guardian*, 1 March 2013).

Alison argues that this is symptomatic of a broader issue: Africa is still not allowed to tell its own stories. The news agenda about Africa is often decided in Western capitals, and foreign correspondents, lacking a nuanced understanding of local complexities, frequently produce distorted or even borderline racist depictions. These narratives tend to reinforce tired stereotypes of poverty, conflict and starvation. Even when the tone shifts toward the positive, such as in the sweeping generalisations of an "Africa rising", the framing remains reductive and externally imposed. The long-term impact is that policy decisions about Africa are often shaped by outsider perspectives.

Alison raises the point that within the continent itself, news coverage about other African countries is a "cut and paste" job from global wire services such as *Reuters*, *Associated Press*, *Agence France Presse* (*AFP*) and the *BBC*. In his view, Africa's failure to tell its own stories to its own people amounts to a serious constraint on the continent's freedom of expression.

He ends on a rather pessimistic note: "Yes, there are solutions, but they are imperfect at best, meaning ultimately that for the foreseeable future, foreigners will continue to craft the African narrative."[17]

I do not share Alison's pessimism. The media landscape will change—and it will change soon, for Africa and India—as both take steps to reinvent their narratives and visual economies.

Presently, media exchanges between Africa and India are largely routed through global hubs in New York, London and Paris. This dependence not only results in the homogenisation of news content but also facilitates the subtle imposition of a foreign mindset and worldview that seeks to impose cultural hegemony and uniformity on the political, economic, social and cultural lives, as well as values, of African and Indian societies and institutions.

On the other hand, direct and close media connectivity between Africa and India will not only strengthen the African–Indian paradigm of diversity and pluralism but also help counter the hegemonic gatekeeping of Western media. New technologies present both an opportunity and a challenge in the effort to create a more balanced and equitable international information and communication order, one grounded in democracy, social justice and pluralism.

17 Alison, *The Guardian*, 2013.

Together, Africa and India account for one-third of the world's current population and are well-positioned to take the lead in this critical process.

The opening of an African Union office in New Delhi, a decision pending since the Second Africa–India Forum Summit in 2011, would definitely strengthen the Africa–India relationship and stimulate greater media connectivity.[18]

As a first step, India should consider appointing a roving correspondent in Africa and leveraging its space programme to enhance Africa–India media collaboration. In the 1990s, as mentioned earlier, India had a roving correspondent of AIR in Africa based in Johannesburg. This position should be reinstated, and with the benefit of modern technology, the correspondent can now produce content across multiple platforms, including radio, television, online portals and print media.

On 5 May 2017, India successfully launched a communications satellite for South Asia from the Sriharikota spaceport.[19] Entirely funded by India, the satellite was designed to help regional countries boost their telecommunications and broadcasting capabilities.

---

18 Adopted in the IAFS-2 Declaration Document, "Second Africa-India Forum Summit 2011: Africa-India Framework for Enhanced Cooperation", 25 May 2011. This recommendation was originally proposed during a seminar held on the eve of the IAFS-2, titled "India and the Rise of Africa: New Strategies and Approaches to Synergy for Sustainable Development" organised at the India International Centre, New Delhi, and moderated by the author on 4 May 2011. Speakers at the seminar included Amb. Shashank, former Indian Foreign Secretary and Chairman of the African Studies Association of India; Vivek Katju, Secretary (West), Ministry of External Affairs; Ethiopian Ambassador Gennet Zewide; Egyptian Ambassador Khaled Aly El-Bakly; South African High Commissioner H.M. Majeke; Nigerian Acting High Commissioner Adebola Labiran; and Indian journalists Vijay Naik (*Sakal*) and Siddharth Vardarajan (*The Hindu*). Subsequently, the recommendation was incorporated into the "Addis Ababa Media Declaration of African and Indian Editors" on 21 May 2011.

19 ISRO, "GSLV Successfully Launches South Asia Satellite", 5 May 2017. Available online: https://www.isro.gov.in/GSLVSouthAsia.html#:~:text=GSLV%20Successfully%20Launches%20South%20Asia%20Satellite&text=India's%20Geosynchronous%20Satellite%20Launch%20Vehicle,(May%2005%2C%202017) (accessed on 5 January 2025).

Analysts have referred to this initiative as an example of Indian Prime Minister Narendra Modi's "space diplomacy".[20] A similar model now needs to be replicated in Africa.

This "gift" from India has no parallels in the space-faring world. All other regional consortia are commercial, for-profit ventures. The South Asian Satellite, cost approximately US$37 million, with total expenses including operational costs and insurance amounting to US$71 million. By undertaking this initiative, India has positioned the Indian Space Research Organisation (ISRO) on a new trajectory, offering a space-based platform that, according to some estimates, would have cost the participating nations nearly US$1.5 billion.

The satellite offers a wide range of services to India's neighbours, including television, direct-to-home (DTH) broadcasting, education, telemedicine, weather forecasting and disaster management support. Beneficiary countries include Sri Lanka, the Maldives, Bangladesh, Nepal and Bhutan, while Pakistan chose to opt out of the initiative.

ISRO took three years to build the satellite, which was launched using its reliable Geosynchronous Satellite Launch Vehicle (GSLV). The South Asia Satellite is equipped with 12 Ku-band transponders, with each participating country allocated one dedicated transponder. However, to utilise the services, each nation must develop its own ground infrastructure. In addition to its telecommunications and broadcasting capabilities, the satellite can also provide crucial and secure communication links between nations to coordinate rescue and relief operations during natural disasters.

India can replicate its South Asian experience of "space diplomacy" in Africa. While a single satellite was sufficient for the South Asia region, ISRO may have to deploy multiple satellites to cover the entire African continent in its footprint. To achieve this, a well-defined roadmap with tangible milestones and timelines is essential.

---

20 Chetan Kumar, "Space Diplomacy: India to set up Ground Stations for Five Neighbours", *The Times of India*, 3 January 2019. Available online: https://timesofindia.indiatimes.com/india/space-diplomacy-india-to-set-up-ground-stations-for-5-neighbours/articleshow/67357464.cms

By taking the lead, India would gain a first-mover advantage in establishing a strategic "space bridge" through dedicated India-Africa satellites, which could undoubtedly transform Africa–India media connectivity. It would also foster linkages across the socio-economic and cultural spectrum, bringing Africa and India closer in ways never imagined before.

References

Alison, Simon. "African Journalism is being Stifled by a Lack of Resources", *The Guardian*, 1 March 2013. Available online: https://www.theguardian.com/world/2013/mar/01/ african-journalism-stifled-lack-resources (accessed on 3 July 2025).

All India Radio. "Languages of External Services Division", n.d. Available online: http://allindiaradio.gov.in/Services/External/Documents/5658d0d27c96472ba6cd5d4c322081b3LanguageServicesofExternalServicesDivision.pdf (accessed on 9 January 2021).

BBC HARDtalk. "John Kani: Art and Activism." 11 February 2020. Available online: https://www.bbc.co.uk/programmes/w3csy993 (accessed on 9 January 2024).

Bhasin, Avtar Singh, ed. "India's Foreign Relations – 2012 Documents". New Delhi: Geetika Publishers, in cooperation with Public Diplomacy Division, Ministry of External Affairs, Government of India, 2013. Available online: http://mea.gov.in/Images/pdf/India-foreign-relation-2012.pdf (accessed on 9 January 2024).

Chatterjee, Sailen. *Mahatma Gandhi the Journalist.* Bombay: Asia Publishing House, 1965.

Chavan, Akshay. "Dadabhai Naoroji: First Indian Member of British Parliament", 2017. Available online: https://www.peepultree.world/livehistoryindia/story/people/dadabhai-naoroji-first-indian-member-of-british-parliament (accessed on 9 January 2024).

Chhabra, Aseem. "Tribute to Dad: A Life spent Fighting Injustice", www.rediff.com, 26 December 2012. Available online: https://www.rediff.com/news/report/tribute-to-dad-a-life-spent-fighting-injustice/20121226.htm (accessed on 9 January 2024).

Das, Kishor Kumar. "AIR External Services: A Critical Analysis of Language Broadcast to Southeast, South and East Asia (1990–2005)" MPhil dissertation, Madurai Kamraj University, 2008.

Gandhi, M.K. *My Experiments with Truth.* Ahmedabad: Navajivan Publishing House, 1948 [1927].

Grover, Vrinda, ed. *Africa and India's Foreign Policy*. New Delhi: Deep & Deep Publications, 1992.

Gupta, Ranjit. "Interview with Indian Ambassador (ret.) Ranjit Gupta: Cairo, Egypt—The First Posting (1965–1968)", 26 February 2013. Washington: Middle East Institute. Available online: https://www.mei.edu/publications/interview-indian-ambassador-ret-ranjit-gupta-cairo-egypt-first-posting-1965-1968 (accessed on 12 January 2024).

The Hindu. "The Hindu returns to Africa", 22 August 2012. Available online: http://www.thehindu.com/news/national/the-hindu-returns-to-africa/article3804615.ece (accessed on 11 January 2024).

Kumar, Chetan. "Space Diplomacy: India to set up Ground Stations for Five Neighbours", *Times of India*, 3 January 2019. Available online: https://timesofindia.indiatimes.com/india/ space-diplomacy-india-to-set-up-ground-stations-for-5-neighbours/articleshow/67357464.cms (accessed on 11 January 2024).

Narasimhan, Bharati. *Making of a Great Communicator: Gandhi.* New Delhi: National Media Centre, 1997.

Pereira, Benegal, ed. "Apa Pant in East Africa: Nehru's Protégé", n.d. Available online: http://benegal.com/pant/apa.htm (accessed 9 January 2024).

Pillai, Manu S. "Dadabhai Naoroji: The Black Man in Westminster', *Mint*, New Delhi, 7 November, 2017. Available online: https://www.livemint.com/Leisure/shVMSA6UkcVLqx6KCUXHhI/Dadabhai-Naoroji-The-black-man-in-Westminster.html (accessed on 9 January 2024).

Saldanha, Ayesha. "Are Indian companies 'land grabbing' in Africa?", farmlandgrab.org, 19 May 2013. Available online: http://farmlandgrab.org/post/view/22099-are-indian-companies-land-grabbing-in-africa (accessed on 5 January 2025).

Sethi, Aman. "Is Bypassing the State the Best Way to Push for Land Reform?", Kafila, 7 September 2013. Available online: https://kafila.

online/2013/09/07/is-bypassing-the-state-the-best-way-to-push-for-land-reform/ (accessed on 5 January 2025).

———. "A Steel Deal not yet Sealed". *The Hindu,* 6 October 2013. Available online:http://www.thehindu.com/business/Industry/a-steel-deal-not-yet-sealed/article5204743.ece (accessed on 5 January 2025).

———. "A broken army lies at the heart of conflict in South Sudan", *The Hindu,* 24 January 2014. Available online: https://www.thehindu.com/opinion/op-ed/a-broken-army-lies-at-the-heart-of-conflict-in-south-sudan/article5610264.ece (accessed on 5 January 2025).

———. "Dispatches from an Unfinished African Revolution", *The Hindu,* 7 September 2013. Available online: http://www.thehindu.com/opinion/op-ed/dispatches-from-an-unfinished-african-revolution/article5101534.ece (accessed on 5 January 2025).

Chapter 23
Locating Technology in India's Engagements with Africa in Contemporary Times

S. Shaji

Introduction

The international system, characterised by the ascendancy of globalisation since the end of the Cold War, has witnessed Asian States such as India and China—often called emerging powers—expand their engagement to other parts of the world, particularly Africa. Such engagements, manifested through various linkages and ties, were mostly shaped by two major developments that unfolded in both Asia and Africa.

First, at the domestic level, there has been a marked shift towards a market economy (i.e., "marketisation" of economies) in the Afro-Asian world, along with a greater degree of democratisation across the African continent (Puddington and Roylance 2017).[1] Second, at

1 There is a common perception among observers that momentum towards democracy is growing in Africa, as evidenced by the holding of referenda and elections across the continent. At the very least, a substantial degree of procedural democracy practices exists. However, apprehensions remain about the quality of these elections and the extent of political inclusion from the standpoint of substantive democracy. Data collected by Freedom House, a leading tracker of

the systemic (international) level, there was an upheaval, following the collapse of the Cold War, and the subsequent dismantling of the prevailing geopolitical and geoeconomic order. These developments, which unfolded on roughly the same temporal scale, had inevitable effects on how emerging states in Asia, such as India, and regions like Africa conducted their international relations in the post-Cold War period.

The dominant perspective in International Relations Studies (IRS) literature suggests that the foreign relations of Asia's emerging powers in the post-Cold War period have been largely driven by their desire to sustain and secure the economic growth they had achieved over a period of time. Consequently, Asian states such as India, with their restructured ("marketised") economies, have increasingly sought access to natural resources, such as oil, and new markets in the Global South. Africa, with its newly discovered natural resources and fledgling markets, became an attractive destination for these Asian states (Leke and Barton 2016).[2] This has given rise to new trends in alliance-building, shaped by the synergy between Africa's politico-economic resurgence and India's strategic repositioning since the 1990s.

Against this backdrop, this chapter examines the evolving trends in India–Africa relations since the 1990s, with a particular focus on technology transfer. The first section briefly analyses India–Africa relations during the Cold War, providing historical context for subsequent developments. The second section explores post-Cold War engagements (since the 1990s)—especially in the economic domain, with a focus on technology transfer. The final section draws inferences from ongoing technological cooperation to assess the future trajectory of India–Africa relations.

---

freedom and democracy, show that around 60 per cent of African states are classified as free or partially free. It may be noted that authoritarian governance systems in Africa, especially in Sub-Saharan Africa, declined from 60 per cent in 1990 to 41 per cent in 2014 (Puddington and Roylance 2017).

2 In 2000–2010, Africa registered an economic growth of 5.4 per cent, adding US$78 billion annually to the economy (Leke and Barton 2016).

India–Africa Relations in the Cold War: Historical Context

In the post-colonial phase (beginning in the late 1940s), India and Africa entered a new phase of friendship and cooperation, shaped by their similar colonial experiences. In this context, one has to look at India's assistance policies since independence, especially towards like-minded regions and states of the Global South (commonly referred to as the "Third World" during the Cold War period). These assistance policies were embedded in India's broader foreign policy objectives, which emphasised maintaining strategic autonomy, respecting the sovereignty of other states, and strengthening South–South cooperation (Saferworld 2012).

In line with these broad objectives, India provided strong political support to anti-colonial and anti-racist struggles in Africa, actively backing liberation movements and standing with African states in multilateral and regional forums on issues of decolonisation, freedom, autonomy and racial equality. Such support was largely materialised through India's initiatives at the United Nations (UN) and its involvement in the Non-Aligned Movement (NAM), which came into existence in 1961. India also supported national movements across the continent, according diplomatic status to freedom organisations such as the South West Africa People's Organisation (SWAPO) in Namibia, and the African National Congress (ANC) in South Africa (Pham 2007).

Furthermore, India supported African countries through platforms such as the Group of 77 (G77), the Commonwealth and other multilateral fora, while also extending bilateral-level assistance. From these developments, one can infer that India's policy towards Africa during the period of the Cold War under the framework of South–South cooperation always had a normative trajectory.

Economically, too, in keeping with its political goals, India provided Africa with resources, aid and technology under the rubric of South–South cooperation. In a way, India assisted the launch of African economies, mostly through developmental aid. In 1964, the Indian Technical and Economic Cooperation (ITEC) was established in a modest fashion in order to assist newly independent Afro-Asian states, with a focus on African nations. Similarly, through another initiative—the AFRICA (Action for Resisting Invasion, Colonialism, and Apartheid) Fund—India donated US$40million of the initial US$70 million investment in 1986. Many of these government-led initiatives reflected the complementary political and economic interests promoted by the respective governments at the time.

At international forums such as the United Nations Conference on Trade and Development (UNCTAD), India and African states supported each other in advocating for a more just and equity-oriented economic system, known as the New International Economic Order (NIEO). When the NAM underwent a radical shift in the 1970s, both India and Africa were at the forefront of championing agendas that would benefit the trade and economies of the "Third World" and get them heard by the rest of the world. It is often argued that India's cooperation with Africa during this period was ideologically driven (Shaji 2014). Accordingly, India's foreign policy was always seen through a normative prism, where certain values and principles formed the basis of its engagement with Africa (Pham 2011). India extended a large number of economic assistance programmes to Africa during this period. In a nutshell, one can argue that India's version of South–South cooperation was perceived as an alternative to the Western model of "developmental cooperation" on the continent.

India–Africa Relations: A Real Turnaround Since the 1990s

Amid the broader processes of globalisation unfolding in liberalised market settings, a dominant regional and middle power like India has assumed a more proactive role in engaging like-minded countries through various development networks. One example is the Techno-Economic Approach for Africa–India Movement (TEAM-9), which includes technology transfer as a key component. The African continent, with its immense mineral wealth, expanding markets and strategic geographic location, is incontestably an important region where India can effectively initiate development cooperation projects, particularly in the realm of technology transfer (Harshé and Seethi 2005).

Furthermore, India's economic turnaround following market-driven reforms has prompted the country to seek natural resources and new markets to sustain its economic growth. An acute shortage of energy on the domestic front has propelled emerging states like India to look towards Africa. Currently, around 75 per cent of India's energy needs are met through imports. With approximately 10 per cent of the world's crude oil reserves, Africa has become an increasingly attractive partner (Carpenter 2020), especially given the geopolitical volatility in traditional energy suppliers like West Asia. Consequently, achieving energy security, accessing natural resources, and tapping into Africa's fledgling markets have become the foci of India's foreign policy vis-à-vis Africa. At the same time, African countries have shown keen interest in India's technology, capacity-building capabilities and investments. This mutual interest has elevated cooperation to a new level, as is evident from trade statistics. For instance, Indian corporations have invested to the tune of US$54 billion in Africa over the past decade, while India's trade volume exceeded US$62 billion in 2015, a 21 per cent increase from the previous year (Prime Minister's Office 2018). Alex Vines, a leading scholar on Africa, has observed that trade between India and Africa has expanded fourteen-fold over the last decade, surpassing US$70 billion (Vines 2015).

India has introduced several initiatives and programmes to deepen economic linkages with Africa. Subsequently, both India and Africa have been building networks of alliances and institutions across public and private sectors to accelerate economic development and cooperation. Notable programmes during this period include the expanded Indian Technical and Economic Cooperation (ITEC), the Focus Africa (2002), India's Pan African e-Network Project (2007), and the India–Africa Forum Summit (which began in 2008).

The next section discusses these developments by mapping broad trends in technology transfer, particularly since the 1990s.

Technology Transfer in India–Africa Ties since the 1990s

Technological cooperation and transfer have become a new thrust area among the economic linkages that India has built in Africa, particularly through the flow of technologies in the modern industry and service sectors. Against this background, it is important to examine the new forms of technological cooperation and transfer that India has been undertaking with African states, along with their nature and specificities. This highlights that India's approach differs from China's resource-based investment, Brazil's focus on agriculture and South Africa's emphasis on governmental capacity. Another dimension of Indian technology transfer is the low level of conditionalities involved, unlike many other aid-providing states that tend to be patronising.

The Government of India has introduced several programmes and initiatives aimed at supporting the African economy through technological cooperation and transfer. A prime example was the Focus Africa Programme, launched in 2002 under the Export-Import (EXIM) policy, which provided lines of credit to various African states. Its initial focus was to build closer ties with countries such as Ethiopia, Kenya and Mauritius, and it later expanded to South Africa, Ghana, Tanzania and Nigeria. The programme primarily sought to enable African states to access services from Indian companies. TEAM 9, introduced in 2004, was a new strategy with a focus on West Africa. J. Peter Pham notes that through TEAM 9, India provided around US$500 million on affordable terms of credit to eight African states—Burkina Faso, Chad, Cote d'Ivoire, Equatorial Guinea, Ghana, Guinea-Bissau, Senegal and Mali)—which facilitated the import of Indian products and services. This success aroused interest from several other African countries (Pham 2007).

Furthermore, in the post-Cold War period, economic engagements like the ITEC have been supplemented by new formal market-driven linkages, especially in technological cooperation and transfer. The ITEC programme comprises credit provision, capacity building, project-specific cooperation, deputation of Indian experts, and disaster relief. India's development cooperation also focuses on education and training in areas such as finance and accounting, information technology, promotion of small- and medium-sized enterprises, languages, rural development, environment and renewable energy (Ministry of External Affairs 2011–12).[3] Additionally, the Pan-African e-Network for Health and Education, managed by India, is active in 48 African countries. Since 2008, India has awarded 40,000

3 See for details https://itecgoi.in/index (accessed on 28 July 2020).

scholarships, with approximately 22,000 African students studying in India (Vines 2015).

Likewise, the India–Africa Forum Summits, held three times so far, have substantially institutionalised multilateral economic and technological cooperation. The latest summit, held in 2015 in New Delhi, placed strong emphasis on technology, especially in renewable energy, agriculture, education and skill development (India–Africa Forum Summit 2015). In addition, India's development partnership with Africa has operationalised 180 lines of credit worth US$11 billion across 40 African states. At the 2015 Summit, India made a commitment to provide a Line of Credit (LOC) worth US$10 billion on favourable terms, along with grant assistance of US$600 million (Siddiqui 2019). Indian aid tends to focus on education, health, technical cooperation and infrastructure development.

In 2003, India entered the African oil sector through its public sector enterprise, Oil and Natural Gas Corporation – Videsh Limited (OVL), by directly participating in oil exploration and production projects in Sudan, alongside companies from China and Malaysia under an equity participation model. This engagement enabled India to share its technologies and expertise in the extraction industry, benefiting all parties involved. It also generated a "positive spillover", with effects on related sectors such as heavy industry, power, railways, telecommunications, information technology and agriculture.

Such collaboration was propelled by India's desire to achieve energy security and promote growth in other economic sectors. It was also motivated by Sudan's interest in accessing state-of-the-art technologies and economic resources from the Global South (Shaji 2007).

The OVL currently has a presence in four African countries.[4] India has adopted a similar model in other parts of Africa as well. In some cases, most notably in India–South Africa relations, alliances have

4 Information from https://www.ongcindia.com/wps/wcm/connect/en/about-ongc/subsidiaries/ongc-videsh-limited/ (accessed on 25 July 2020). See also https://ongcvidesh.com/

been formed in the defence sector through experience sharing and capacity building.

While discussing India's role in the African economy, specifically in the field of technology, the contribution of Indian companies deserves emphasis. In addition to the OVL, state-run companies such as Bharat Heavy Electricals Limited (BHEL), National Thermal Power Corporation (NTPC) and IRCON International Limited (formerly Indian Railways Construction Company Limited) are providing technological support in several African countries, thereby contributing to infrastructure development.

A similar trajectory is discernible in the education and health sectors, where India is supporting African nations through digital platforms and health system technologies. Indian software companies such as Wipro, TCS and Infosys also maintain a substantial presence in the African market.

Parallel to public sector involvement, there has been a high degree of institutionalisation of economic and business partnerships at the private level, aimed at deepening trade ties (Shaji 2003). One example is the FICCI Africa Desk, established by the Federation of Indian Chambers of Commerce and Industry. FICCI also formed an alliance with apex chambers of commerce in various African countries through a newly institutionalised initiative—the Joint Business Council (JBC)—which offers business facilitation services through close coordination with government bodies and business promotion agencies in both India and its partner countries (Shaji 2003). Similarly, the Confederation of Indian Industry (CII) has set up the CII Africa Committee to strengthen economic and business linkages with African states (Shaji 2003).

In general, infrastructural and logistical support, along with involvement in extractive industries, has become the hallmark of emerging powers such as India in Africa (Taylor 2014). In policy and scholarly debates, it is often argued that linkages among middle-ranging powers, through the sharing of developmental experiences, capital and technology, have the potential to neutralise the asymmetric North–South ties that continue to dominate the Afro-Asian world.

Such cooperation also has the capacity to challenge the hegemonic and unilateral strategies traditionally advanced by powerful Northern states at multilateral trade bodies like the World Trade Organisation (WTO). In this context, alliances formed by India and African states, along with like-minded countries, are particularly noteworthy. One prominent example is the India–Brazil–South Africa Dialogue (IBSA) Forum. Similarly, multilateral initiatives such as the Indian Ocean Rim Association for Regional Cooperation–Southern African Development Council (IOR–ARC–SADC) forum are perceived as strategic efforts to achieve economic growth and technological cooperation across the Afro-Asian region (Shaji 2007).

However, there has been growing criticism of Asian involvement in Africa in recent times. Asian oil companies are frequently criticised for their policies in African countries; for example, the ONGC-VL was embroiled in controversy in Sudan during the first decade of this century. Indian agricultural companies operating in Kenya and Ethiopia have also come under scrutiny, particularly regarding land acquisition practices.

More broadly, concerns have been raised about labour rights, the appropriateness of transferred technologies, resource exploitation and environmental degradation (Henning 2007; McLure 2010). In response, several Asian states have defended their engagements by citing official treaties and agreements to establish their legitimacy, while also asserting a principle of non-interference in the domestic affairs of African nations.

Conclusion

In the post-Cold War period of globalisation, India's relations with the Global South, notably Africa, underwent dramatic transformation. The shift towards "market" economies in India and Africa supported democratisation in Africa, which had an impact on the way they engaged with one another. Technology transfer and cooperation took centre stage in these interactions, propelled by India's pursuit of energy security and access to new markets and by Africa's interest in India as a new source of technology and investment.

These technological engagements, marked by a certain degree of mutuality, were notably different from those seen during the Cold War period. Since the 1990s, Indian involvement in Africa, through both public and private corporations, has become much more emphatic and tangible, by way of a high degree of institutionalisation.

In sum, it can be argued that India's engagement with Africa in the realm of technological cooperation and technology transfer has had largely positive effects, while also attracting critical scrutiny regarding the broader role of emerging Asian powers in the continent.

References

Carpenter, J. William. "The Oil Producing Countries in Africa", *Investopedia*, updated 25 November 2024. Available online: https://www.investopedia.com/articles/investing/101515/biggest-oil-producers-africa.asp#:~:text=The%20African%20continent%20is%20home,about%209.6%25%20of%20world%20output. (accessed on 2 January 2024).

Harshé, Rajen and K.M Seethi, eds. *Engaging with the World: Critical Reflections on India's Foreign Policy*. New Delhi: Orient Longman, 2005.

India–Africa Forum Summit. "India–Africa Framework for Strategic Cooperation", 2015. Available online: http://www.mea.gov.in/Uploads/PublicationDocs/ 25981_framework.pdf (accessed on 10 July 2020).

Leke, Achankeng and Dominic Barton. 2016. "Three Reasons Things are looking up for African Economies", World Economic Forum on Africa, 5 May 2016. Available online: https://www.weforum.org/agenda/2016/05/what-s-the-future-of-economic-growth-in-africa/ (accessed on 31 March 2020).

McLure, Jason. "Africa's Failing Democracies", *Newsweek*, 12 July 2010. Available online: http://www.newsweek.com/africas-failing-democracies-74717 (accessed on 2 June 2013).

Melber, Henning. *China in Africa*. Uppsala: Nordic Africa Institute, 2007.

Ministry of External Affairs, Government of India. "Civilian Training Programme: Indian Technical & Economic Cooperation (ITEC) & Special Commonwealth Assistance for Africa Programme (SCAAP)

2011-2012". Available online: https://www.dpsa.gov.za/dpsa2g/documents/hrd/2011/Civilian%20Training%20Programme%202011-12%20ITEC.pdf (accessed on 2 January 2024).

Pham, J. Peter. "India's Expanding Relations with Africa and Their Implications for U.S. Interests", *American Foreign Policy Interests* vol. 29, no. 5 (2007): pp. 341–52. Available online: DOI: 10.1080/10803920701681378

———. *India in Africa: Implications of an Emerging Power for Africom and US Strategy*. Strategic Studies Institute, US Army War College, 2011. Available online: www.jstor.org/stable/resrep11446 (accessed on 8 March 2020).

Prime Minister's Office. "Prime Minister's address at Parliament of Uganda during his State Visit to Uganda", posted on 25 July 2018. Available online: https://pib.gov.in/PressReleasePage.aspx?PRID=1540025 (accessed on 28 July 2020).

Puddington, Arch and Tyler Roylance. "Populists and Autocrats: The Dual Threat to Global Democracy". Freedom House, 2017. Available online: https://freedomhouse.org/report/freedom-world/freedom-world-2017 (accessed on 1 December 2019).

S., Shaji. "India's Involvement in Africa since 1990s: Emerging State Business Relationship", in *India–Africa Enduring Partnership: Emerging Areas of Cooperation*, ed. Aparajita Biswas. New Delhi: Gyan Publishing House, 2003.

———. "Transfer of Technology and India's Foreign Policy: A Study of Changing Trends". Unpublished PhD Thesis. University of Hyderabad, 2007.

———. "Asian Involvement in Africa: A Perspective on Emerging Binaries in the Global South", *South Asian Survey* vol. 21, nos. 1 & 2 (2014): pp. 151–63.

Saferworld. "Rising Powers and Conflict", Issue Paper 3, 24 November 2012. Available online: https://www.saferworld.org.uk/resources/publications/710-issue-paper-3-rising-powers-and-conflict (accessed on 28 July 2020).

Siddiqui, Huma. 2019. "Focus Africa: Why India needs to accord High Priority to Relations with World's Second Biggest Continent", *Financial Express*, 28 May 2019. Available online: https://www.financialexpress.com/economy/focus-africa-why-india-needs-to-accord-high-priority-to-relations-with-worlds-second-biggest-continent/1591573/ (accessed on 30 June 2020).

Taylor, Ian. "Emerging Powers, State Capitalism and the Oil Sector in Africa", *Review of African Political Economy* vol. 41, no. 141 (2014): pp. 341–57. Available online: DOI: 10.1080/03056244.2013.864630 (accessed on 1 December 2019).

Vines, Alex. "India's Interests at the Africa Forum Summit: From Deals to Delivery?", Expert Opinion, Chatham House, 25 October 2015. Available online: https://www.chathamhouse.org/expert/comment/india-s-interests-africa-forum-summit-deals-delivery (accessed on 30 June 2020).

Wagner, Christian. 2019. "India's Africa Policy", SWP Research Paper 2019/RP 09, July. Available online: https://www.swpberlin.org/fileadmin/contents/products/research_papers/2019RP09_wgn_Web.pdf (accessed on 5 July 2020).

Afterword

Two words—continuity and change—capture the essence of India's historical and current engagement with Africa. As a diplomat, one of my most enriching experiences was my stay in South Africa. Thereafter, my direct association with Malawi and Mozambique gave me valuable insight into our extraordinarily diverse and mutually beneficial relationship with these countries.

The continent of Africa—the many nations, the multiple and diverse cultures, and ethnicities of Africa—has been familiar to India since the dawn of history. Some of our most ancient trade routes mark the passage of goods and ideas from the Indian subcontinent to the heart of Africa. While the political, and more recently, economic and developmental exchanges have often been commented on, the cultural aspects of our relationship are equally striking and grand. If I may be bold enough to say so, there is a little bit of Africa in every Indian, and a little bit of India in every part of Africa.

There is a Xhosa (Bantu ethnic group) proverb that is shared by many African cultures and languages: "Umuntu ngumuntu ngabantu" (meaning, "A person is a person through persons"). This has resonance for every Indian. It suggests that whether in the many nations and regions of Africa or the many states and regions of India, there is abiding faith in the power of communities and the strength of togetherness. This suggests a common embrace of cooperation and harmony—with fellow human beings and with nature alike. This is the African way, and it is the Indian way.

In the 20th century, both India and Africa experienced a common struggle: a fight for liberation, for freedom from colonialism and racial prejudice, and for the rights of every man and woman. The same fires and the same tests shaped us. India was a steadfast and longstanding supporter of democratic development in Africa and stood in solidarity against colonialism and apartheid. The struggle for Africa's liberty was our own struggle.

India placed apartheid on the agenda of the United Nations in the very first session of the General Assembly. Even as a poor, newly independent nation, we did not think twice to impose a trade embargo on the apartheid-era South Africa. This happened when trade with South Africa accounted for nearly 10 per cent of India's international trade.

During the Namibian liberation movement, India hosted the first South West Africa People's Organisation (SWAPO) embassy in 1986, catalysing international support for Namibia's independence. India also established diplomatic relations with Nigeria, Ghana and Madagascar even before their independence. India was at the forefront of convening the momentous Afro-Asian Conference in Bandung in 1955.

Our most emotional link with Africa is through Mahatma Gandhi, who worked and strove in South Africa for many years. As he once remarked, "I may have been born in India, but I was made in South Africa." For this "making" of the Mahatma, India owes Africa an eternal debt. More recently, the magnificent life and legacy of Nelson Mandela, or Madiba as he was known, have united us in a spirit of inspiration and shared purpose.

As waves of freedom and democracy swept across Africa, India stood by to help secure these hard-won gains and maintain peace. India contributed actively to United Nations peacekeeping missions in Congo, Somalia, Liberia, Burundi and Sudan. India also supported African Union initiatives to restore peace in Somalia, Mali, and other regions. We have a tradition of training African military officers at Indian institutions as well as by deploying training teams to partner countries. India has helped set up defence academies in countries such as Nigeria, Ethiopia and Tanzania.

India's policy of being a first responder in crisis situations across the Indo-Pacific extends to Africa. For instance, Operation Sahayata was launched to assist cyclone-hit Mozambique in 2019, and Operation Vanilla was initiated by the Indian Navy to provide relief to flood victims in Madagascar. These are just two examples of the humanitarian assistance and disaster relief (HADR) missions India has undertaken on the African continent.

Thus far, I have focused on the "continuity" of the India–Africa relationship—our shared history, our common political and developmental struggles, our togetherness in celebration, in sorrow, and in response to humanitarian crises. This remains constant and perennial. India was there for Africa, with Africa, and in Africa before others came, and we will remain there even if others choose to leave.

Yet, amid this continuity, there is also change. A new energy and electricity is seen in the India–Africa equation in recent years.

The Indian and African economies represent two of the world's most dynamic economic growth stories. Many of the world's fastest-growing economies today are in Africa, and the continent's combined GDP is US$2.4 trillion. By 2030, Africa is projected to represent nearly a quarter of the world's workforce and consumer base. With 54 countries, over a billion people, a youthful demographic, and an abundance of resources, Africa will count for a lot and will carry the hopes and responsibilities of our planet.

Reaping the benefits of democracy and political stability, countries in Africa have made major strides towards economic integration through initiatives such as the African Continental Free Trade Area (AfCFTA). Once fully implemented, AfCFTA is expected to raise intra-Africa trade by 52 per cent and create one of the largest and most ambitious economic spaces in the world. India wants to be a part of this exciting journey and is committed to helping Africa realise its potential—on Africa's own terms and in line with its priorities.

India's relationship with Africa has been strengthened through consultative and responsive mechanisms under the rubric of the India–Africa Forum Summit. The 2015 Summit was a landmark event, with participation from all 54 African countries. It infused a new dynamism in our partnership and I am confident that the next Summit will take us even further.

Under the leadership of Prime Minister Narendra Modi, our political engagement with Africa has intensified as never before. There have been over 34 high-level visits to African countries by the President, Vice President and Prime Minister of India. There is not a single country in the continent that has not been visited by at least one Union Minister. India has also had the privilege of hosting more than 100 African leaders for various bilateral and multilateral events, including 41 leaders for the India–Africa Forum Summit. To further enhance diplomatic engagement, India is opening new embassies in Africa.

The picture of trade and investment between India and Africa is encouraging. In 2019, India–Africa trade was valued at US$69 billion, reflecting a 12 per cent annual increase. The Duty-Free Tariff Preference (DFTP) Scheme, announced by India, has significantly benefited African nations by extending duty-free access to 98.2 per cent of India's total tariff lines. Thirty-eight African countries currently benefit from this scheme. India has become the fifth-largest investor in Africa, with cumulative investments of US$54 billion. These investments have created thousands of jobs for local citizens.

In terms of development cooperation, over two-thirds of India's Line of Credit (LOCs) in the past decade has been extended to African countries. At present, 189 projects across 42 African nations—valued at US$11.4 billion—are being implemented under Indian LOCs. These projects span a wide range of sectors, including drinking water supply, irrigation, solar electrification, power generation, transmission infrastructure, cement production, technology parks, and railway systems. Notable examples of our cooperation include:

- Power projects and dams in Sudan and Rwanda
- Water treatment in Tanzania
- Sugar factories in Ethiopia
- Technology parks in Mozambique and Swaziland
- Construction of the Presidential Palace in Ghana, the National Assembly building in The Gambia, and the Mahatma Gandhi International Convention Centre in Niger

The International Solar Alliance (ISA), an international organisation incubated by and headquartered in India, seeks to support the implementation of the Paris Climate Agreement through the rapid and massive deployment of clean energy. It provides a collective platform to address the key challenges to solar energy expansion—in terms of technology, finance and capacity.

The ISA's ambitious goal is to raise the trillion dollars needed to develop 1 TW (terawatt) of solar energy capacity by 2030. African countries are expected to play a vital role in achieving this target. The ISA Secretariat is setting up large-scale solar projects of 500 MW each in several African countries. It is also installing solar-powered water pumping systems in at least nine African countries and establishing Solar Training Application and Research Centres (STAR-C) in six African countries.

More than digital pathways or brick-and-mortar projects, India's association with Africa is about the human touch—about facilitating the capacities of the African people, particularly the youth. For over half a century, India's flagship initiative—the Indian Technical and Economic Cooperation (ITEC) programme—has offered training and skill development to countries across Africa. At the India–Africa Forum Summit in 2015, India announced the doubling of scholarships to 50,000 over a period of five years, including the introduction of new schemes exclusively for African students and scholars. At any given time, thousands of African students are studying in India. We are proud of the fact that 13 current or former Presidents, Vice Presidents and Prime Ministers in Africa have studied in India. Each African student arrives as a scholar, stays as a friend, and returns as an ambassador of India. The goodwill that our country draws from such linkages is unimaginable.

Thousands of Africans have also been taught by Indian teachers in their countries. In Washington, D.C., it is not uncommon to meet migrants from Ethiopia who turn nostalgic while remembering their Indian schoolteachers. Our partnership with Africa goes beyond strategic interests and economic benefits—it is based on the emotional bonds we share and the solidarity we feel.

To paraphrase what Prime Minister Narendra Modi said in his address to the Ugandan Parliament in 2019, "India's priority is not just Africa; India's priority is Africans—every man, woman and child in Africa."

I must mention that Africa is home to over three million People of Indian Origin who are settled all across the continent and contribute meaningfully to their adopted homelands.

I congratulate the IIC for encouraging these important deliberations that have added intellectual lustre to the India–Africa story. From the age of colonialism to the age of globalisation, India and Africa have done much together. Yet, there are still challenges to be addressed and frontiers to cross.

As Madiba once said: "After climbing a great hill, one only finds that there are many more hills to climb." India and Africa have scaled heights together, and will continue to climb even higher—hand in hand—in the years to come. Our shared values and friendship represent a bond that is constant and one that will ignite continuity. May this always be so.

Harsh Vardhan Shringla

Index